Understanding NLP

Principles and Practice

Peter Young

Crown House Publishing
www.crownhouse.co.uk

First published by

Crown House Publishing Ltd
Crown Buildings, Bancyfelin, Carmarthen, Wales, SA33 5ND, UK
www.crownhouse.co.uk

and

Crown House Publishing Company LLC
6 Trowbridge Drive, Suite 5, Bethel, CT 06801, USA
www.chpus.com

British Library of Cataloguing-in-Publication Data
A catalogue entry for this book is available
from the British Library.

10-digit ISBN 1904424104
13-digit ISBN 978-1904424109

LCCN 2003103579

Printed and bound in the UK by
Cromwell Press, Trowbridge, Wiltshire

Contents

Acknowledgments

I would like to dedicate this book to Alison Lang, in appreciation of her support and her continuing ability to present me with the problems and challenges that I need for sorting out my own thinking. My thanks also go to my brother John for his comments, and to the staff of Crown House Publishing for their help in this project.

Preface

Changing NLP

Neuro-Linguistic Programming (NLP) works by changing the way people perceive and make meaning of the world they live in, how they understand their experience, so that they may intervene effectively. Although NLP is renowned for its rapid and dramatic changes, it also creates subtle changes over the longer term, on all levels of Body, Mind and Spirit.

When it first appeared, NLP offered a radical shake-up of traditional therapy and change techniques. Although some rejected its ground-breaking approach, there were many who welcomed NLP's innovative way of working, and over the last three decades NLP has expanded greatly. New techniques and therapeutic procedures are constantly being developed; the number of training courses and books grows all the time.

Although NLP works well when used by skilled practitioners, there is always room for improvement. The body of knowledge known as NLP has accumulated such a huge amount of material that there is now a need for this to be consolidated. This can be done by generalising, sorting, finding similarities, noticing patterns, and so on. The aim is to find a model or set of principles for change. Generally speaking, the simpler the working principles, the easier it is to apply them in practice. NLP needs a unifying model if it is going to advance, if it is going to be more than the sum total of what a whole host of different practitioners are currently doing. And, therefore, it needs a paradigm or theoretical basis that will streamline it, and enable it to evolve to the next stage. *Understanding NLP* is my attempt to provide such a paradigm for NLP. I present this model in its basic theoretical form in Chapter Two, and provide numerous examples of it in practice throughout the book. This paradigm will enable NLP to reinvent itself and move forward with a clearer structure, and with increased power to meet its own future requirements. The challenge for NLP practitioners to reframe and reorganise their current understanding, to rethink their own practice, and to become part of the next phase of NLP's development.

NLP is surprising

When someone else seeks your help as a skilled practitioner, and tells you that they are experiencing a limitation in a part of their life, you already know that they have tried to change consciously and have failed. They are requesting that you intervene because you can offer a different point of view, and may therefore see what is hidden from them. To 'intervene' is to deliberately choose to act in a way that will produce a difference, that will assist someone in changing themselves. In a therapeutic context this means with their permission and willing co-operation. Because your intervention gets them to do something they have not thought of doing themselves, it will therefore be unexpected. NLP interventions surprise the other person into perceiving their world differently! Surprise effectively overcomes resistance to change. (The fact is that some people do resist change, because their anticipated discomfort outweighs the possible benefits of actually changing. Change does have its consequences.) If the person does not know what to expect, they cannot resist or defend themselves against it.

When you first do a particular NLP exercise and it delivers a desired change, it is often a profound learning experience. However, with repeated use, the surprise factor may wear off and that particular exercise becomes run-of-the-mill—the so-called Law of Diminishing Returns. Those NLP processes will still work in surprising ways for naive persons, but as the techniques become better known, they are likely to lose some of their potency. From time to time therefore, NLP Practitioners need to update the way in which they think about and use the techniques. And that includes keeping up with the latest ideas, not only in NLP but in other relevant fields.

Being aware of this need for innovation, NLP practitioners can use their creativity to find new ways of surprising people or of reframing their understanding, by developing new techniques or customising existing ones. Otherwise, you could find yourself being outwitted by the ever-smarter people who appear in front of you. The test of how well you understand and can utilise the generative power of NLP thinking is to continue to come up with alternative ways of perceiving reality and novel ways of creating change.

To meet this need, *Understanding NLP: Principles and Practice* will enable you to enrich your understanding of the basic patterns discernable in NLP. This will take you into big chunk generalisations, recognising paradigms which run throughout our civilisation's endeavours to explain what it means to be a human being. This book is a complete revision of the first edition of *Understanding NLP: Metaphors and Patterns of Change*. Since the first edition was published in 2001 my own thinking has moved on, and I have extended and refined many of the ideas which that book explored. This revised edition is more specifically for those people who wish to re-examine their existing knowledge of NLP and enhance their understanding of it. It also offers suggestions of ways forward in developing their own style of doing NLP.

I show how it is possible to bring all the pieces of NLP together using a new paradigm which I call the *Six Perceptual Positions model*. After the groundwork has been laid, this is made explicit in Chapter Eleven. In the process of arriving there, the book takes a critical look at many of the original ideas of NLP, their later modifications, and considers the appropriateness of the models and metaphors used to explain them. It also provides numerous examples of the new paradigm in action. There are guidelines on how to do NLP with a client from the practitioner's or therapist's point of view. As a result, you will be able to gather useful insights about someone else's model of the world, and about how best to intervene in order to help them change in a surprising way.

Because there is now so much NLP material, there is a limit to how much can be included in one book. Therefore a further volume *Understanding NLP: Language and Change* is planned. This continues the exploration of helping people change by explaining the linguistic aspects of NLP, guiding you through using the NLP model of language (the 'Meta-model') and demonstrating how different kinds of language are appropriate in different contexts. It also considers the art of using metaphors and telling stories.

Peter Young
Exeter, May 2004

Chapter One

Understanding NLP

A story is a doorway through which the imagination enters another reality. Every book or film offers the reader or viewer an opportunity to visit a different world, to see what is familiar from an alternative point of view.

Some children's books and films show this transition quite explicitly. For example, Alice finds her way to Wonderland down the rabbit hole; the Bastable children discover Narnia through the back of a wardrobe. I can remember a story I once read as a child, in which a travelling theatre arrives at a town. The protagonist of this story, whose name I have long forgotten, is initially entranced by the performance, despite the crudely painted scenery, the tawdry costumes, and so on. At the end of the show our principle character decides to explore this theatrical world, climbs up on to the stage and discovers the false nature of the cardboard cut-out trees and bushes. However, by going deeper into the recesses of this particular stage, it transpires that there is no back wall to this theatre so that this imaginary world goes on forever. As it does so the scenery becomes increasingly realistic and trans-forms into a reality somewhat different from the one in front of the curtain. Somehow our hero has made a transition into an alternative universe.

My interest in drama sometimes means I find myself performing on stage in a theatre. I feel at home with the technology of that magical space, the mechanics of illusion. The fabricated plywood flats, the shabby drapes, the painted scenery—nothing is quite what it seems to the eyes of the audience. Scenery is frequently reused, repainted, repositioned. I prefer minimalistic sets: a plat-form, a ramp, a flight of stairs. If the setting has been constructed in a neutral way it can represent whatever the director of the play wants it to be, and in this way the actors and the audience have to do the work in providing meaning. A trapdoor can lead to a dun-geon, a nightclub or an air-raid shelter. A flight of steps can lead to a throne, to a tower or to the top of a mountain. In this way you create your own world in which the story can unfold.

As a way of exploring some of the complexities of human understanding, remember a time when you had just finished seeing a play or movie, or reading a book that you enjoyed, and a friend asked you, "What was it about?" What happens in your mind as you seek to answer that question? It seems straightforward, and yet it may lead your thinking not forward but off in all directions or around in circles. My guess is that you engage in a frantic search for anything that will allow you to formulate an appropriate answer. Finding such an understanding often takes a little time, and it may seem remarkable that you can do it at all. Think about what you have to do. You are confronted by a complex assemblage of words, pictures, sounds, which were probably worked on, refined, transformed into the finished book or film for a year or more. You have to extract the essence of this so that you can arrive at a succinct yet relevant description, and all in a sentence or two.

Of course, the quest may be easier if you have some way of directing your thoughts. How well you do this will be helped by your existing understanding of how books, films or, indeed, human life works. This will be influenced by your previous experience of similar stories, the level to which you can see beyond or beneath the surface details of the experience and identify some kind of pattern, theme or familiar plot that enables you to classify this story according to some kind of criteria. If you are not used to thinking this way, such a task could be well nigh impossible.

The story of NLP

Now turn your attention to another complex accumulation of information about how people change themselves and their behaviour in order to improve their ability to achieve the results they want: NLP or Neuro-Linguistic Programming.

Historically, the founders of NLP, Richard Bandler and John Grinder, noticed that some therapists were achieving outstanding results and so they inquired into what they were actually doing that produced significant change in their clients. Having found contemporary theories and explanations somewhat lacking, they began asking questions that no-one had asked before. As a result, they formulated a series of principles, working practices, models for change, and so on, which they called Neuro-Linguistic Programming. Since the advent of NLP in the 1970s, it has been expanded to include a vast amount of knowledge about the different ways in which people perceive their reality and how they change. However, all this accumulated information about NLP currently appears more as just a collection of ideas rather than having any obvious unifying theoretical model or paradigm. So what is NLP about? Is it possible to organise it into a recognisable story? *Understanding NLP* seeks to answer these questions by taking you on a journey through the realms of NLP, using a set of guidelines that will enable you to interpret your experience in a new way.

The puzzle

Imagine NLP as a jigsaw puzzle. You open the box and tip the pieces out onto a table. You look at the jumbled heap and contemplate your strategy for arranging them into some kind of meaningful whole. Some pieces show bits of a picture, whilst others are face down and show nothing at all. Even with the picture on the box, it is not always possible to unerringly fit each fragment into the whole.

Now NLP is far more complex than that. With a jigsaw puzzle you know ahead of time that there is actually a way of putting the pieces together. However, with NLP, you do not have this certainty. And what would the picture on the box be? Perhaps some kind of impressionistic image, a sketch or a diagram rather than a finished composition. Maybe there is no coherent picture at all! Nevertheless, you set yourself the goal of understanding how NLP works; you are going to put the puzzle together as best you can. It would make the job easier if you could devise some general principles for sorting and connecting the pieces. For example, you could find pieces with similar themes—whatever similar means in this context. Once you have clarified that, you could, by joining similar areas together, create small sections with a broader meaning. Eventually, you have enough of these sections to give you an idea of the big picture. Having a preliminary sketch enables you to test your ideas against it, and to modify the picture accordingly. Once you find a pattern, it immediately tells you how to incorporate other sections and to fit new material into that design.

My intention in this book is to demonstrate one way of transforming the jumble of pieces into a coherent and structured pattern. This will give you not so much a picture on the box but rather a plan or set of guidelines to help you make your own picture. Although this might seem rather vague, it will serve you well enough, and, importantly, it will help you deal with the continuing growth of NLP. Unlike a real jigsaw puzzle, even as you are fitting existing parts of NLP together, other people are adding new pieces, developing new areas outside of the original frame. This puzzle is forever changing its size and shape. Fortunately, you are well-practised in creating order out of chaos.

Understanding

When things are going well, you have the feeling that you understand what is happening, that you are somehow on top of events, or in control of your life. Understanding is more an emotional response that lets you know that your interpretation of events— the story—makes sense, and that, for the moment at least, issues are being resolved satisfactorily. However, just because a story is reassuring, there is no guarantee that it has greater applicability to life in general. Think of all the obsolete notions of how the world works that have been abandoned over the centuries. All of our stories and theories about human existence are only ever our best attempts so far. At some point they will be challenged and possibly improved.

4

However, if you have a set of procedures or processes that consistently deliver results, there is no urgent need to change them. It is when you become dissatisfied, believe there has to be a better way, want to enhance your expertise, find new ways of intervening to create change, and so on, that you will need a greater depth of understanding in how things work. Understanding is more an ongoing process of interpreting and reinterpreting your experience, rather than a once and for all 'truth'. Therefore, understanding is paradoxical in that instead of moving towards an ultimate truth, you are developing the mental flexibility to entertain multiple, sometimes contradictory views about the nature of your reality.

Understanding NLP not only means you will be able to enhance your own competence and achieve excellence in those areas of life that you choose to develop, it also means that you will gain a sense of many alternative worldviews and beliefs about the nature of human existence. You will be able to intervene more appropriately and effectively in helping other people deal with the problems and issues in their lives. To do that, you first need to be sufficiently in rapport with them so that you may gather information about their model of the world and about how they are stuck. Your flexibility of thought will then suggest ways for them to move beyond their current limitations, so that they have further options and opportunities for action.

Metaphors

People use metaphors for making meaning of experience. You compare what you know about the everyday experiences of life and apply that way of thinking to the new material you want to comprehend. Metaphors are useful in that they draw attention to what two disparate domains of experience have in common by focusing on certain similarities. For example, the jigsaw puzzle metaphor offers a way of perceiving NLP as a jumbled collection of pieces, but little else about it. Every metaphor has its limitations.

Exercise 1.1: A Metaphor for NLP

- Think about how you would describe your current understanding of NLP. What kind of metaphor would you use to describe your present thinking?

- Consider how your thinking and behaviour have changed as a result of learning about NLP. What metaphor would best describe the changes you have made?

- What does NLP mean to you now? Again, find an appropriate metaphor.

Make a note of your answers, so that you can refer back to them from time to time and notice how your ideas change. When these metaphors seem no longer appropriate, what other metaphors would you use instead?

Metaphors are easily changed, revised or updated. However, when you find a metaphor which really does its job, then there is always the danger that it takes on a more permanent quality, and you forget that it was made up, or that it only deals with a particular aspect of that experience. For example, it has become a cliché that people "fight cancer" or that the immune system "guards against alien invasion forces". These military metaphors may not actually work in the person's best interests. Many of the metaphors used in NLP have acquired this taken-for-granted quality. Therefore, it will be worth checking them to see if they are still communicating what was intended, and are in line with advances in thinking.

You will notice the preponderance of visual metaphors. For example, you are going to be seeing things from many different points of view as you adopt different perceptual frames and focus on a variety of aspects of your experience. The visual sense is very important to most people (even blind people), and we use visual metaphors to talk about our views and to illuminate a kaleidoscope of subjects. When you understand, you say "I see what you mean". The key metaphors used in this book are those of seeing things from various points of view, adopting perceptual positions or ways of perceiving things.

Although this book contains much 'how-to' material, it could be seen as more of a 'how-else' book. It is intended to take you to the next stage of your search for meaning by presenting some alternative ways of perceiving what you already know. It presents metaphors, paradigms and models that will provoke you into seeing things from other points of view. Now a point of view is just a point of view. No point of view is more true or valid than any other. What makes certain points of view special is what they enable you to *do* in a particular way. The Six Perceptual Positions model (see Chapter Eleven) will enable you to enhance your personal excellence in using NLP.

Aims and challenges

Given the huge amount of material subsumed under the label of 'NLP', elucidating its underlying patterns and structures might seem a daunting task. However, NLP does not exist in isolation from other attempts by human beings to understand themselves. Those attempts are part of our history, and show how many individuals have debated and described human nature over thousands of years. Drawing on their wisdom and observations, my aim is to seek patterns and regularities in NLP by finding what its operating principles have in common with other explanations of human nature. If we can see the similarities, this will enable us to fit the pieces together, find a unifying paradigm—and could even indicate the kind of picture we have on the box.

Paradigms

'Paradigm' is a rather loose term which refers to a way of understanding the world, to a framework that gives meaning to experience, to a distinctive way of perceiving a set of phenomena. A paradigm offers an explanation often in the form of a narrative or story. Any paradigm is a best attempt so far at accounting for how something happens. What matters is whether the paradigm is useful: does it explain what happens, does it predict what will happen, and does it suggest an appropriate course of action to take? A paradigm does not claim to be some kind of ultimate truth, because our understanding depends upon the language and metaphors we are using. To create a paradigm we need to generalise from our experience and find underlying patterns and regularities in the world. The art lies in learning to see beyond the superficial evidence of the senses, and to notice abstract patterns which organise experience in a meaningful way.

Systems of thought change over time. New paradigms are introduced because they offer greater utility and also suggest further avenues to explore. Historically, we have noted such milestone events; they mark the boundaries of epochs. Scientific explanations have shifted because of developments in astronomy, geology, quantum physics, genetics, technology and so on. Artistic movements such as Polyphony, Jazz, Impressionism, Art Deco and Postmodernism have all affected the way we perceive, enjoy and make meaning of our experience.

When new ideas or information arrive which do not fit the old pattern, the old ways of thinking are overthrown—or get revised. Any evolving body of knowledge benefits from a periodic shakedown in which its principles and paradigms are assessed and updated. Thomas Kuhn (1970) called this kind of restructuring a "paradigm shift". When Bandler and Grinder originally introduced NLP to the world, this paradigm shift offered a better model for understanding therapy and personal change.

So, given the jumbled state of NLP, we need some organising principles or a new paradigm for clarifying what currently lies within its extensive territory. Such a paradigm would show how all the various sections and pieces can be brought together. In practical terms it would offer an understanding of where other people are coming from—their models of the world—and would empower practitioners to become more proficient in creating effective interventions that would respect those worldviews when implementing change.

What is NLP for?

If all systems of thinking exist in order to meet a need then it seems reasonable to assume that NLP meets some deep need of humanity. Therefore, it is in order to ask what this need is. There are several ways of asking this question: What is ...

   ... the problem to be solved?
   ... the issue to be addressed?
   ... the conflict to be resolved?
   ... the block to be overcome?
   ... the outcome to be achieved?
   ... the mystery to be revealed?

Even though they cover a range of attitudes, I shall treat these questions as more or less equivalent, as they indicate how people refer to aspects of life which they would like to be different somehow. They each suggest an intention to intervene in the world in order to create a change. You intervene in order to break a pattern or habit; your intended result is a change in behaviour. NLP's aim is to increase choice of behaviours. If your "programming" (your collection of acquired habits) is not giving you what you want, then you need ways of creating alternatives. When people do not know how to change, they often describe this situation as "being stuck". It is when people get stuck that you need to have some general paradigms or principles that suggest ways of getting moving again.

NLP techniques are primarily concerned with *process*—what people *do*: "How do you do that?" For example: How do people consistently achieve their outcomes? How do people 'unstick' themselves? How do they establish and maintain good relationships? Finding out *how* means firstly identifying someone who already does whatever it is effectively and then paying sufficient attention to what they do so that you may copy them successfully. By systematically studying their actions and intentions, patterns emerge, from which you can devise the principles of "what works". One thing you will discover is that effective people are often breaking existing patterns and 'doing something different'. Therefore, the kind of paradigm we seek will take this need for surprise into consideration, and will suggest unexpected ways of creating change or getting things moving again.

NLP addresses the question—not a new question by any means—how is it possible for two people to engage, interact, communicate in such a way that one is able to help the other one change their understanding and, therefore, the meaning of their experience?

Essentially, we tell ourselves and each other stories. We learn to intervene in the world using the strategies and stories we have acquired through our own experience and the strategies and stories we have learned from others.

Stories and understanding

Life must be lived forwards, but it can only be understood backwards.

Søren Kierkegaard

Learning involves reflecting on the past and noticing where you can make improvements. The purpose of examining what you know about NLP is to challenge your beliefs in order that you may revise any which are no longer serving you. A second aim is to provide you with practice in those two qualities so prized by NLP developers: curiosity and flexibility, and in particular, a greater flexibility in perceiving your reality from different points of view.

Change results in different behaviour, but does not necessarily produce insight. Insight is the "Aha!" phenomenon which produces a feeling of understanding when things 'fall into place'—you have structured your ideas about the world into a story which makes sense to you. The film-director David Mamet (1991: 60) neatly sums up this storytelling ability: "It is the nature of human perception to connect unrelated images into a story, because we need to make the world make sense."

You have spent a great deal of your life learning to anticipate what other people will do, and how they are likely to respond to the events in their lives. You are continuously, and often uncon-sciously, monitoring patterns of behaviour, noticing preferences, making generalisations and checking your predictions against what actually happens. There are few circumstances where you have no expectations. Although people's lives are full of unique details and idiosyncrasies, there are commonalities and regulari-ties in what they do, and these can be described in terms of sto-ries. Such stories help you imagine possible futures, anticipate "what happens next". Given the state of things now, you know how stories are likely to turn out in the future.

Stories are the basic units of understanding and tell us *how things happen*. They are a product of hindsight. Because lives are messy—many things happen unintentionally or simultaneously—you look back and interpret your experience by organising your per-ceptions of what happened into a story with a beginning, a mid-dle and an end. In putting together a story (sometimes called a *schema*—plural *schemata*—by philosophers and psychologists), anything that appears irrelevant to the final outcome (where you are right now) is disregarded, at least for that particular story. In describing your personal history of learning NLP, information about what you had for breakfast or how you got to the training venue is probably irrelevant.

Thinking in stories

A story starts with an inciting incident or precipitating event: something happens to interrupt your habitual way of doing things or to disturb the status quo in some way. The middle of the story explores attempts to resolve the issue, often with several set-backs or complications. The ending marks the return to equilib-rium: the goal is achieved, the problem has been solved. You know it is the end because the tension of unfulfilled expectations disappears. There are no loose ends and you have a feeling of closure. For example:

• You lose your job, are made redundant. You apply for other jobs, attend several interviews and eventually get another job.

- You meet someone and fall in love with them. You do whatever it takes to build the relationship. Depending on how well you get on together, you either part or move in with them. Traditionally, such stories end with "they lived happily ever after".

The story of NLP starts with that observation that some therapists were achieving consistently good results with clients, and the questions: "What are they doing that is different?" "Is it possible to learn to do that, too?" NLP expands as answers are obtained by those people whose curiosity impels them to seek out and observe best practice in many different areas of life, especially where people are dealing successfully with problems, or are maintaining a balance in their lives. Looking at the history of NLP, we can see various lines of inquiry materialising, techniques being recorded, adapted and generalised. Gradually, some of these change processes became the major cornerstones of NLP. Each process describes a story: from upset to resolution. You might wonder: "How many different stories of change are there? Are most problems variations on a theme? How many different techniques do we need to have?" If we can identify the common patterns of change, then maybe our task will be easier.

Because life is uncertain, people become very adept at revising their personal beliefs and stories in order to make sense of the unexpected happenings in their lives. As you learn, you amend your stories. In this way, nothing stays the same for ever. When your stories fail you, or you do not get the results you expected, then you need to examine their validity. The job of the NLP practitioner or therapist is to assist clients in making changes through rewriting those strategies or stories which do not work. If you are going to influence other people effectively, then you need to know something of the stories they are using to explain their experience and for anticipating their future. Because they are not often expressed as such, it is useful to identify the underlying stories as they offer essential clues about that person's model of the world. In recognising the patterns in someone else's behaviour, you know where they are coming from, and you can then adjust your communication style to influence them appropriately. Frequently, your intervention will get them to change or revise the story of "what happens next", especially if that anticipated future is limiting them in some way or preventing them from acting now.

By making the person's stories explicit, you can assess how well the elements of their story are related or connected. Very often, to your eyes, the connections will be tenuous or nonexistent, and you fail to see how they arrived at a particular meaning for those experiences. However, it is important to remember that it makes sense to them, or did once. The Linguistic aspect of NLP offers a systematic way of challenging the meaning and saliency of those explanations and stories. Your task is to help the person find ways to re-frame, edit or re-write their own stories so that the meaning changes, and so that they have greater flexibility in how they perceive their reality, and more choices in the way they may intervene to achieve their desires.

The story of NLP itself is not finished, and will probably never be complete. It will remain an enigma because it arises from a sense of curiosity. It has the whole of human nature in its scope, and that has already kept us busy for millennia. Although we seek truths, we also know that the truths we find are ephemeral.

Unfinished stories

Many of the events in your life which have been satisfactorily resolved have become part of your "life-story". However, not every story reaches a conclusion. You may wait to see what happens in the end, or you could ignore those issues until such time as you feel competent to deal with them. Or you may never know. Having 'unfinished business'—stories as yet unresolved—creates a mental tension which sustains your desire to end them. Unresolved issues stay potent, cause you to worry, and this can affect your everyday functioning. In academic psychology this is known as the Zeigarnick effect. Briefly, when people are interrupted in a task, or when a story is not completed, they tend to remember it better because closure has been denied and they are mentally aroused. Delaying the ending is a frequent plot-device in storytelling; you want to know how it turns out, but are denied resolution. Closure is frustrated by a cliff-hanger: will the hero survive, will the couple get together? Uncertainty holds your interest until the story is satisfactorily completed.

When a story ends, and makes sense, you feel satisfied, and you stop being curious because the tension disappears and the puzzle is complete. However, this says nothing about the story's validity as a generalisation. Throughout your life you acquire a great number of stories which have varying degrees of meaning, utility, and logic. Although those found wanting get updated or replaced, others, such as "It is possible to communicate with those who have died", are difficult to test and tend to linger. What matters is that you act as if your stories are true. When the validity of a belief is questionable, when a particular story becomes irrelevant, or limits your options, it can be changed. NLP is the art of changing such stories so that they serve you more effectively.

If you are stuck, then it helps to make your stories, beliefs, assumptions and expectations explicit. Once you can see the pieces in front of you, it is much easier to see the pattern and then edit or rearrange them. Often though, you may need someone else to help you who can see what you are not seeing. This could be a friend, a mentor, a personal coach or an NLP practitioner—someone who can spot alternatives to your habitual way of doing things. Then, as you shift your perception, you alter the way you do things. This kind of change often requires skilled help because you have to be surprised out of what has become deeply ingrained in your sense of who you are—that bundle of habits which you think of as 'me'. And then you will possibly need ongoing support to maintain the new you—until that too becomes habitual.

How NLP helps

NLP has produced a vast number of techniques and processes designed to help people move from being stuck. These techniques can be applied in various contexts to help people achieve what they want. If someone is unclear about what they want, then NLP offers ways of clarifying their needs and outcomes. Knowing which technique to use comes from recognising general patterns. However, NLP is often presented in terms of a recipe book: in this situation, technique X or process Y is the one to use. Therefore, having a general model or paradigm will enable you to think beyond that, and find new examples based on the general principles of change. Your interventions will continue to be effective because you can focus on the essence of change, which is to surprise the client into going where they have not gone before.

This notion of examining the stories people use to construct and interpret their reality offers an insight into how NLP works. By looking at the stories that NLP itself has generated, in terms of the processes, techniques, explanations and so on, we find that there are a few basic paradigms and models which apply generally to human thinking. These abstract patterns appear widespread, at least in Western cultures. Because they manifest in a huge variety of ways, it is not always easy to see what they have in common. The next chapter examines three basic paradigms that will improve your ability to notice underlying patterns in many different contexts.

Chapter Two

Patterns of Change

I have come to believe that the whole world is an enigma, a harmless enigma that is made terrible by our own mad attempt to interpret it as though it had an underlying truth.

Umberto Eco

Noticing patterns

Imagine that you are walking through a bustling city. At any time this can be an overwhelming experience, but suppose you are seeing it for the first time. There is just no way that you can identify, categorise or make meaning of what you see. You have no way of knowing what is important or what is likely to happen next. For example, there are a great number of coloured lights, but you do not know which ones you need to pay attention to if you are going to remain safe. What is the significance oif the different colours? Ignoring some of these lights could put you in danger—but which ones? Only when you understand your environment can you interact with it appropriately.

Human beings are born pattern-makers. The world is infinitely rich in sensory experiences, but we only have the mental capacity to pay attention to a small portion of it at any one time. Therefore, to maintain a meaningful sense of permanence and continuity we need to simplify our experience. We do that by generalising what we perceive, and by organising it into patterns. We then interpret the world in the light of these patterns. For example, having created the concept of 'traffic light' and given meaning to the different colours, then regardless of where we encounter any particular example we know what to do and what we expect others will do. At least, this is the general idea! In some cultures our expectations will not be fulfilled and we will be surprised at what actually happens!

A pattern comes from noticing what disparate things have in common. In what way is this like that? How are they similar? Pattern emerges from these relationships. Pattern allows us to arrange things into categories or groups of the same kind. For example, you mentally arrange your perceptual world into groups (or *gestalts*) of similar objects, such as a row of paintings on an art gallery wall or a circle of chairs in a training room. You see not only the objects themselves, but appreciate the generic quality ('pictures', 'furniture') as well as their spatial relationship to each other. Pattern organises a mass of information and enables you to perceive things in terms of identity, type, structure, sequence, organisation, relationship, similarity, intention and so on. Seeing such patterns both reduces your mental load, and provides some stability in a constantly changing world. For example, even if the chairs are replaced by cabbages or kings, the notion of a circle persists.

To generalise, you need only pay attention to those aspects or qualities which appear to stay constant. Ignore any variability in your environment, any superficial or ephemeral details. Ignore your physical relationship to it, that is, the way your perception changes as you move around, in terms of the perceived size, distance, qualities, orientation, perspective and so on. For example, you probably think your room looks 'the same' in daylight as in artificial light. You still see the furniture and decor as having the 'same' colours that they had in daylight, even though electric light gives them a different spectral appearance. As you move around the room, the table top constantly changes its apparent shape, ranging from a rectangle, to a trapezium or a line, depending upon your point of view. However, to you it is still the same rectangular table. It would be hellish living in a world without continuity, forever reinventing the meaning of everything around you.

Abstracting patterns

Perceiving sameness in behaviours usually means looking beyond superficial appearances. For example, the action of loving can manifest in many different ways. When one person "loves" another, there can be a variety of evidence; such as producing bunches of flowers, kissing, laughing or holding hands. None of those actions is sufficient of itself, but is part of the story you are creating in your mind about that behaviour. You build your model of the world by abstracting such patterns from a mass of experience. However, because it can be quite challenging to work in this abstract way, it is usually helpful to have some pointers or guidelines which direct your attention to certain aspects of what you perceive.

I am going to draw on Victor Fleming's 1939 film *The Wizard of Oz* to demonstrate some of the points I want to make. For example, how would you answer the question raised in Chapter One: "What is it about?" Each description would require varying degrees of abstraction based on the experience of actually watching the movie. You could give the title and author, the director, the actors or characters, and describe the sequence of events. You could explain what the various characters were each trying to achieve. You could classify the film in terms of *genre*: fantasy, musical, maturation plot. You could describe the *theme*: an adventure in an unknown land where things happen differently. You could state the *moral*: "You have within you the power you need to achieve what you want." And so on. Describing something in terms of a genre or theme, requires that you are familiar with other movies which exhibit a similar pattern.

In describing what NLP is about, we need some patterns which relate to the general ways in which people change. We are looking for similarities across a range of behaviours, seeking generalisations about actions and intentions. Eventually, we arrive at a highly abstract set of principles—a paradigm—that offers a basic model or story of "how things happen". The paradigms I am exploring in this book are such generalised patterns. However, they are not new. They have been around for thousands of years, presumably ever since people began to reflect on their experience. And these patterns are continually being rediscovered and renamed to meet the changing needs of society. There is no shortage of human experience to be noticed, observed and interpreted. Our culture has a huge collection of recorded observations of its thinking and activities: in books, paintings, sculptures, sound recordings, films, photographs and so on.

Of the many paradigms that can be identified in human behaviour generally, some have a more basic quality. Once you have some idea of what to pay attention to, you improve your ability to see beyond the immediately apparent, to read between the lines, as it were, and notice patterns, affinities, themes and paradigms in what is happening at a deeper level. Once you have noticed a pattern, made a connection, seen the hidden picture in the puzzle, it is almost impossible *not* to see it thereafter. Your knowledge has increased, you perceive the world differently.

To understand how NLP works, it appears that we need only three paradigms which when combined generate a model of the basic change process. This model can be represented in its simplest form by the following diagram (Figure 2.1 and on the front cover):

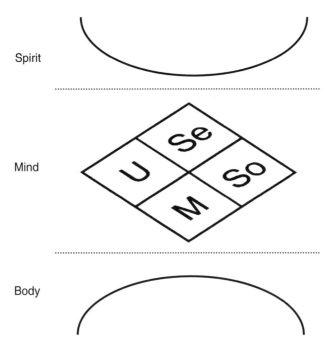

Figure 2.1 The Six Zones

This model divides human experience into three major zones: Body, Mind and Spirit. The central zone, Mind, which is about perception and cognition, has been further divided into four boxes. A major part of this book explores these four essentially distinct modes of thinking, the ways people perceive reality. I will explain the four abbreviations in a moment.

Although the diagram might seem rather stark at first, it will become more relevant as you cover these bare bones with the flesh of your wide knowledge and experience, with your existing expertise in the art of successful change, with those aspects of life that you find important, and with your ever-extending network of associations and ideas. As you allow your imagination to play with this paradigm, you will go beyond this "cardboard cutout" model which is on stage as the curtain rises. It will start triggering ideas in your mind and enable you to venture into the rich backstage world of your own imagination, further and deeper into a familiar yet unknown territory.

The model will gradually take on a life of its own to such an extent that you will begin to notice the pattern in many different and surprising places, and that it is somehow there in the background, guiding change processes, not only in NLP and therapy, but in management theory and in Hollywood movies! Eventually it will seem so obvious to you that you'll wonder why you never noticed it before.

Once we have examined the three basic paradigms, we can then find out what emerges when they are brought together.

Paradigm #1: The Three Levels

The first paradigm illustrates how we categorise reality into different kinds or levels. We are used to organising things, concepts and ideas into hierarchies. For example, a familiar distinction is: Body—Mind—Spirit (Figure 2.2).

Spirit	Level III	what you *aspire to*, the meaning of your life
Mind	Level II	what you *think*, your perceptions, intentions and actions
Body	Level I	what you *are* in a physical or physiological sense

Figure 2.2 The Three Levels

All three levels are aspects of what it means to be human. We have a physical body, the bones, nervous system, organs and so on. We also are thinking creatures, able to manipulate our environment and influence others; and we have some awareness of the meaning of our lives in a much wider sense.

We use the hierarchy metaphor as a way of understanding the world. NLP uses the terms 'chunking up' and 'chunking down' to refer to the process of describing things with greater or less generality (see also Chapter Eight). One kind of hierarchy is based on the idea that we attribute greater weight to certain notions because they have wider application, because they are more complex or encompass a wider domain. The *Body—Mind—Spirit* hierarchy is of this kind. There are also hierarchies based on the notion that each level 'transcends and includes' the levels below it. It is also possible to create hierarchies based on personal value systems or according to the number of connections each item has across a network. As with many of the concepts we will explore in this book, there are alternative definitions according to your particular point of view.

Paradigm #2: The Two Pulls

The central zone, Mind on Level II, consists of a four-box diagram, which represents four different kinds of thinking. In order to understand how this four-box model has been created, we first need to explore the simplest kind of discrimination that we can make: that based on opposites or *polarity*.

Think of a line stretched between two mutually exclusive or opposing ideas, such as Light and Dark. It's possible to experience total darkness in a deep cave. As you approach the outside daylight, the illumination gradually increases from Stygian gloom to dazzlingly bright in the midday sun. Between the two extremes there are places along the continuum which represent different light levels. Apart from using this kind of description for physical qualities, we can also think of a gradual transition between any two states or attitudes, such as *curiosity* and *apathy*, or *dominant* and *submissive*. We can then indicate the degree to which we feel able and motivated to find out more. When we come to decide on a course of action, we may feel drawn more to one direction than to another. For example, looking at the programme of what's on at the local cinema, we might prefer to see a *thriller* rather than a *love story*. Some movies can be classified somewhere in between. For example, *Casablanca* could be described as being both a thriller and a love story to some extent.

We can think of this basic paradigm as relating to what we move towards and what we move away from. The two ends of the continuum can be perceived as opposing *pulls* or *attractors*. For example, one important human dilemma is how we balance the pull for stability with the pull for change. We want to live in a world which is consistent and predictable. To a large extent we want things to stay the same. If we can 'take something for granted' then we only need to pay attention to variations; it is the deviations from the norm that make life interesting. Because living in a steady, unchanging environment would soon become utterly boring we also need and enjoy novelty and stimulation. We demonstrate a frequent desire to be creative and do things we have never done before, to perturb the system to see what happens. We engage in challenging physical activities, show great interest in other people's stories (real or fictional) and constantly seek to improve our personal performance in many of the things we do.

Imagine a line stretching off towards infinity, a continuum (Figure 2.3). At one end is the pull towards closure. It urges us to reduce all options and arrive at a definite description of the world. It offers certainty and permanence. At the other end of the continuum there is a pull towards openness. This attracts us to explore the infinite variety of existence. It offers novelty and excitement. Life is the continual dynamic of trying to balance these two opposing pulls. This polarity influences everything we do; the only escape from it is to stop living!

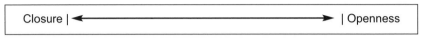

Towards closure:	Towards openness:
Certainty, maintaining the status quo, the way things are.	Creativity, and the possibility of doing something different.

Figure 2.3 The Two Attractors

Somewhere along this continuum there is a place which represents your position of relative comfort between these conflicting attractions, a moveable spot that oscillates between greater closure and greater openness.

Life in the balance

Somewhere between the two extremes of total chaos and total certainty you find a place where you can cope satisfactorily with this polarity, where you feel more or less at ease. However, should life become too comfortable, you may deliberately tilt the balance and seek new experiences, for example, going white-water rafting, moving to a new country, starting your own business, or going on a training course that promises to change your lifestyle.

This polarity pattern permeates all of our mythologies. In Egyptian mythology, Horus, the god of light (depicted as a man with the head of a falcon), eventually vanquishes Seth (depicted as a man with a head rather like an aardvark with upstanding ears and a curving snout), the evil god of chaos—the lack of structure and order. This eternal conflict between order and chaos lives on in our current mythology. It is depicted in popular movies such as *Star Wars*, *Lord of the Rings*, *Harry Potter* and so on. These stories depict the battles between the forces of light (order) and the forces of darkness (chaos). The struggle continues forever, because it is unresolvable, because this is how we create the meaning of life. We are always somewhere between the two—in all our endeavours—engaged in a balancing act. It is only when it veers too much towards one extreme that we feel we must do something about it.

Wherever we look at human endeavour we see these two forces being played off against each other. For example, you may want a safe, economical and reliable car for driving along roads which are smooth and clear, and at other times you may want to go as fast as possible, to test your car at the extreme end of its performance capability, and to drive it off-road to places where no vehicle has gone before.

Balancing your life is like walking: you are perpetually off-balance because you are on only one leg, moving, and temporarily unstable. But then you change the configuration and become unstable on the other leg. By maintaining a forward momentum you manage to achieve a 'dynamic equilibrium'; as long as you keep moving the system stays more or less stable.

Noticing preferences

Given these two pulls, you can notice, in any situation, whether someone is attempting to narrow things down, define or specify terms and conditions, reduce uncertainty, get down to brass tacks; or wanting to open things up, to find creative solutions, alternatives, engage in blue-sky thinking. In many situations you will be using each pull in turn. For example, if you are designing a new garden layout or a new company logo, you start with creative, divergent thinking and explore a range of ideas. Completing your project means using convergent thinking as you finalise the design and specify precisely how it will be.

To be able to predict something about other people, it helps to know something of their preference: to what extent do they want to control things; how open are they to alternatives? There are very definite biases here, and we have several descriptions for different 'types' of people (Figure 2.4).

Convergent	Divergent
Towards closure:	Towards openness:
"Procedures"—Sequential	"Options"—Simultaneous
Normative	Creative
Limiting	Expanding
Controlling	Laissez-faire

Figure 2.4 Polarity Typology

Exercise 2.1: Your personal preference

You have probably been thinking about your own preference here, where you would locate yourself between the two extremes. Indicate your preferred place on the line below.

Closure/Convergent | | | | | | | Openness/Divergent

This may vary according to the context. You might be very strong-minded or authoritarian at work, and more liberal and easy-going at home with your friends or family.

Using polarity thinking

Although this polarity is vital in understanding people and change, it is only one of a huge number of distinctions that we make every day. Indeed, all of our measures and assessments of personality—both formal and informal—are based on "Does X exhibit a certain quality, tendency to act in a particular way, have a certain set of beliefs ... or not?" NLP calls these kinds of distinctions 'metaprograms', and has assembled a number of useful descriptive patterns which indicate how people are likely to behave (see, for example, James & Woodsmall, 1988; Bodenhamer & Hall, 1996).

Establishing polarities, or category-thinking, is one way of defin-ing the world. For example, "Do you tend towards Options or towards Procedures?" How do you rate according to John Gray's popular psychology book, *Men are from Mars, Women are from Venus* (1993)? Most of the time this works reasonably well. However there are many instances where it is not at all clear how to make the decision. For example, "Are you a winner or a loser?" "Are you a good husband/wife, parent, lover ...?" Thinking in terms of polarities does not provide a particularly deep psycho-logical understanding, and may lead to simplistic thinking, such as: "If you're not with us, you are against us", and so forth.

There is an ancient debate concerning whether or not human beings have free will. However, this tends to force the issue and pushes people to the ends of a polarity by insisting that this is about being either 'true' or 'false'. This is a limiting way of under-standing the world and is ultimately frustrating as it creates con-flict, generating heat rather than light. You do not have to believe in free will or that you live in a deterministic reality. Think of these positions as points of view, each of which provides a way of understanding the world. There will be times when it is appropri-ate to use a deterministic approach; at other times you are going to be expressing your personal freedom to create your reality the way you want it.

Thinking in polarities is useful at times, but can be rather limiting when it comes to describing the richness of human types and behavioural preferences. Therefore, we need something with more distinctions. There are already a great many ways of classi-fying people, depending on what you want the information for. Do you want to know if they will be good at a job, or if they will make a good partner in a relationship? Do you want to know how they will vote in the next political election, or whether they will do well at school? It is always challenging to define which aspects or measurable qualities might lead to reasonably accurate predic-tions. However, for our purposes, these multi-faceted analytical tools are too complex. We want a simple enough pattern that will give us information useful for understanding people's world-views, but not have so many distinctions that we cannot use the categorisations in a practical sense. This brings us to the widely used four-box model. Such models define four types of people, four styles of behaving, four modes of making decisions, four ways of understanding experience.

Paradigm #3: The Four Realities Model

We create a four-box model by combining two separate polarity dimensions. This gives us four spaces or domains to which we can allocate things or people which exhibit the four combinations of qualities. For example, if you are interested in people who are Optimistic/Pessimistic and how they rate according to Rich/Poor, then you can sort each individual according to the four types: Optimistic and Rich; Optimistic and Poor; Pessimistic and Rich; Pessimistic and Poor, and then look for significance in the relative distribution.

The next step is to find some useful dimensions for understanding how NLP works. I am grateful to Will McWhinney for providing an answer to this (see McWhinney, 1997: 27). I shall be using his names for the four distinctions.

McWhinney studied the patterns and paradigms which are discernable running through our cultural ideas over the millennia and suggests that when we combine the two basic polarities: One/Many, and Determinism/Free Will, the result is a four-box model of very wide applicability. First, we need to understand these two dimensions separately. Then we can bring them together and explore how these four thinking styles facilitate our understanding of NLP.

One—Many

The domain of *attention*: do you perceive reality holistically or as consisting of parts? Do you focus on the *Self* and your needs and wishes, or on what *Other* people want? At a very early age babies learn to distinguish between *Me* and *Not-Me*. It is assumed that very young babies do not make this distinction, and live in a universal sense of 'all is one'—a state that we, as adults, often try to re-achieve through spiritual disciplines. During the period of socialisation, we learn to take account of other people.

McWhinney uses the term 'monistic' to describe this undifferentiated realm, and 'pluralistic' to refer to the multiple alternative ways of perceiving reality. Figure 2.5 lists some other similar distinctions.

One	Many
Self	Other
One	Many
Monistic	Pluralistic
Individual	Society
Home	Away

Figure 2.5 The One—Many Dimension

Determinism—Free Will

The domain of *intention*: the extent to which you believe you can influence what happens in your life and in the world. Which aspects of your life can you control? And which seem to be determined by your genetic make-up, your upbringing, the influence of your family, peers, authority figures and so on? Determinism suggests that your life is governed by your genetic inheritance, the laws of nature, the rules of society.

In terms of developmental psychology, this polarity is sometimes referred to as the Nature/Nurture issue. Figure 2.6 shows some other common names for this polarity.

Determined	Free Will
Objective	Subjective
Scientific	Humanistic
Impersonal	Personal
Complying/Conforming	Challenging

Figure 2.6 The Determinism—Free Will Dimension

Will McWhinney suggests that when these particular dimensions are combined into a 2 × 2 grid to form a four-quadrant model, the resulting pattern can be identified as the foundation of a fundamental paradigm which has been in use in our culture for over three thousand years. He calls this the *Four Realities model* (Figure 2.7). (See also Figure A.2 on page 280.)

	One	Many
Determined	**[U]** **Unitary** *Truths* *Rules*	**[Se]** **Sensory** *Facts* *Logic*
Free Will	*Ideas* *Metaphors* **Mythic** **[M]**	*Values* *Feelings* **Social** **[So]**

Figure 2.7 The Four Realities model (based on McWhinney (1997) with permission)

Each box describes *a type of thinking* or *reality mode*. McWhinney names the "pure" types: *Unitary, Sensory, Social* and *Mythic*. I will use these terms (and their abbreviations) throughout this book.

[U]   Unitary: The pull towards One + Determined

[Se] Sensory: The pull towards Many + Determined

[So] Social: The pull towards Many + Free Will

[M]   Mythic: The pull towards One + Free Will

As they stand, these labels probably don't mean much. When you know what each reality mode focuses on, and how each one works, then the model comes to life. An indication of what each type pays attention to is given in Figure 2.8.

In real life, no one is a pure type. We each have all four modes as options, and use all four thinking styles in different contexts. However, it is usually the case that people have one mode of thinking as a strong preference. You could think of the Four Realities model as a set of Metaprogram distinctions, in that at any one time a particular worldview will be evident in the way a person is thinking about what they are doing. That particular preference will be a major influence in their model of reality. When, I refer to 'Unitary types' or 'Sensory-mode thinking', and so on, I am referring to that mode which is most apparent or which indicates the dominant preference.

Exercise 2.2: Your preference

In order to get some idea of your own preference, look at the four Focus and Motivation descriptions in Figure 2.8, and decide which you find yourself most drawn to.

Focus	Motivation
Truths, Principles, Rules	Authority: I do what is right. I do what I am told. trust the people who tell me what to do.
Facts, Details, Logic, Strategies	Logic: I follow procedures. I use the strategies that work for me and others.
Feelings, Values, Judgements	Values and criteria: I need social approval. I want to stay within the norms of my group, my social networks and society.
Ideas, Creativity, Metaphors	Curiosity: I want to do my own thing. I am curious about what this would be like, so I create opportunities to find out.

Figure 2.8 Focus and Motivation

If your preference is not clear, because you think in all of these ways, then consider:

- Which is the one you do least of?
- Which one are you least attracted to or find most challenging?
- Which kind of motivation preference do you have most difficulty with in other people?

To get to know something about another person, it is often more useful to know which way of thinking they are *least* familiar with or least happy using. In my experience, most people have one mode which is under-represented. They may find ways to compensate for this in their relationships. Rather than team up with someone who matches their preferences throughout, they find a partner or colleague who fills in their gaps. (In my experience it seems difficult to bring the under-represented mode up to the same level as the others, but this could be because I have not yet found how to do it!) Therefore, if you work with teams, you might want to include people whose preferences cover the range of modes.

Convergent—Divergent

A third polarity emerges when we consider the two diagonals of this four-box model. This is the dimension we have considered above, which relates to convergent and divergent thinking.

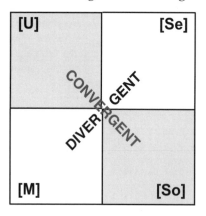

Figure 2.9 Convergent and Divergent diagonals

McWhinney refers to the Convergent diagonal as *Normative*. These terms give the sense of narrowing down options, of providing definitions intended to remove ambiguity, of arriving at a particular definition, answer, decision or judgment.

Convergent (Normative)

[U] Right/Wrong. Defining what exists.
   Upholding principles. Maintaining the status quo.
[So] Values. Defining what is important.
   Prioritising according to perceived value. Judging according to moral and other criteria.

One distinction between Ethics and Morality is that Ethical thinking is Unitary, about right and wrong, obeying the rules; whereas Morality comes from the Social realm, concerned with choosing to act according to your or the group's value system.

McWhinney refers to the Divergent diagonal as *Creative*. These terms suggest a widening of choice, of going beyond the existing boundaries, of thinking outside the box, and of finding connections and associations which have not been created before.

Divergent (Creative)

[Se] Analytical thinking. Breaking things down into ever smaller parts. The details.
   Small chunk thinking. Nit-picking, procedural, meticulous. Leaving no stone unturned.
[M] Synthetic thinking. Exploring associations. Creativity. Flights of fancy. The big picture.
   Big chunk thinking. Inspired, Associative, Intuitive. Going with the flow.

Models of the world

One of the eternal questions is: "What is the nature of reality?" NLP refers to a person's 'model of the world' but does not define what would constitute one, or provide details about what features it would possess. Bandler & Grinder (1975: 7) refer to understanding the client's model of the world:

> No two human beings have exactly the same experiences. The model that we create to guide us in the world is based in part upon our experiences. Each of us may, then, create a different model of the world we share and thus come to live in a somewhat different reality.

However, they do not explain the qualities of such a model of the world other than to explore how people use language to refer to it. Therefore, one approach would be to use the Four Realities model as a first step for exploring the nature of models of the world, worldviews, or models of reality (I use these terms interchangeably). Each reality mode offers a description of a way of thinking, a way of intervening in the world. According to this schema, being aware of these different modes is vital if we are to understand how to communicate with and to motivate other people who have a preference for a particular worldview.

A four-part model may seem simplistic, but it is better than making no distinctions at all and then treating everyone as essentially the same. It is also a step up from the two extremes of polarity thinking. Integrating two appropriate dimensions provides a serviceable way of profiling someone's 'personality'. Having four basic distinctions for identifying "where someone is coming from" is an extremely useful tool. However, as this way of thinking does not form part of a conventional NLP Practitioner training, much of what follows will provide an elegant reframe of what you have learned.

Apart from offering a practical typology, a further benefit of the Four Realities model is that it also provides a model for change. McWhinney suggests that all change can be seen as moving from one quadrant to another, which is equivalent to changing someone's perceptual frame. This simple paradigm is a great way of understanding what to do when you need to change. McWhinney and his colleagues have outlined a number of *paths of change* which are used in all kinds of management and therapeutic change processes (see Figure 3.1 on page 42). Most of the change processes described by NLP can be perceived as variations on this theme.

Using these patterns

Versions of the Four Realities paradigm have been used to define human behaviour and thinking styles for thousands of years. This abstract pattern is constantly being reinvented, with new versions frequently appearing in management and self-help books. There is a list of some of these in Appendix A. Usually, all four parts already exist. However, it is not necessarily the case that all four aspects are perceived as belonging to the grouping. Sometimes only three parts are described. If the fourth part is 'missing' there is usually no need to invent it. You simply go and look for it.

This abstract pattern can also be found—in the way that the plot of a story can be found—within Neuro-Linguistic Programming. When you look beneath the surface of NLP you find examples of these paradigms because they are part of the way human beings organise their experience. The Six Zone model (Figure 2.1) pro-vides a way of sorting out the mass of material that NLP has absorbed into its domain, of fitting the pieces together into a sim-ple paradigm. There is no need to reinvent the wheel when you can use the existing wisdom our society already possesses. In Chapter Eleven I will show how the six zones can be understood as Perceptual Positions. Remember that these paradigms are metaphorical and that they also have their limitations as ways of describing and interpreting human experience. What makes this particular model useful is that it is extremely general and therefore can manifest in a multitude of ways.

The next stage is to move from the *content* of the four boxes—what the world consists of, how we sort and categorise reality—and explore the *process* of moving from one box to another—how we intervene in the world to change things. There are twelve simple 'paths of change' and many more complex ones. You will recog-nise many of these change processes if you are familiar with what happens not only in a therapeutic context, but with management techniques (see McWhinney et al, 1997: 30–85). By journeying through several reality modes, a story of change emerges. It is from these stories that we develop our understanding of how the world works, and of how people achieve (or fail to achieve) their desires. If a particular story does not work, then we have a means of analysing and then editing that story. The revised story will change the way someone thinks by showing them how to intervene more effectively.

In other words, by using these paradigms to think about NLP, it becomes possible to organise a great deal of the material, to find basic therapeutic change techniques, and to generate ways of helping yourself or others move from stuckness to flow.

Chapter Three
How Change Happens

God grant me the serenity to accept the things I cannot change, the courage to change the things I can, and the wisdom to distinguish the one from the other.

Reinhold Niebuhr (1892–1971)

There are two different types of change: one that occurs within a given system which itself remains unchanged, and one whose occurrence changes the system itself.

Paul Watzlawick: Change

This chapter explores how we manage change and describes some basic principles for achieving it. These ideas will be picked up through the rest of the book, as we see how they manifest in NLP techniques.

When it comes to changing, what people want to know is:

- How can I deal with the changes that happen to me?
- How can I make changes in my life?
- How do I change myself, my behaviour, my habits?
- How can I change other people?
- How can I help other people change?

Finding answers to these questions is what NLP is all about.

You will have arrived at your own answers to these questions from your personal experience of changing. You also have access to the collected wisdom on change gathered over many centuries. However, despite all that knowledge, you only have a set of practical guidelines. There are no guarantees, because it is not possible to know exactly how change works. This is not a matter of incompetence or "just give it time, and we'll have it sorted". Despite brain-scanning technology, what happens in the *mind* is not open to scientific scrutiny. Although we can see the results of learning, in the form of new neural connections, we cannot directly observe learning taking place. This is a fundamental philosophical issue. Put simply, we are part of the system under investigation. To know how it works we would need to 'stand outside' of our own minds to observe the processes, and this we cannot do. We can, however, set up favourable conditions for achieving change, although when human beings are involved, we cannot specify exactly what will happen. We can project scenarios into the future as far as we like, but we still do not know what will actually happen. It is wise, therefore, to bear in mind Heraclitus's dictum to "expect the unexpected".

Why change?

Sometimes change is thrust upon us. Lives are interrupted, so we take action to put things right again. At other times we have choice. People make changes of their own volition because they want to improve themselves, have more fulfilling lives, achieve their desires, become happier, or balance their various activities. A traditional motivation metaphor refers to carrots and sticks: we change because we imagine something that will give us pleasure—a carrot—and then move towards it; or we do not like the way things are, want to avoid further pain—a stick—and so move away from it.

When you are not getting what you want from life, you act in order to improve your state, to solve problems, to resolve conflicts, or to overcome difficulties. There are times, however, when despite your motivation to change you do not know what to do. This could be through lack of knowledge, or you may already have the appropriate know-how but you do not interpret the present situation in a way which allows you to transfer your knowledge to what appears to be an unfamiliar context. Because you do not recognise the underlying pattern you cannot see how what you know applies. In either case, if you believe that there are no options available, you will feel 'stuck', or that possible action has been 'blocked' in some way. This also happens when you cannot choose between alternatives. Maybe there are too many choices open to you and you have no way of making a decision. Or you might imagine the consequences of taking action will be so terrible that you 'freeze' or retreat from taking any action.

One benefit of thinking in terms of the models introduced in the previous chapter is that they offer ways for overcoming blocks of this kind. The basic theory is that change occurs when you shift your attention and change your point of view. Shifting your polarity, reality mode and level can all lead to a different point of view, as each offers an alternative way of perceiving any situation. This then affects your behaviour, as you now understand your reality in a new way. This process is called 'reframing'.

The way you relate to the world depends on your previous knowledge and understanding, and on your particular motivation or intention: are you curious and want to gather information; do you want to become more flexible by learning a new skill? Your attitude or specific need alters the way you perceive the world, and you focus on different qualities or aspects of what is happening. Frames change as you shift the focus of attention. For example, if you want to post a letter, you start noticing post offices or post boxes, which are usually out of your awareness. Reframing is a way of deliberately changing how you perceive things in the same context. For example, when you are driving, instead of seeing other car-drivers as competing with you for road-space, look upon traffic behaviour as a kind of a dance, with its own rhythms, conventions and so on. Reframing often leads to a change in your physiological state; suddenly encountering the unexpected often produces laughter.

Doing something different

People get stuck when they do not believe that, or cannot imagine how change is possible. Their existing beliefs or stories about their world limit their options. This is a consequence of the pull of convergent thinking, the need to 'fix' the world in a more-or-less stable form. However, the restrictive side of 'being certain' is that you reduce your options to one—to stay as you are. You then feel stuck because you can see no way out. As Bandler & Grinder (1975: 13) put it:

> Our experience has been that, when people come to us in therapy, they typically come with pain, feeling themselves paralysed, experiencing no choices or freedom of action in their lives.

One answer to such an impasse is: "If what you are doing is not working, then doing *anything else* will be an improvement." However, being stuck may be so debilitating that doing something different is easier said than done. The difficulty arises because people may not believe that there is a way out or a way forward. They have become trapped by the very language they are using to interpret their situation. A sensible strategy for finding a way out is to examine in detail the language and the metaphors someone is using to describe their reality. Language is intimately connected to change, which is why the Linguistic aspect of NLP is so important. Identifying the kinds of linguistic tangles people get themselves into indicates something of their model of the world, and suggests how you can intervene appropriately to extricate them.

Using NLP on yourself, and particularly on your own use of language, is a great way of improving your communication ability. However, it is tricky being your own therapist because of the challenge of surprising yourself, or of finding interventions that will get you to do something you have never done before. Exploring your reality with an open mind and altering your usual way of thinking can lead to surprising insights. For example, you could set up some 'random input' devices (such as tossing coins or rolling dice), or physicalise your metaphors using NLP techniques such as Timeline (see Chapter Ten) or the Metamirror (see Chapter Twelve). However, it is usually easier to have on hand a skilled practitioner who can identify and then interrupt your patterns.

People are creatures of habit, and have strong preferences. They are often reluctant to let go of the familiar and embrace an alternative point of view. This is why using a surprising methodology —which is what NLP is for many people—often shifts the person's perceptual frame, and consequently, their behaviour, thinking and possibly their understanding. The three patterns presented in Chapter Two present schemata for noting where someone's preferences lie, and suggest possible paths of change. If you are working with clients, consider using the three paradigms as the basis for making interventions. Essentially, you start by identifying where your client is currently stuck and then consider moving to somewhere different according to the particular model you choose. Taking someone to a less familiar place will definitely create choice.

Polarities

Using the Polarity model, change comes by shifting your location along a particular dimension. For example:

- *Flip the polarity.* If you are of a gloomy nature, try 'thinking positively' by eliminating the negatives in your speech. So instead of saying "Don't forget …" say "Remember to …." See the glass half full rather than half empty. Learning to think flexibly and divergently gives you more choices, and enhances your autonomy.

- *Move along the continuum.* If you are somewhere in the middle of the continuum, you might be hesitant or wavering, unsure what to do. So deliberately choose a direction to go in, or move to one extreme, just to clarify the issues. For example, flip a coin and then treat that as a basis for potential action, and consider the consequences. It is a way of focusing the mind. You know you are going to make a decision one way or the other so do it first in your imagination and check things out before you do anything in reality.

Changing your reality mode

Once you have identified which reality mode someone is in—and there are plenty of clues about how to recognise this throughout the book—you can then choose which other mode to shift them to. You could see change as moving from one box to another.

With four reality-modes there are three alternatives to move to, and twelve possible paths between the four boxes (Figure 3.1). Every path is a familiar way of changing.

U = Unitary   Se = Sensory   So = Social   M = Mythic

Shift	Typical Action	Examples of Movement or Change
U → Se	Add choice, Analyse, Break apart	Shift point of view, way of perceiving: chunk up or down, analyse the elements, components, qualities (submodalities)
U → So	Evaluate	Explore value systems, priorities, decision making processes
U → M	Express	Find new metaphors, make new connections orassociations
Se → U	Define	Find "what works"—an effective strategy, theory or paradigm
Se → So	Prioritise	Evaluate different strategies, procedures, flowcharts
Se → M	Explore	Consequences and "what if …" scenarios
So → U	Persuade, Align	Define moral values, align people to their purpose
So → Se	Allocate	Allocate resources and assign roles to people
So → M	Evoke	Set outcomes, prioritise personal goals, check ecology
M → U	Establish, Reframe	Name, categorise, find a symbol, icon or logo
M → Se	Connect, Implement	Brainstorm, sort ideas, put into practice
M → So	Motivate, Facilitate	Tell powerful stories that invoke values and emotions

Figure 3.1 Twelve Change Paths (adapted from McWhinney et al, 1997)

If all that matters to the person is that they get a change in their behaviour or thinking, they do not need to be aware of such a model. However, when people make a significant change they may want to understand what happened so that they can use a similar process again. If you are teaching the principles of change, then you could explain some of the thinking behind your interventions, so that the person can learn the process or strategy and thus be able to generate their own solutions in future. In other words, they will be able to model you.

It is in Unitary mode that we *define* and *fix* the nature of our reality. Generally speaking, people get stuck in Unitary mode because they think that particular truth or perception is the only one there is. The monolithic belief that "This is the way I am, this is how the world is—and there is nothing I can do about it" is limiting because it removes choice. The way out of this is to find alternatives, and the usual route is to change to Sensory-mode thinking. This is the metaphorical shift that Dorothy makes in the movie *The Wizard of Oz* when she is transported by the whirlwind from Kansas to the Land of Oz. She leaves behind the limiting monochrome world of Kansas, and finds herself in the alternative Technicolor world of Oz where she eventually comes to understand herself better, and to fulfil her own destiny. Your role as NLP Practitioner or therapist is to be the whirlwind! You lift the person up and deposit them in some alternative reality which for them is relatively unexplored. This way of changing focuses more on the process of shifting from having no choice in Unitary to an abundance of choice in Sensory. This is also a move from convergent to divergent thinking.

These twelve single-step moves can be combined into sequences. Many NLP techniques start by getting the person to shift from Unitary to Sensory mode where they can explore options. Then they evaluate and prioritise their choices in Social mode. It is as though the person has stepped out of their stuck state, analysed the situation and broken it down into its component parts, for example, using techniques involving Parts (Chapter Ten), Submodalities and so on.

Traditional counselling techniques tend to shift the client's point of view directly from Unitary to Social mode by asking about their emotional response to their stuckness. This move gets them to take responsibility for their position, but keeps them in convergent thinking mode, which does not necessarily suggest options. By going first into Sensory mode the person becomes aware of the choices they have. Then is it possible to move to Social mode in order to evaluate and prioritise courses of action, and set outcomes.

Creative change happens in moving to Mythic reality. Ask for a metaphor for their condition: "That's like ...?" "What does this remind you of?" and so on. Or get the person to free-associate, or use the 'random object' technique to stimulate the imagination. For example, you want to get moving again. Use the word 'penguin', say. Instead of walking, you lie down on your tummy and slide across the ice. Or think of how awkward penguins are on land, but how graceful they are in the water. How do these ideas help you? Other creative techniques such as Mindmapping (see Buzan & Buzan, 2003) and brainstorming involve divergent thinking in order to generate ideas. *Brainstorming* creates options through the association of ideas. The aim is to get as many ideas as possible by building on the ideas of others, while refraining from criticism or judgment (Social-mode). *Mindmapping* is more about making connections between ideas and noticing patterns. At the end of the creative process there needs to be an evaluation (Social-mode thinking) of the ideas created, in order to decide on which is to be implemented.

Those who prefer convergent thinking may find difficulty in moving into a divergent thinking mode. For example, you may encounter resistance or incomprehension if you try to get strongly Social types to think in Sensory-mode terms. They are reluctant to let go of their moral beliefs or values, and they see scientific or 'objective' thinking as 'cold' or 'sterile'. For example, I once encountered some care-workers (strongly Social) whose primary role was to help their disabled clients improve their life-skills. However, in order to get their funding, they had to meet the targets set by the accountants (strongly analytical and Sensory). The accountants assumed that everyone else would see the logic of needing to conduct controlled assessments that measured improvement in skill-level to check that the targets were being met. However, the carers were more concerned with building supportive relationships with the clients, and doing whatever was possible to improve their lives. To them, such changes were qualitative, rather than quantitative, and they were not interested in doing experiments or making statistical analyses to prove that their clients were improving. However, to get the financial support they needed, the carers had to meet the accountants' conditions. Until these two groups learned how to understand each others' very different worldviews, their mutual incomprehension would lead to entrenched positions, and increasing frustration.

People who prefer Mythic mode can often be dreamers, living in a world of free-range ideas, quirky associations, and 'what if' scenarios. A useful shift for them is to ask them to 'get real' by moving them into Sensory mode, which requires they find a strategy for implementing their ideas, and a detailed action plan for bringing the fantasy into physical reality.

NLP's preferred shift is the move into Sensory-mode analytical thinking. A great many NLP techniques involve breaking things down into smaller parts, and then modifying them or rearranging them. In many cases this works well because it multiplies choice. However, concentrating on detail can have the disadvantage that the overall picture or purpose gets lost, and big-chunk, abstract thinking disappears. This way of working may not suit those people who look for the underlying essence or the patterns that become apparent when you 'stand back' and see things from a global perspective. As the great Bengali writer Rabindranath Tagore succinctly puts it: "By plucking her petals you do not gather the beauty of the flower' (1916: *Stray Birds* #154).

Combining single shifts

A single move may be all that is needed to change someone's behaviour. However, making several sequential shifts can create a more thorough change, and offer a sensible strategy for dealing with a group of people whose preferences cover the range of reality modes. There are two major sequences of basic moves which provide a better sense of how you can implement change. Each covers all four modes, but in a different order.

The Hero's Journey—The Path of Renaissance

This path starts from the Unitary position of 'stuckness' and moves into the 'alternative world' of Sensory, thus changing the way reality is perceived. This pattern is frequently used in Hollywood movies, such as *The Wizard of Oz*, *The Cider House Rules* and so on. Once Dorothy has got her bearings in the land of Oz, she then moves into Social mode and makes friends with some of the inhabitants: the Scarecrow, the Lion and the Tin Man (who can be seen as representing different parts of the personality). Together they establish their priorities and set a goal of visiting the Wizard in the Emerald City. After a number of adventures, Dorothy and her companions return to Oz and discover that Oz himself is a sham, merely the man behind the curtain pulling the strings. Dorothy then changes the meaning of what happened (in Mythic mode) and 'rewrites the story' of her transformation in the Land of Oz. The four companions have achieved their desires without realising it. This is one way of interpreting the 'magical' aspect of change. To complete the story, Dorothy returns home to Kansas with her new understanding, bringing a new truth into her improved Unitary reality.

This path, [U] → [Se] → [So] → [M] → [U], is one you will frequently encounter in NLP, as it fits the basic paradigm of change used in many kinds of change-work and therapy. Joseph Campbell (Campbell, 1949) called this *The Hero's Journey*; Will McWhinney (1997: 132) refers to this cyclic journey as the *Path of Renaissance*. There are examples of this journey in mythology, ancient and modern, from Homer's *Odyssey*, to the *Star Wars* series (see Vogler, 2000). The final transition from [M] back to [U] represents returning home after the adventure has been completed, or returning to the beginning of the cycle, ready to start again. In *The Cider House Rules* (1999), the young Homer Wells leaves the orphanage, grows into manhood, and finally returns to fulfil his destiny by taking over as the resident physician. Hollywood movies frequently use this story format (thanks to Chris Vogler) as the metaphorical 'return home' effectively produces a sense of completion. In other cultures, such as French cinema, this kind of formulaic plot is less important, as they feel no compulsion to tie up the loose ends.

The Leader's Journey—The Path of Revitalisation

The Leader's Journey describes another cyclic path: [U] → [M] → [So] → [Se] → [U]. This cycles the opposite way to the Hero's Journey. McWhinney (1997: 127) refers to this as the *Path of Revitalisation*. Leaders become dissatisfied with the current 'truth' and create new visions of alternative truths which they wish to bring into reality. Working in Mythic mode, the vision is explored, clarified, and becomes a rich and compelling story, which is then used to motivate the team in Social mode. The team decides how to apportion roles and resources, and follows best practice in order that the vision becomes implemented in Sensory reality. Its completion results in a new order.

This metaphor provides an elegant differentiation between the role of the Leader and the role of the Manager. Although Leaders can arise within each mode (McWhinney 1997: 186), charismatic Leaders follow the *Path of Revitalisation* (see Young 2003: 165). They start with their vision in Unitary reality, enrich their vision by telling motivational stories to their managers in Mythic reality and then generally oversee the project as it unfolds. Managers are more often engaged in Sensory/Social roles, and deal with the complexities of implementing the Leader's vision by working with teams, maintaining motivation, deciding priorities, planning strategies and allocating resources.

Changing Levels

We also have great experience of moving from to different Levels, to experience the sensations of physical exercise, to meditate, to enjoy arguments and discussions. The first step is to identify the

Level from which someone needs to move. Then there are two options.

At Level II or Mind, NLP is predominantly concerned with the effects of language. Many problems or difficulties arise from the way you think about the world, and how you put your experience into words. One way of looking at the Four Realities model is to see it as providing four cognitive aspects of Mind. When people get stuck in thinking about things then the most appropriate change is to move out of Level II altogether. As Fritz Perls, the creator of Gestalt Therapy, would say, "Lose your head and come to your senses." Has anyone ever said to you that you think too much? Do they suggest you forget the 'headstuff' for a moment and ground yourself? People often know when to move from Mind to Body. They feel the need for physical exercise—a run or a good work-out—which helps them change their emotional state. Better to use your energy, or let out your frustrations in a way which will do you good, than to take it out on other people. At other times people need to become more aware of what they are doing with their bodies in order to develop physical skills or just to stop knocking the furniture over!

People get a more balanced understanding of life by acknowledging their spiritual needs. They want the benefits that come from changing their state, through meditation, by going on a retreat, or by reconnecting with nature by visiting beautiful and inspiring places. This benefits you on all three levels of body, mind and spirit.

Moving from Body to Mind

If you ignore the messages that your body is sending you, you may be missing information about impending illness, stress, and possible physiological damage.

Exercise 3.1: Increasing Body Awareness

Use this exercise to become more aware of your body. I assume you are probably sitting down to read, and are relatively motionless. So without doing anything else, just start to check in with the different parts of your body:

- Start with your feet and work up. Pay attention to the feeling in your feet. Do they feel comfortable? Or is there something not OK, that you want to change?

- Now check your legs. How do they feel? Any pressures, tensions, aches? Just notice these feelings, whatever is true for you.

- Now notice the feeling in your bottom, the contact between you and what you are sitting on. How does that feel? Is it a feeling of comfort, or would you want to shift your position?

- Check your stomach area. Are you feeling hungry? Or have you eaten recently and feel pleasantly full? Or perhaps you ate too much and are regretting it.

- Move up into your chest area, and notice how you are breathing. Until now you have probably not been aware of your breathing at all. But now you are paying attention to it, just notice whether you are breathing low in the abdomen and moving your diaphragm, or high in the chest so that you breathing is rather shallow and your shoulders are moving.

- Put your attention in your head. What sensations do you notice here? Any tastes or sensations inside your mouth? How do your eyes feel having been reading for a while? Any pressure or noises in your ears? Finally, your brain: any tightness, headaches, or discomfort here?

That was a quick tour of your body. Were there any parts that you are not normally aware of? Now that you are aware of them, do you get the sense of integration, that all parts are working well together? Or are there are any messages from your body that you need to attend to?

You may want to try this exercise at other times—when you can do it safely. Just check in with your body, notice what is going on. Do you feel 'together' or are there conflicts? For example, you may have been engaging in vigorous exercise, and your body wants to rest, and yet other people—your children perhaps—are demanding that you engage in even more activity when all you want to do is relax....

If a person appears to engage in 'unthinking behaviour' or possesses habits that seem odd, and they seem unaware of this, then you could draw their attention to it. One way would be to wait until they are behaving in this way, and then tell them to "Stop. Just take a moment to become aware of your body, and what it is doing." You are asking them to reflect on what is happening. Interrupt what they are doing by saying: "Stop what you are doing." You want them to physically change their point of view. If they are sitting, ask them politely to stand up and walk round behind their chair. If they are standing, have them take a few steps backwards, that they can "See that 'you' over there, and pay attention to what that 'you' has been doing and thinking." By 'stepping back' you can 'get things in perspective', and decide what to do next.

Exercise 3.2: Observing yourself

You might try this now. When you have read this instruction, put the book down, and change your state by doing something different to what you have been doing.

- If you are sitting down, stand up and move round behind your chair so that you can look down on the 'ghost' of you who has been reading the book.

- If you are standing, then take a few steps back, far enough away so that you can 'put yourself in context', as it were. Look at the space you have just vacated, and again focus on your ghostly presence as if you are still there.

- And from that height or distance, consider: "What do I notice about that me and the way I have been responding to this material?"

If the person is unaware of how they come across, and if you have access to the technology, you could video what they do and then show it back to them. Tell them what to pay attention to as they watch themselves in action, because if they are unaware of what they do, they simply may not 'see' anything untoward, or appear to deny what is obvious to you. Then ask them to think about what they have seen themselves doing. Their reaction could be surprise, or embarrassment, because they just didn't realise they did that!

Moving from Mind to Body

Some people seem to spend much of their time thinking, but seldom take action. They get caught in what is sometimes known as the 'paralysis of analysis'. This can also occur in therapeutic situations in which the client is encouraged to talk about their 'issues' and examine the details of their 'past'. Exploring these in detail may be fascinating, but are not guaranteed to produce change.

When using NLP processes with a client, there is a danger that if they spend all their time sitting and thinking about things, they could become 'anchored' to the chair they are sitting in. That is, they link the feelings associated with their problem with *you, that chair*, in *that office*. Although their mental point of view may change, their physical position stays the same. This can make permanent change more difficult. Therefore, it is a good idea to have the client physically move as part of the changing process. Some therapists arrange their office so that the door the clients enter by (when they are carrying their 'baggage') is not the same door that they leave by when they have made the change, to symbolise moving to a new state. Physicalising metaphors can be a powerful change technique.

If someone is stuck in their thinking, one solution is to have them shift more into their body by engaging in some physical movement or exercise. Anything different from sitting in a chair will do. Bodily movement is the easiest kind of change of state to make: shake your arms and legs, jump up and down, take some deep breaths, roll on the floor, kick your legs in the air!

A version of this approach figured in Judith DeLozier and John Grinder's *New Code NLP*, which appeared in the late 1980s. Based on their existing knowledge of NLP, they asked: How would we do it differently if we had to start again? New Code thinking offers some exercises ('edits') which engage the person's physiology, for example, by getting into a good state—walking in a flowing, relaxed way, or breathing deeply and fully. As long as the person maintains this good physiology, it becomes virtually impossible to simultaneously entertain a negative problem state.

Somehow the mind-body chooses the positive, and 'problems' disappear.

Therefore, to make change more effective, include physical shifts as well as mental shifts. NLP techniques which involve physically moving around and exploring metaphorical realities certainly seem to make change easier and more fun!

There are many therapies around which involve treating the person on a physical or physiological level, regardless of how they are thinking. For example, we may derive great benefits from acupuncture, massage, reflexology, or some form of deep body work such as osteopathy, shiatsu or acupressure. The premise is that we store our tensions in our bodies, and our muscles become knotted or tight, or that our habitual way of being blocks energy flow in the body. We usually need assistance from skilled practitioners to change these physiological conditions. Alternatively, by doing yoga or t'ai chi both the Physical and the Spiritual become engaged.

The t'ai chi master, Chung-Liang Al Huang (1973: 80–81), says:

> I very seldom work on personal problems with a participant because I usually don't find it's necessary. In t'ai chi we do not recognise problems. There is no problem. The minute you recognise it, it emerges, and then you may get stuck in it. I find that if I don't focus on a problem it has a way of settling by itself—without my disturbing it and pushing it by saying, "Why do you do that? How come you are so resistant?" Then t'ai chi is not working for either of us.

In other words, when you do your t'ai chi, problems disappear. Dancing can have the same effect. Something similar happens with actors and singers who are feeling ill, and yet still manage to produce a great performance—which they attribute to Doctor Theatre. Life flows when you are engaged body and soul.

From Mind to Spirit

Alternatively, have someone rise into the realm of Spirit through some kind of 'letting go'. You could take them on a guided meditation, or engage in some form of spiritual discipline. In certain ways, Body and Spirit have things in common, which is why in the diagram (Figure 2.1) they are represented as semi-circles. If you were to fold the diagram round they would join to make a circle.

Another way out of being trapped by your thinking is by learning to meditate, or to be in a state where you are 'above all that'. To get an overview of a problem you must rise above it and allow your thinking to expand into a bigger space. Whatever you think your limitations are, think to yourself that "I am bigger than that".

Remember that whatever you think you are, or do … you are more than that. Whatever you think you are in terms of the four realities, your preferred metaprograms, your personality factors, or even your star sign, you are always more than that. These are only descriptions, metaphors, which have limited usefulness in certain contexts. We are more than our metaphors and linguistic descriptions of ourselves. The spiritual realm is open, beyond language.

These mental exercises take you out of your usual thinking. Move from a stuck state by expanding the frame, by becoming bigger than whatever that limitation may be. By moving up to a higher level and letting your mind fill the universe, as it were, it is possible to look down on that limitation or problem from a universal perspective. Seeing your reality this way allows you to put things into perspective. It also reminds you of the results of *your* creativity: this relationship, this problem, this opportunity to learn. It also empowers you to do something different, in whatever way you choose. The further your imagination expands your domain of consciousness, the more alternative versions of reality you have, and the easier change happens.

Working with other people

> Atticus was right. One time he said you never really know a man until you stand in his shoes and walk around in them.
> *Harper Lee (1960) To Kill a Mockingbird, Chapter 31*

Insisting that other people change is often a waste of time. It creates resistance, resentment, even revenge, and you end up with the opposite of what you set out to achieve! Rather than trying to control or manipulate other people, a better strategy is to find ways of getting inside the other person's mind to gain a sense of where they are coming from or what makes them tick. Because that is going to be different for different people, you need to be familiar across the range. But first you need to find out where you are coming from. The more you explore the Four Realities frame in every aspect of your own life, and notice the different ways of thinking and behaving, the easier it becomes to recognise someone else's habit or preference.

When you are using NLP with other people, you need to know that your interventions are effective. Do this by comparing the *before* and *after* states, to notice what has changed. This is known in NLP as 'calibration'. When you start, before changing anything, make an assessment of how that person is in terms of body, mind and spirit. What is their posture like? How are they breathing? and so on. Noticing how these indicators change as the person shifts their perception will let you know whether or not your interventions are working.

Where to start

> Change is an act of the imagination. Until the imagination is engaged, no important change can occur.
> *Robbins & Finley (1997)*

Change happens not just to part of you, but to your whole being. The distinctions made above are essentially arbitrary, but still useful for knowing where to start. A useful metaphor is to see people as *systems*. A system comprises parts which are intimately linked, where everything is connected, and functions are integrated. If you treat the person holistically, then it doesn't really matter where you make the intervention, because the effects will spread throughout. This partly explains the proliferation of different change systems and techniques, each with its own particular and often surprising focus which will break the habitual patterns of thought and behaviour.

We have already seen that physical therapies affect someone's mental and spiritual state. If the key piece is to do something the client does not expect, then using the Four Reality mode distinctions, you could …

[U] Change the *name*. "A rose by any other name …"? Actually, it could make a big difference.

For example, people sometimes give the 'wrong' name to their emotional experiences. If before giving a presentation, the presenter tells you they feel 'nervous' or 'afraid', it could be that they are misinterpreting their experience, and using a label which limits them. In such a case it would be valuable to explain to them that they are actually feeling 'excited' or 'more alive' about appearing in public, and that this is something all good presenters experience.

[Se] Break the problem down into its component *parts*. NLP uses many analytical interventions, which examine the structure of experience. For example, find out how the person imagines something in terms of its physical qualities (submodalities) and then have them change what they see, hear and feel so that it changes its meaning.

For the nervous presenter, explain that the adrenalin their body is producing keeps them alert, and thus enables them to respond quickly to whatever happens.

[So] Check the person's *values*. What really matters to them? How can they do what is their highest priority? How important is it that they remain part of their group or organisation? What kind of criteria would be relevant if they were to change their behaviour?

Remind the presenter that the audience is on their side, wants them to succeed, because they want an enjoyable presentation.

[M] Find out what would make something *interesting*. Interesting ideas are those which are richly connected to other ideas, produce many associations and possibilities for further exploration. Find a metaphor which gets the imagination flowing.

Suggest to the presenter that they might think of what they are doing as leading an expedition into an unknown land, and that in their role as a guide they will be pointing out relevant features, and helping the audience members to relate their experiences to other parts of their lives.

Maintaining change

Even though change can sometimes be swift and dramatic, and you experience a breakthrough, there is no guarantee that the change will last. The sad fact is that without support and nurturing most change fades away, often quite quickly. Your innovative ideas are unwelcome because they will upset the status quo and disturb its routines. Other people do not welcome such interruptions because they perceive them as creating problems for them. They then make adjustments which will bring the system back into equilibrium. Given the usual inertia, the system will not change that much. In reality, it does not take long before the changes that you have made have been undone. You may have had the experience of going on a training course and achieving a personal transformation. Then, when you return home to the family environment or work context, even though you are buzzing with new ideas and increased vitality, you encounter 'resistance' rather than enthusiasm from those who didn't go and who don't understand what has happened to you. The 'new you' may have to struggle to survive.

Who are your allies?

To maintain your changes, you are going to need some allies and ongoing support. Start with yourself. Ensure that you recognise all the good things you have going for you: your skills and resources, your ability to change, your more effective ways of dealing with the world, and your greater understanding of who you are and what you are doing. Put up some reminders, practise your new skills, consolidate your learning.

Changing yourself could mean altering your social context. Consider the environment you are moving into. Think about: "Who will acknowledge and accept the new me?" "Who will support me?" Make a list of your allies, both personal and pro-fessional. Choose to be with people who have a positive, creative, life enhancing, expansive attitude to life, where everything is possible, and learning is fun. Who are the people who will be pleased with the changes you will be making? Avoid anyone who wants you to sink down to their level of complaining and blaming, in their gloomy world where "It'll never work" is the rule. You might also want to list those people you think may be unsupportive, and develop some strategies for dealing with them.

What does knowing these patterns do for you?

The Three Levels model and Four Realities model offer some use-ful guidelines for making appropriate interventions when you want to create change. You still won't know exactly what is going to happen, but at least you can get moving again when you are stuck in any particular worldview. The great advantage of using linguistic interventions is that the mind will follow them and make sense of them even as you read the words, or hear them spo-ken. Someone only has to say "When I was at school ..." and you are probably back in your own schooldays. This is how minds—and stories—work. You just need some words, and your mind will conjure up appropriate memories, images, associations. Choose the right words, and you can shift someone's point of view. NLP is the art of finding words that change minds.

Now, even when you understand the ideas in this book, it is not going to be the case that you know how NLP works! NLP is one way to make sense of the world, but it too is just a story—maybe a powerful story, but a story none-the-less. There are many NLP practitioners who claim to be practical folk who don't need theories or models (though in reality they are using models and paradigms without being explicitly aware of what they are!). They are happy to use what they have learned in their NLP training, follow the procedures, and get results. That's fine. On the other hand, if you want to be a creative NLP practitioner, you do need to know some basic principles, so that you can invent your own techniques, using whatever your client offers you.

These models are thinking tools, that assist you in seeking order in chaos. Finding patterns is something human beings are good at. So play with these ideas—as you played with many other ideas when you were a child—and find exemplars in the world around you. It doesn't all have to be serious. For example:

Exercise 3.3: Clothes maketh ...

For fun, think about how the Four Realities thinking might apply to kinds of clothing.

Try this on for size:
[U] Formal clothing, such as a uniform, which has to be 'correct', and obeys the dress-code.

[Se] Practical clothing, such as a wetsuit, or protective clothing, which is fit for the purpose.

[So] Designer clothing, high fashion or designer labels which shows your taste; clothing that indicates that you belong to a certain group, organisation, or part of society—a dark suit and tie, a national costume, or a strip that identifies you as part of a sports team.

[M] Fun clothing, stage costumes, fancy dress, or the one-off fantasy creations that are paraded at fashion shows.

This is not about 'right' or 'wrong' answers; it is about making connections and finding real-world examples of the four-reality types that you are now aware of. Because this pattern underpins a great deal of human understanding, you will find examples if you look for them.

Chapter Four

Definitions of NLP

They sought it with thimbles, they sought it with care;
They pursued it with forks and hope;
They threatened its life with a railway-share;
They charmed it with smiles and soap.
Lewis Carroll: The Hunting of the Snark

Defining reality

It is human nature to want to define reality: to know what things *are*, what is happening, to have a life which is comprehensible. All definitions are attempts to 'fix the world', to create some stability, even if just for a moment. Given that 'all is change', this is an unceasing task. Similarly, producing definitions of NLP is a challenge comparable to that of those apocryphal blind men describing an elephant. Each encounters different parts of the elephant—a leg, a trunk, an ear and so on—and thus arrives at a very different understanding of what an elephant is. However, combining these partial glimpses enables us to build up some kind of overall picture. Therefore, we can get an idea of what NLP is by examining some of the variety of definitions that have appeared during its history. No definition can ever be absolute or complete, because such things are not possible, and besides, NLP is still growing and revising itself.

What does NLP mean?

There are several 'standard' definitions which you will encounter in NLP books and on NLP websites. However, should someone ask you for your definition, you might enjoy creating an *ad hoc* answer for that particular questioner by considering your own ideas. This is a useful exercise for clarifying your current thinking, and I would recommend doing this from time to time in order to notice how your understanding is changing. The more you practise NLP, the more often you will need to integrate new information and revise your perception of it. Putting your understanding into words may help things to fall into place, as you reorganise your experience and find new meanings emerging. It will also remind you of the inadequacy of words to communicate ideas!

When you want to talk about NLP to people who are unfamiliar with it, you need to be flexible in the way you explain it. Expanding the initials to 'Neuro-Linguistic Programming' might remind them that they have already heard these terms before, but the name itself does not usually produce insight. Because each person will interpret your answer according to their own model of the world, creating some definitions that describe NLP from each of the four realities points of view would enable you to provide definitions that will better match different audiences' preferred way of learning. What kind of definition of NLP would work for you? Do you want a dictionary definition and an outline of its fundamental principles? Or perhaps your preference is to analyse the three parts of the name and explore how these fit together to create effective change processes? Do you want to know about the benefits that NLP has to offer? Or would you prefer some metaphors that inspire you? There are examples throughout this book of words and metaphors that will be acceptable to the various preferences and worldviews.

If you are starting cold, because you don't know how much your questioner already knows, you could begin by providing the information at a big-chunk level, the broad principles: "It's about better communication and change ..."—and then begin to add further details. You could tell them about the kinds of problems and challenges that NLP is designed to solve: "It's helping people get unstuck." Or you could do a simple exercise by having them notice how they perceive the world, and then getting them to do something that will change their point of view: "Imagine you're a world-class tennis player, or brilliant entrepreneur, and that you want to teach other people how to match your level of ability ...."

History of NLP

Some people like to know how things came to be as they are now: the origins and history of NLP, the order in which NLP ideas evolved, and how later developments came out of the earlier thinking. Nothing comes out of thin air. Sir Isaac Newton said, "If I have seen further it is by standing on the shoulders of giants." Some of the giants in the origins of NLP were three extremely effective therapists: the founder of Gestalt Therapy, Fritz Perls; the family therapist, Virginia Satir; and the hypnotherapist, Milton Erickson. Together with the psychologist and thinker, Gregory Bateson, another 'giant' in the history of western thought, Richard Bandler and John Grinder (a professor of linguistics) established the foundations of NLP in the 1970s. They were curious about what these people were doing that made a real difference. Using a linguistic model (which they called, somewhat inaccurately, the 'Meta-model'), Bandler and Grinder began to analyse what each of those innovators said and did to help other people change, and assembled the fundamental principles of NLP. These were based on the essence of what seemed to be working for those effective therapists: the descriptions, practices, philosophies, and ways of being which they were using to great effect. Much emphasis was placed on the power that language had to change people.

Since then, NLP has been constantly revised, expanded and reinvented. Some practitioners and trainers along the way have absorbed NLP and then followed their inclinations and developed their own particular variation. For example, Tad James placed more emphasis on a particular metaphorical understanding of time and created Time Line Therapy™. Others have found practical applications for sports, health, education and business management. This is a common pattern of growth of any body of knowledge. Some NLP practitioners take a pragmatic view and claim that "Does it work?" is the only thing that matters. However, few have inquired into the underlying patterns and models from which the techniques and processes can be generated.

Some definitions of NLP

Given that people have their own preferred ways of understanding, you need a variety of answers. One approach is to look at an analytical definition of NLP, and explore the meaning of the three parts of Neuro-Linguistic Programming:

Neuro   The mind-body system and how it functions. Physiological and mental states. The nervous system through which you experience, interact with, and make sense of your world, through the sensory systems of vision, speaking and hearing, and through touch and feeling.

Linguistic The language you use to describe, categorise, and analyse your reality. How you make sense of your world and communicate your experience to others. How you can use language to create change in your own and others' models of the world.

Programming The thought patterns and habitual ways of perceiving and behaving. You learn to interpret the world based on your experience, according to your needs. You develop repeated sequences of behaviour and strategies that get you what you want, and create stories to explain those experiences. Because these are of your own making, it is possible to re-program them.

This definition was provided some time ago by Richard Bandler:

> NLP is an attitude and a methodology that leaves behind a trail of techniques.

That is, given the intention to change, you need both a particular attitude or state of mind (which involves curiosity and the capacity for self-reflection), and some effective practical strategies for intervention. Because people are creatures of habit, NLP has been able to identify a number of general processes and techniques which are consistent and effective in creating change for a variety of people.

Developing curiosity

Richard Bandler has suggested that an essential quality of being an NLP practitioner is that you are curious (he calls this 'wanton curiosity') about yourself, your talents, your expertise, how you do what you do. Curiosity is not something new to learn. Appreciating your natural curiosity is a way of restoring your sense of wonder about the world. Curiosity is often socialised out us when we are children, and is negatively associated with 'poking your nose in where you're not meant to go'. As a result, many people lead very incurious lives, in which they unquestioningly do what they are told, and keep their heads down so that no one will pick on them or mark them out as 'troublemakers'.

Here are some definitions from two experienced NLP trainers:

- NLP is about replicating success, achieving success consistently (John McWhirter).

- NLP is the answer to the question "How is it possible …?" (Eric Robbie).

Ask the question: "How can I …?" and notice the kinds of answers that then present themselves to you. Because the *process* of change is hidden, you are constantly going to be surprised.

The *How* question is a key piece of NLP thinking. If you know *how* change happens then you can use that understanding to change yourself and improve your own capabilities. Being curious means becoming intensely inquisitive about how other people achieve excellence in what they do. To find out "How do they do that?" you need to discover as much as you can about their model of the world. You need to pay attention to their state, their intentions, their motivation, to how they are in themselves, to what they do, and to what they say. As you gather this information about them, you can try those things for yourself, and begin to find out what it is like thinking and behaving in that way. When you model someone else, you begin to get a sense of their world, its expectations and consequences. Curiosity is the key that opens the door of your imagination. As you try on someone else's way of being, you experience how things could be different.

If you are working with other people to help them change, you need to be curious about how their thinking contributes to their capabilities, and to their current stuckness. By also wondering about what they want instead, the direction their desires take them, you can begin to formulate ways of assisting them in shifting towards their desired alternative reality.

Self-reflection

Self-reflection is the ability to stand back from yourself and notice what you are doing and thinking. In NLP this is referred to as 'going meta', or seeing things from a 'meta-perspective'. (The prefix *meta* comes from the Greek word meaning *across, with, beside, after*.) You act as if you are taking a mental step back and shifting your point of view by thinking outside of the existing context and going into an 'objective' observer mode (see Chapter Eleven). A physical way of doing this was described in Exercise 3.2.

Exercise 4.1: Reflecting

Use the technique described in Exercise 3.2 at any time for taking 'time-out' to consider what you have been thinking or learning, or when you are getting 'bogged down' in a subject and need a fresh perspective. Simply stop whatever you are doing (however busy you are) and decide to reflect on what is going on.

For example, you might want to find your own latest ideas about NLP. Adopt an observer state, either mentally, or by shifting your physical position. Appreciate your existing knowledge about NLP and briefly consider the history of how you obtained your present wisdom. You may find it useful to consider:

- How would you define NLP right now?
- Complete the sentence: "The purpose of NLP is to …"
- What has NLP enabled you to do that you probably would not have done otherwise?
- What are the key points, the most important things about NLP for you?

- What does NLP currently mean for you?
- What does learning about NLP remind you of? What metaphors come to mind?
- How would you see your own use of NLP developing in the future?

Answer any other relevant questions that you can think of in this curiosity-based investigative role. Give yourself time to get clarification. You may not get answers directly; they may just pop into your mind at an odd moment. Simply breaking the routine creates an opportunity for new ideas, change. When you have some, return to your previous activity with your new understanding.

Another definition

A broadly disseminated definition of NLP is:

> NLP is the study of the structure of subjective experience.

The emphasis here is on 'structure'. (Sometimes this definition refers to *structures* in the plural in order to draw attention to the fact that each person has their own way of structuring reality.) 'Structure' is a metaphor belonging to Sensory-mode thinking. The term 'subjective' refers to the way that each individual structures their own reality, based on their personal history.

This definition presupposes that people organise their experience into meaningful patterns or stories. Even though we do not know how they do this, we can be curious about the results—their model of the world. It is in this interpretation of reality that people get stuck, because it has become their 'truth': "This is the way things are!" To get out of the impasse, it is necessary to dismantle that 'truth', restructure, reevaluate and reinterpret the experience. Doing that leads to a change in behaviour, and in that person's understanding of their reality, based in the Free Will positions of Social and Mythic-mode thinking.

The Computer metaphor

One metaphorical definition of NLP is that it is 'the software of the brain'. This is based on the metaphor of 'the brain is a computer'. The composite metaphor of 'software' carries the ideas of being a *program* or set of instructions written by someone in order to achieve certain ends, and of *soft* in the sense that it is flexible and can be changed. However, only certain aspects of the metaphor will be appropriate. For example, the brain appears to be better able to deal with 'malfunctions' than a computer does; it neither 'crashes' nor requires replacement parts. However, the programming aspect—providing a series of processing instructions—does have a parallel, though there are vast differences between conventional computer programming, which is a strongly Sensory-mode activity, and working with the human brain, which is more systemic and holistic. We need other kinds of metaphors for understanding the brain.

The Building Block metaphor

Developing the 'structure' metaphor, we can perceive NLP as being akin to a set of building blocks, which can be assembled in a huge variety of ways. Each individual thus builds up a model of the world in their own unique configuration. Having a 'modular' structure, it is always possible to take the components apart and reassemble them in a different arrangement.

No model or structure is 'correct' or 'absolute'. A model is only an attempt at a description, and at some point it will fail. We know when this happens because we will get stuck (or use some other metaphor for describing failure). Our choices are then limited, and we are unable to predict what will happen because of our inadequate beliefs and limited understanding of the world. However, by breaking apart the old structure (it doesn't have to be done neatly or systematically, it can just be scrambled) we will make meaning of the new configuration and experience a new way of interpreting the world. Every new structure brings with it new associations, further choices and opportunities. To explain it, we will create a new story that incorporates our revised perceptions of how things appear to us now.

This 'building block' metaphor offers an account of our learning and development. From birth, we are making incremental shifts, adding blocks to our pile of knowledge. However, we do not just build bigger and bigger heaps. We organise our knowledge, our 'closures', into structures, by finding similarities, organising principles, explanatory schemata and so on. We understand that some terms are more general than others: the names of classes, rather than individuals. For example, young children take great delight in visiting the park and feeding the ducks. When a child learns to speak, they are just 'ducks'. Over time children learn to discriminate various kinds of birds, such as mallard, moorhen, coot; the males from the females; the residents from the migratory. Each new piece of learning depends upon previous knowledge. In this way, your model of the world expands. At any time, all you know is the accumulated knowledge built upon layers and layers of previous understanding. Each version of reality then becomes your 'truth': "This is the way things are." But it is true only temporarily. The learning process is open-ended; there is always more to know.

As you continue to learn, you develop expertise in certain areas, which means you have the ability to differentiate details, and describe differences which other people who do not have the same background experience literally cannot see. For example, if you are taken to see a football match but have no idea about how the game is played, then all you see are people running around, some of whom get to kick a ball more often than others. It is only through making generalisations about your experience that you learn to perceive the moves and tactics, to recognise when a player is 'off-side' and so on. Then you can appreciate the subtleties of the game.

You can choose to restructure your building-block edifice at any time. A particular structure you enjoyed in the past may become obsolete or irrelevant as you explore new interests. You take the wisdom from that creation, and use your growing expertise to form new patterns and stories that suit your present context. You may never challenge the truths you created in the past until you realise that they are contributing to your present stuckness.

Then you need to rewrite that story in the light of your current knowledge, and rearrange the building blocks to create another model of the world which offers you more choice, and better understanding.

Story metaphors

You can also use stories, metaphors and analogies to explain the basic change process. For example, most people are familiar with the movie *The Wizard of Oz*. It has been around since 1939, and each new generation of children gets to see it. In the previous chapter, a key metaphor of change was making the transition from one state to another. In *The Wizard of Oz*, Dorothy moves from the stifling grey world of Kansas, which symbolises being stuck in a place she is unhappy with, to the very different and colourful Munchkinland which offers adventure, new people, new thinking, and so on. This altered state represents choice: the people look different, and things happen in magical ways. You could use this story as a metaphorical way of talking about the purpose of NLP: to help people move from one reality to another; from being stuck to having choice.

Magical definitions and transformations

In the early days, NLP was perceived as 'magical'. Bandler & Grinder wrote *The Structure of Magic*; their *Frogs Into Princes* (1979) also alludes to magic. Many subsequent books by other writers also use this word. Judging from the first chapter of *The Structure of Magic*, the notion of magic is prominent in Bandler & Grinder's thinking. They quote the psychotherapist Sheldon Kopp in *Guru* (1971:146) referring to the magic of Fritz Perls. Bandler & Grinder (1975:5) begin *The Structure of Magic* by quoting the German philosopher Hans Vaihinger (1852–1933), who wrote about:

... operations of an almost mysterious character, which run counter to ordinary procedure in a more or less paradoxical way. They are methods which give an onlooker the impression of magic if he be not himself initiated or equally skilled in the mechanism.

H. Vaihinger (1924: 11) The Philosophy of As If

A more frequently cited example of 'magic' comes from Arthur C Clarke's Third Law in *Profiles of the Future* (1962, 1982: 36): "Any sufficiently advanced technology is indistinguishable from magic." In other words, when we are amazed or surprised by technology, we perceive it as magical. To the uninitiated, technology can appear quite magical if you are unfamiliar with the mechanical or scientific principles of how things work. However, when you understand the principles underpinning that technology, it becomes more ordinary.

Although every metaphor has its limitations, that has not prevented the notion of perceiving NLP as a 'technology' from being taken beyond its limits to produce some philosophically naive notions. The technology metaphor might suggest that it might eventually be possible to have a sufficiently detailed mechanical understanding of how the mind works, and it would therefore be magical no longer. However, human beings are not just mechanical or biochemical devices, and we cannot have a 'technology of mind'. Knowing exactly how change occurs has to remain a mystery for us. All explanations, however scientific they seem, are only ever metaphors or stories. What could be construed as magical is the linguistic power of NLP, in the way that language can reframe perceptions, influence actions, and transform meaning.

Magical thinking is often linked to Mythic mode. In this sense, the magic applies to the ability to reprogram or reconstruct reality, or to the effects of rewriting the myth. When, as a consequence, the behaviour changes, this may seem magical in that it is unexpected and often transformative. For the person who is stuck, what matters is that they can now move again, they have choices.

Pragmatic approaches

"NLP is 'what works'."

"If it works, it's NLP!"

"NLP is modeling excellence."

These broad definitions relate to the modeling aspect of NLP. Bandler and Grinder introduce this concept in *The Structure of Magic I* (1975: 6):

> ... we would like to present the simple overview of the human processes out of which we have created these tools. We call this process modeling.

By modeling how the people who demonstrate excellence and achieve success do what they do, NLP has been able to reveal the relevant strategies in their thinking and behaviour. The assumption is that it is possible to emulate anyone's abilities by developing appropriate models and language for describing their beliefs, attitudes and frames of mind, and then using them for yourself. This has worked to the extent that it is possible to improve your performance in a number of skilled behaviours. However, to find out how people achieve outstanding performances in more general abilities, such as being a successful entrepreneur or a charismatic leader, is not so straightforward. Although it is possible to observe and copy certain *behaviours*, this may be insufficient for changing your own way of being in the world. If it were that easy, we could all 'think and grow rich' and be millionaires by now, as there are numerous accounts of how rich people achieved their wealth. People are more than just their behaviours. They also have value-systems, attitudes, and so on. The NLP focus on small-chunk details is useful at the level of behaviour, but leaves many gaps when describing the whole person. Using some big chunk concept of models of the world (such as those described in this book) might offer a definite improvement in this endeavour, although this may still not give us The Compleat Modeler—the *how-tos* for modeling excellence.

You can model people on the level of Body by using the evidence of your senses: what you can see, hear and feel; and at the level of Mind by inquiring at a cognitive level into what they are thinking, focusing on, paying attention to, expecting to happen. However, much of what might be useful is not open to observation, and we have to rely on their verbal descriptions, which are open to bias and imprecision. Or it could be that the only way of achieving excellence is to find your own way of doing it. Having the benefits of others' wisdom helps, but in the end, it is your own journey towards understanding that is more important.

The point about definitions ...

There can be no definitive single description of NLP. Any definition, although giving the illusion of being 'eternal', is really only a snapshot view of an evanescent process, it vanishes like vapour even as we look at it. Essentially, as a practitioner of NLP, you will be creating your own definitions, finding what works for you, finding your own way of explaining your own understanding of the nature of reality at that particular time. The more you make NLP your own, the more it will work for you, and the more enjoyment you will have in using it.

Having looked at several definitions, you may find it a useful exercise to think about the challenge in terms of the Four Realities way of thinking. This will increase your familiarity with the essential nature of these worldviews, test your flexibility in using them, and provide explanations that will be satisfying to the range of people you will encounter.

Using the Four Realities model:

[U] **What it is:** The definitions, principles, presuppositions that underpin NLP, based on current definitions of the terms, jargon and concepts.

[Se] **How things happen:** An analysis of the elements of NLP, the techniques and processes, the ways of sequencing behaviour in order to achieve goals. The strategies that people who are deemed 'excellent' use consistently for achieving success.

[So] **What matters:** evaluating the emotional impact of change on people, finding out the motivation that drives action. An assessment of someone's values and priorities in terms of setting desired outcomes.

[M] **What might happen if …:** forecasting the future, considering and exploring the consequences of intervening in the world. What NLP enables you to do, and the consequences of that: What might happen if you were to intervene in the world in certain ways.

Some metaphors, analogies, stories that indicate what NLP is like, and how it has been applied. For example, using the *Wizard of Oz* story suggests that change is like the whirlwind transporting someone from Kansas into the Land of Oz. Using the metaphor of 'writing the story of your life, and then editing it' NLP enables you to create a future that turns out how you want it.

Over and above this, you also need to find a way of integrating and balancing all aspects and parts of yourself so that you are fully aligned with whatever you perceive your purpose to be.

Chapter Five

The Philosophy and Presuppositions of NLP

Reality is contradictory. And it's paradoxical. If there's any one word—if you had to pick one word to describe the nature of the universe—I think that word would be paradox. That's true at the subatomic level, right through sociological, psychological, philosophical levels on up to cosmic levels.

From an interview with Tom Robbins in January Magazine

A philosophical understanding of NLP

How does NLP work? Is its methodology coherent, logical, in line with current best thinking on learning and personal change? To answer these questions, we need to know a little of the philosophical foundations of NLP, as that will enable us to assess how well its formative ideas hold up. We can also see what NLP has in common with other disciplines such as learning, education, cognitive psychology, various kinds of therapy and so on.

One way of elucidating the theoretical underpinnings is by examining NLP's 'Presuppositions'. These Presuppositions cover the principles, values, and beliefs about how human beings function, communicate, and change. These Presuppositions were formulated during the early days of NLP, and are listed and discussed in many NLP practitioner trainings and books (for example, Bodenhamer & Hall, 1999: 61–86). However, some of the statements have become slogans, which suggests that perhaps they are being used unthinkingly.

Even though NLP has things to say about human understanding, during its lifetime there has been little or no mention by NLP practitioners of the various debates that philosophers have engaged in, such as Realism, Structuralism, Postmodernism and so on. There has been little discussion on the problems associated with assessing competence in NLP, even though NLP can be seen in part as a form of competence-based training.

Many practitioners and developers take a pragmatic approach and treat the Presuppositions as useful guidelines about how to 'do' NLP. As a result, they end up with a collection of stories, rules and heuristics (rules of thumb or practical short-cuts formulated through trial and error) which they have accumulated through experience. This has produced a multitude of elegant change sequences and detailed processes, but there has been relatively little analysis at the 'big chunk' level of the philosophical basis of their ideas. Every NLP practitioner will inevitably bring their own philosophical and spiritual beliefs into their practice or their teaching, but these may neither be made explicit, nor clearly defined.

If you are in the business of advocating a system of attitudes, beliefs and methodologies for producing profound changes in other people's lives, then it is important to assess your own beliefs, thinking and communication. The deeper philosophical issues do need to be examined, otherwise you might find yourself using a homespun wisdom which is internally inconsistent, based on incompatible principles and dubious beliefs. However, providing a comprehensive account of the philosophical underpinnings of NLP is beyond the scope of this book. Instead, I will point out some of the relevant ideas as they appear in the Presuppositions, and offer alternatives when they are found wanting.

The philosophical basis of NLP

In Chapter 1 of *The Structure of Magic I*, Bandler & Grinder (1975) offer some indications of the source of their ideas. Again they quote Hans Vaihinger:

> It must be remembered that the object of the world of ideas as a
> whole is not the portrayal of reality—this would be an utterly
> impossible task—but rather to provide us with an instrument for
> finding our way about more easily in the world.
>
> *H. Vaihinger, The Philosophy of As If, p. 15*

Humanity is forever attempting to understand the nature of its
reality: Is it possible for us to truly know and understand the universe? Over thousands of years innumerable solutions have been
proposed. In the scientific community especially, there is a commonly held belief that final explanations *are* possible, that eventually we will construct a universal theory of everything. The
philosopher Hilary Lawson (2001a: xxvii), with a hint of irony,
calls this quest *The Great Project*, which "in its unmodified form
has consisted in the belief that it is possible to make steps, however small and painstaking, towards a true, final, and complete
account of the world".

The simple answer to "Can we have complete understanding of
our universe?" is that it is not possible. There are no ultimate theories of everything. We cannot ever know the true nature of the
universe. We only experience the universe through our own
unique perception, which is based to a large extent upon the accu-
mulating knowledge and understanding of our experience.
Lawson explains why such a quest is bound to end in a self-refer-
ential paradox, and proposes a different kind of account of how
we make meaning of reality, in terms of what he calls 'a theory of
closure'. This is similar to the building block and story metaphors
described in Chapter Four: we create many levels of closure,
which we understand as stories. Because each person has structured their experience differently, using a different set of building
blocks—'closures'—their universe is unique to them. (For a brief
summary, see Lawson, 2001b.) Lawson's philosophical ideas provide an illuminating insight into how human perception and
thinking can be explained without resorting to, or falling into the
traps of traditional philosophical thinking. Lawson's philosophical argument, although mentally demanding, is relevant to the
understanding of NLP.

People describe their reality through language, and the nature of
the relationship between language and reality has produced
intense debate in philosophical and psychological circles for

many centuries. In this matter, the founders of NLP appear to have 'hedged their bets' and have adopted a mixture of philosophical approaches to the nature of language. However, there are some patterns which can be discerned which influence the early writing of Bandler and Grinder. The view they adopt is based on the notion put forward independently by Jeremy Bentham (1748–1832) and Hans Vaihinger (1852–1933), suggesting that all our attempts at explaining the universe are, to use Vaihinger's term, 'useful fictions'. This is part of his philosophy of 'as if': if you imagine that something would be beneficial to you, you act *as if* it were true. This also fits with the notion that our models of the world are based on stories. Unfortunately, NLP developers have been inconsistent in their linguistic understanding, and can be found adopting a Realist philosophy, which holds that science does indeed provide truthful descriptions of nature, and assumes that ordinary objects that we perceive through the senses, such as books and chairs, have an existence independent of anyone perceiving them.

Practical philosophy

The philosophy of the Four Realities model (see Figure 2.7) is concerned with the cognitive spaces constructed from two dimensions or polarities. In one sense these are arbitrary 'useful fictions', but they are also familiar and useful in our way of understanding our humanity. The top half of the diagram indicates moving towards a deterministic view; the bottom half, more towards a belief in free will. In Unitary-mode there is no choice; in Sensory-mode there are alternatives but they are not under your control. On the other hand, in Social and Mythic modes you have the freedoms to evaluate and to alter your perception in any way you choose.

One of the key presuppositions of NLP is that 'reality is all made-up', that every individual creates their own reality or model of the world, which is unique to them. This is one way of understanding the key presupposition underpinning NLP, the notion that no version of reality is 'true' in any absolute or ideal sense; each version is one person's current thinking about their own life experience. A fundamental belief held in NLP is that you are always in a position to change your worldview (even if you believe that that is not possible) because you created it in the first place. A worldview comprises your current collection of beliefs, stories, and explanations about how things work; it is continually being updated as you learn from your experience. Even if you think of your worldview as fixed, by questioning "Has it always been like this?" you will discover that how it appears now is not the way it has always appeared. Because it is your *perception* of reality which creates limitations or difficulties, NLP works by changing those perceptions.

Although a worldview takes on a sense of truth, permanence, indivisibility, this is more a result of the language we use to describe our experience. Although it is useful to talk in terms of things and define categories, and so on, this is a function of our thinking, rather than a description of reality. Recent philosophical thinking rejects the notion that things can be defined uniquely (Lawson 2001a: xl). Nothing is uniquely identifiable, one and the same, as there are always alternative meanings for experience. Unitary perception sees a seamless holistic reality, whereas in Sensory mode there are alternative ways of perceiving things: nothing is uniquely defined; everything can be analysed into parts, chunked up or down, seen in terms of different classifications. There are multiple descriptions of everything. For example, a chair is not simply a chair, but can be seen as furniture, wood, a Chippendale and so on. The chair consists of parts (seat, arms, back), and also a part of a greater whole, such as a constituent of an auditorium, or reframed into other interpretations. Other modes of thinking change the meaning of the fixity of Unitary reality.

The NLP Presuppositions

The NLP Presuppositions are stated using abstract nouns or nominalizations such as 'communication' or 'failure', and metaphors such as 'map' and 'filter', and these need to be examined. How appropriate are these metaphors? Do they help people

77

understand themselves? How well do they match the way people actually think and behave, or do they merely offer alternative perceptions which will trap people into thinking this is the 'truth'? If so, you may be advocating change techniques which in the long term could prove detrimental to clients. One consequence would be that having led them down a blind alley, they become stuck within a different yet limiting belief system. For example, the psychiatrist R D Laing promulgated the view that in some way parents were 'responsible' for schizophrenia in their children. Blaming the parents condemned them to a lifetime of guilt about which they could do very little. Therefore, in order to avoid such problems, we need to be clear about the basis of NLP and why it employs the kinds of change techniques that it does.

No philosophical explanation of human perception is 'correct'. There are an infinite variety of descriptions of reality. However, using the four major distinctions enables us to think more productively. The model suggests that all four general points of view (and their combinations) will be encountered, and all play their part in making sense of the world. People are constantly and deliberately changing their perceptions. For example, updating their beliefs, rewriting their explanatory stories, revising their paradigms. Thinking about your own life, it is easy to see that you have done this. For example, most adults do not believe in the childhood realities of tooth-fairies, or in the ursine dangers of walking on cracks in the pavement. When such stories and beliefs no longer support a reality system, they fall away. As you mature, you rewrite your personal manual for living. Beliefs adapt to meet new circumstances.

Exercise 5.1: 'Reunited'

Given the relative ease of contacting old school-friends using the internet, you may have caught up with people you have not seen for many years. If so, then based on your updated knowledge, consider:

- How has your memory of your schooldays changed?
- How has your perception of your class-mates altered?
- To what extent have the personal relationships changed?

As you think about your school-days, and recall your own memories of that time, you may find that in discussing what happened with others, there are discrepancies between your accounts. You may have forgotten some things completely, or different events may have merged into a composite. You may even have 'remembered' things that never happened, perhaps prompted by other people"s stories, or your own dreams and desires. These different versions of the 'truth'. suggest different experiences at the time, or that your memories and beliefs have changed in the intervening years. You may have found that you did not recognise some of your erstwhile friends because your memories and the present reality are at odds. (If you discover some unresolved problems with certain relationships, and you would like to change them, then the Metamirror process, in Chapter Twelve, will enable you to do this.)

So how would you describe what happened in the process of forgetting? How does 'memory' work? Human abilities such as memory are usually couched in terms of metaphors which have varying degrees of utility. If you assume a storage metaphor then the mind becomes an archive or library. 'Forgetting' may then mean that certain data has been 'lost' or is temporarily 'inaccessible', or that the catalogue entry is missing. If you think of information as flowing, then your memories could have dried up or evaporated over the years. However, the mind is not a library, and information is not a fluid. Although using these metaphors is useful at times, they do not tell you how memory works. Neither does combining the library and liquid metaphors produce further enlightenment. Therefore, recognising the limitations of a metaphor is important. When a metaphor doesn't work, you can always find or invent another one. In other words, there are no limitations to perception; you can reperceive your reality in any way you choose.

In the same way that mixing metaphors can result in bizarre images, mixing philosophical realities can also produce mental confusion. This would suggest that we may need to take care when using certain NLP terms and metaphors in order to avoid mismatching other people's models of reality.

Representation

Finding ways of explaining 'perception' has given rise to a number of mutually incompatible theories and metaphors. In particular, the assumption that there is a knowable reality separate from us, of which we construct a 'representation' in our minds. The 'representation' metaphor suggests a Realist philosophical stance by assuming that there is a separate 'objective' reality of which we create our own mental version or depiction. Because the mind is creating a 'copy' of the world, that implies that somehow it can be more or less 'correct' or truthful in that perception. A similar Realist position also arises in Bandler and Grinder's explanation of the language Meta-model, in which the 'deep structure' is taken to be some kind of 'objective' truth about the world which the speaker is 'representing' using the words they utter—the 'surface structure'.

The term 'representation systems' is a cornerstone of NLP. The phrase refers to the ability to perceive the world in terms of physiologically-based sensory systems: what you see, hear, feel, taste and smell. There are actually more than five sensory systems in the human body, but the notion of having five senses is common in our culture. In terms of working with people to change their perception, using this familiar notion is appropriate. Paying attention to the three main senses—visual, auditory and kinesthetic (VAK)—will usually suffice for most purposes.

I prefer to use the term 'imagination' instead of 'representation'. Imagining is the process of constructing an image of the world based on your current experience, your accumulation of closures, and can be a completely novel way of perceiving reality. An image does not imply that it is a copy or representation of anything else.

Perceptual filters

A common metaphor for understanding perception treats information as a fluid: information flows through channels, it may swamp you, or merely trickle or percolate through an organisation. It can leak out, or even cause your brain to become rusty—which is a kind of forgetting. However, when this metaphor fails, it can lead to philosophical confusion.

Using the perceptual filter metaphor, perception results from the imagined flow of information from the outside world, through the sensory channels, into the mind. If you want to avoid being deluged with information you need to have a dam or sluice as a way of limiting or screening what arrives. A 'filter' system will reduce the flow, and leave you with only what is relevant or important. This filter metaphor suggests some kind of gateway or entry point at which you can control the flow, and also that you have in place some rules or principles for selecting what comes through, so that you only get the information relating to your current needs. This metaphor presupposes some kind of 'objective reality' which you, through the process of filtering, manage to re-present in the mind as some kind of reduced, less complete version (because of all the information that was rejected), in the way that a model car may resemble an actual one, but is on a smaller scale, less detailed and with fewer features.

The notion of the mind controlling or filtering the flow of information appears to be rooted in the ancient Greek Atomistic theory, which proposed that perception is accomplished by the form (*eidola*) of objects entering the eye. (It seems that the Greeks were never totally clear about how perception worked. Euclid imagined a kind of 'scanning' metaphor, where rays of light (*pneuma*) were emitted from the eye to gain an impression of things. A modern version of this metaphor was used in the *Star Trek* TV series in the form of their various scanning devices.)

The poet and mystic William Blake used the filter metaphor in his poem *The Marriage of Heaven and Hell*:

> If the doors of perception were cleansed everything would appear to Man as it is: infinite. For man has closed himself up, till he sees all things through narrow chinks of his cavern.

The gateway metaphor also suggests some way of deciding what is to pass through. The writer Aldous Huxley used it in *The Doors of Perception* (1954). Huxley's view was that:

Each person is at each moment capable of remembering all that has ever happened to him and of perceiving everything that is happening everywhere in the universe. The function of the brain and nervous system is to protect us from being overwhelmed and confused by this mass of largely useless and irrelevant knowledge, by shutting out most of what we should otherwise perceive or remember at any moment, and leaving only that very small and special selection which is likely to be practically useful.

A diagram depicting the 'filtering' metaphor of perception occurs in James & Woodsmall (1988: 4) under the title of *The NLP Communication Model*, and this diagram has been repeated in many other NLP books and course materials ever since. (They also use the term 'filter' to refer to what are commonly known in NLP as *Metaprograms*.) This model seems to assume that people are more or less 'passive' recipients of information from the external world, rather than treating them as creators of their own experience who have the ability to choose what they pay attention to.

In my own experience, I am not aware of 'filtering' my experience. However, I am aware of how I am paying attention to the world. What I notice is influenced by my intention or need at the time, and is influenced by the background questions that I am interested in. For example, I am always checking my perceptions of the world to see if I can identify further examples of the Four Realities model. In other words, it is my desire which enables me to perceive certain kinds of things in the world, so to speak. I perceive the world using a particular 'frame' or mindset which produces certain kinds of closure according to my intentions.

The map is not the territory

"We actually made a map of the country, on the scale of a *mile to a mile!*"
"Have you used it much?" I enquired.
"It has never been spread out, yet," said Mein Herr: "the farmers objected; they said it would cover the whole country, and shut out the sunlight! So we now we use the country itself, as its own map, and I assure you it does nearly as well.

Lewis Carroll, Sylvie & Bruno

Another influential philosopher of the early part of the twentieth century was Count Alfred Korzybski. Bandler & Grinder (1975: 7) quote what has since become an NLP slogan, based on:

> ... important characteristics of maps should be noted. A map is not the territory it represents, but, if correct, it has a similar structure to the territory, which accounts for its usefulness ...
>
> *A. Korzybski, Science & Sanity, 4th Ed., 1958, pp. 58-60*

"The map is not the territory" seems easy to understand. A map is not the same as the landscape it relates to. It has abstracted and emphasized salient features and relationships for a specific purpose. Mental maps only offer a snapshot of one aspect of your reality at a particular time. Other illustrations of the Zen distinction between the Finger pointing at the Moon, and the Moon itself, point out that a thing and its name are not the same thing, with the corollaries, "Don't shoot the messenger" and "Don't eat the menu". Maps, messengers and menus are means to ends. They are useful for specific purposes, and guide your thinking and behaviour towards achieving your goals.

The metaphor of 'the map and the territory' acts as a useful reminder that people have created and are referring to aspects of their personal reality which is inevitably different from yours. An important presupposition is that people act as if their maps of reality are true. This is not to say that their map of the world is an absolute truth, but just a current model that guides their interventions in the world, a personal truth which is subject to change and evolution. The original statement has also been transformed into: "People respond to their map of reality, but not to reality itself." This has the corollary: "NLP is the art of changing these maps, not changing the reality." By changing your point of view or Perceptual Position (see Chapter Eleven), your understanding of reality changes, or, using this metaphor, your map of reality changes.

However, the implicit Realist position of the *map* and *representation* metaphors could lead you erroneously into assessing how 'accurate' someone's map of the world is, or how well it represents some kind of 'territory' or objective 'truth' which is 'out there'—and this is inconsistent with NLP's overall philosophy.

The initial challenge facing an NLP practitioner is the need to comprehend someone else's model of reality. Working with another person involves exploring their model of the world to elucidate its internal conflicts and inconsistent or limiting beliefs. However, if you are going to maintain rapport, remember that it is *their* world, which is meaningful for them. Part of the therapeutic process may be to indicate any incongruities to the client, or to find appropriate interventions that enable the client to examine and revise them. The hypnotherapist Milton Erickson suggested that you take what the client offers, rather than deny their reality because you need to be 'right' or because you do not understand how their model of the world works.

Some models of psychotherapy have been built around trying to make the client enter the therapist's model of the world. This is often difficult for the client to do, and generates resistance. If the therapist first enters the client's model of the world, it then becomes easier to see how that model works, and then, from an outside or visitor's position, as it were, offer ways for the client to change the way they perceive their reality.

Therefore, take a pragmatic stance and work with the metaphors the person gives you, and then take them to the limits—because at some point every metaphor will fail. For example, the psychotherapist Raj Persaud adopts an unconventional approach by working at the level of beliefs. He says (Persaud, 2003: 414):

> … I do not distract a patient from their delusion by asking them to examine the evidence; I distract them from the central idea by asking them to assess what the future may hold if their concepts are correct. If the natural consequences of their thinking raise their anxiety sufficiently, this will usually provide the necessary drive for a reconsideration of their philosophy.

His general strategy is to "consider their notions more earnestly than they do themselves, which is why I see implications they themselves have not considered." This is indeed a powerful way of changing someone's behaviour. In some contexts, then, it doesn't seem to matter whether the underlying rationale of someone's belief system makes sense to you, or accords with the best philosophical thinking, or not. What matters is matching the client's model of reality, and testing that to the point where it fails.

There is no failure, only feedback

What is your attitude towards failure and making mistakes? Believing that you have made a mistake affects your state, and could possibly lead to you making further mistakes. This presupposition shifts your thinking from judgmental and evaluative Social mode, to the factual and logical Sensory mode. A parallel shift comes from thinking "There is no *success*, only feedback"! It is a common piece of wisdom that we learn from our mistakes, not from our successes.

Tom Robbins, novelist:

> Success eliminates as many options as failure.

Bill Gates, founder of Microsoft:

> Success is a lousy teacher—it seduces smart people into thinking they can't lose.

The inventor Thomas Edison:

> Many of us grow up thinking of mistakes as bad, viewing errors as evidence of fundamental incapacity. This negative thinking pattern can create a self-fulfilling prophecy, which undermines the learning process. To maximise our learning it is essential to ask: "How can we get the most from every mistake we make?"

The Head of Sony, Akio Morito:

> It's OK to make a mistake, but don't make the same mistake twice!

Putting a positive spin on this, Richard Bandler says that "All results and behaviours are achievements, whether they are desired outcomes for a given task/context, or not." It is hard living in a culture of 'right first time' and never making mistakes (or at least, not getting caught). The inventor James Dyson made

5,127 prototypes before he got his cyclone vacuum cleaner to work. Thomas Edison tested a thousand filaments for his electric lightbulb before one would work successfully. His attitude was: "Results? Why, man, I have gotten lots of results! If I find 10,000 ways something won't work, I haven't failed. I am not discouraged, because every wrong attempt discarded is just one more step forward ...."

By removing all the emotional, evaluative responses to your actions, you can operate in a neutral, objective Sensory-mode analytical way, treating whatever happens as 'just information'. (You could also see this as an example of Visual-Kinesthetic (V–K) dissociation: you keep a clear separation between your (kinesthetic) emotional responses (Social mode) and your (visual) perceptions of what happened (Sensory mode) in order to maintain an effective state when dealing with fears and phobias and so on.) Reducing the emotional charge or abandoning your judgmental attitude enables you to become more objective, and probably more resourceful. Then you can find uses for that information and work out alternative strategies for achieving your goal. It is also worth shifting to Mythic mode to explore some of the *What if*s, because otherwise you may be closing down options too soon because you do not know the consequences of your actions. The inventor Edwin Land offers such a move to Mythic-mode thinking: "A mistake is an event, the full benefit of which has not yet been turned to your advantage." Bandler & Grinder (1982: 33) say something similar: "... any time you fail, there's an unprecedented opportunity for you to learn something that you wouldn't otherwise notice."

Exercise 5.2: Attitude towards mistakes

Whatever you call those things that happen which do not give the results you wanted (mistakes, errors, failings ...), what is your attitude towards them? How do you respond?

- "Avoid them at all costs."
- "Bury them as quickly as possible."
- "I'll never do that again!"
- "They're just part of the learning process, and to be welcomed."

- "That was interesting. I wonder what it means."
- "I need time to work out what happened so that I can make improvements."
- "They're not 'mistakes'—just 'opportunities for learning something new'.

Surfers, skateboarders, acrobats, and so on, are happy to practise tricks and manoeuvres often for hours on end, and it would seem that they do not entertain the notion of failure. With any sports or perform-ance skills, you need to *practise* until you achieve competence, or move towards excellence.

If you work in a culture which has the expectation that you should always be right and know everything, then how do you deal with those impossible demands? One way is to switch off judgment, and 'obey orders' in Unitary mode. When things go wrong, you could attribute blame to other people (or 'world events') claiming that errors are evidence of lack of talent, or poor genetic material, or sinister planetary conjunctions. Such an approach is limiting because it is through making mistakes that you learn best. By wanting to avoid failure at all costs, you never get to try anything new, and that means no learning. When things don't work, rather than dwelling on your immediate emotional response, far better to engage your curiosity and analyse your plans, and think through "How else could I do X?", or use your imagination to explore some alternative scenarios to find out "What would happen if ...?"

One attribute of genius may be the ability to persist with mistakes; but deliberately making mistakes is not necessarily going to make you a genius. What matters is how you respond to what happens, and this will be reflected in your commitment to find out, to learn, and to understand. As you continue learning, you will find paths that become boring, fizzle out into dead ends or go off in direc-tions you no longer want to explore at this particular time. Because it is easy to become disheartened along the way, you need a strong vision or clear goal which will remind you of what you are working towards, and will revitalise your efforts.

The 'feedback' metaphor comes from the Sensory realm of mechanical engineering. Originally applied to engineering and heating systems, it had little to do with human communication. However, feedback became associated with the response you got resulting from your actions and interventions in the world. It has also become a euphemism for criticism or an unwelcome response.

If one person can, anyone can

NLP has an egalitarian attitude, and barring physiological impairment, assumes that every person is capable of being the best. Although this is unrealistic, it still provides a positive spur to be better than you currently are. We could all agree that there is always room for improvement. NLP would further claim that by modeling some other person's excellent performance, it would become possible for anyone else to achieve excellence in a similar way. This is not proven. However, adopting a Sensory-mode analytical mindset, the argument runs: "If one person can do something, it is possible to model it and teach it to others. However, you may need to break the task down into small enough chunks." This kind of reductionist approach may work well for some tasks, but is not universal.

There is more to 'excellence' than just a set of performance skills. It may be necessary to have information relating to the other cognitive reality modes, such as how well someone gets on with others, how they think creatively, and so on, together with a spiritual understanding of what they are engaged in. In other words, although a task and outcome orientation may be sufficient for some basic tasks, modeling someone's overall capability requires a more holistic view. You need to understand what is happening from as many points of view as possible in order to reproduce the activity sufficiently accurately. But even then, you cannot be sure that you will find the key piece (the *key-stone* being the wedge-shaped stone that completes the arch and holds it up—if that metaphor is appropriate). For example, you may be able to analyse how a car functions by examining its components, or by taking it to pieces, but you may not be able to build your own car from scratch, nor really understand the function of the driver, why people want to own cars in the first place, or why they are willing to spend so much time and money on them.

Basically, this Presupposition works as a simple injunction to do better. However, it raises wide-ranging philosophical issues when fully expanded.

The meaning of your communication is the response that you get

This is quoted in Bandler & Grinder (1982: 34). They go on to say: "Most people don't think that way at all. They believe that they know what the meaning of their communication is, and that if somebody else doesn't realise it, it's the other person's fault." I have heard this Presupposition being yelled as a term of abuse at another person who was having difficulty getting their point across! You want the other person to respond to you, and yet they don't. They blithely continue doing whatever they were doing before. You call it 'not listening'; they think you are being 'difficult'.

This Presupposition is a reminder that you need to notice your listener's response. It is the feedback that counts. The attitude is that you want to communicate to them to the best of your ability, to convey what is in your mind into their minds. This is a daunting task at the best of times. There is little point in adopting the Unitary-mode view that 'words mean what it says in the dictionary' or complain: "Why don't you understand? I'm using plain English!" Instead of blaming them for their inadequacies in making sense of your language, take it upon yourself to make it easy for them to understand what you want them to hear. You need to know something of their preferences in receiving linguistic information, and something of their experience, because much of the time you cannot be sure of the effect your communication is having. Misunderstandings are common: they may not know the meaning of the words you use; their state may affect their ability to hear what you are saying. You don't know whether other people will understand what you are doing or saying, or how they will make meaning of your intervention. You can be sure that they will interpret what you say according to their own model of the world, and to complete the picture (in their imagination) they will fill in the gaps to make a coherent story—or give up, bewildered.

The more attention you pay to how they respond, the better you will become as a communicator.

Therefore, regard what you see by way of response as 'feedback' or 'evidence of your ability to communicate what you intended'. Even no response is a response, and might suggest that you choose to do something different.

You cannot not communicate

This Presupposition addresses the fact that people, as long as they are alive, are expressing intention—even though this may be indifference or inaction (an intention to stay the same). Understanding other people includes learning to 'read between the lines' and drawing conclusions based on the evidence of their actions. We infer others' intentions because we are used to interpreting as stories the various patterns of behaviour that people engage in.

Even though you may think that you can remain 'neutral', other people will inevitably derive meaning from your behaviour according to their model of the world. The actual words you use to communicate will be accompanied by nonverbal signals. These can be deliberate or habitual gestures and facial expressions. Trying to suppress your body-language is almost impossible, and other people will notice your involuntary movements. This is referred to as 'leakage'.

Albert Mehrabian's 7% 38% 55%

This is one of the prevailing myths, not only in NLP but in communication seminars in general. There have even been television advertisements quoting these numbers. The myth continues in NLP despite explanations of where the figures came from (for example, Smallwood, 1997: 13).

Mehrabian has commented:

> This work of mine has received considerable attention in the literature. *Silent Messages* contains a detailed discussion of my findings on inconsistent and consistent messages of feelings and attitudes (and the differential importance of verbal vs. nonverbal cues) on pages 75 to 80.
>
> Total Liking = 7% Verbal Liking + 38% Vocal Liking + 55% Facial Liking
>
> Please note that this and other equations regarding differential importance of verbal and nonverbal messages were derived from experiments dealing with communications of feelings and attitudes (i.e. like-dislike). Unless a communicator is talking about their feelings or attitudes, these equations are not applicable.

There is value in the notion that non-verbal communication (body-language and tonality) is very important, often more so than the words themselves, but the numbers are spurious.

Every behaviour has a positive intention

Similarly: People make the best choices they can, do the best they can, given the choices they believe are available to them. They act according to their model of the world, and act as though it is effective, it works. This is stated in Bandler & Grinder (1979: 137).

You may not understand why someone else is doing what they do, because it is at variance with your way of doing things. Become curious and gather information about their intentions, their expectations of what should happen. In other words, find out how their model of the world works. Instead of thinking of behaviour as 'wrong', 'irrational' or 'futile', NLP assumes that people are doing the best they can within the limitations of their worldview. Is there any reason to suppose that people would not want to do their best? This presupposition presumes that people act purposefully, even though what they want differs from your notion of good, beneficial or desirable.

Your challenge is then to elicit their reason or purpose for doing what they do (but be cautious about asking *Why* questions—see Chapter Nine). They may not be aware of what this intention is until you ask. If you assume that there is some kind of eventual benefit, then find out what it is. Even if they appear to be set on a course of self-destruction, there could also be some 'higher' purpose or positive gain. For example, killing yourself could be interpreted as a way of achieving 'peace of mind' if you do not have other options open to you. If the eventual benefit would result in harm or pain, then once you know what they are trying to achieve, it becomes possible to help them find other ways of achieving it.

Be tenaciously curious until you get to the desired end result (for example, see Bandler & Grinder, 1982: 148–151). Ask: "What is your intention in doing this?" Each time they provide an answer, ask a further question along the lines of "And what would that do for you?" or "What would be the point of that?" If they give answers which suggest avoiding something negative or unpleasant, then ask them to switch the polarity and provide you with a positive spin. "OK, that is what you *don't* want, so what *do* you actually want?" If you continue to ask questions about someone's intentions, you eventually arrive at big chunk generalisations about their ultimate desires—which are often positive expressions of human existence.

This could be seen as a Mythic-mode shift. Asking "What happens next?" is a way of extending the current story into the future. To find an answer, they enter the realms of their imagination and clarify their long-term goals, wants, and desires. Having such a personal vision then acts as a spur to finding ways of achieving them.

Actors are sometimes asked to take on the role of the villain, or a character who is perceived by an audience as 'evil' or 'wicked'. However, if an actor tries to act 'villainously' or behave 'wickedly', they will come across as inauthentic. Regardless of anyone's opinion about the morality of their intentions, the villain has to believe that what they are doing is right, and is in accord with a coherent worldview. To be believable you have to behave as though every action is for the best, otherwise you will appear incongruent.

Most learning and change takes place at the unconscious level

Bandler & Grinder (1979: 135). This is a corollary of the statement that we cannot know how we change, only notice the consequences of doing so. This was covered in Chapter Two.

People already have all the resources they need to change

Bandler & Grinder (1979: 137) also point out that these resources have to be seen as being available in the current context. Too often, people compartmentalise their lives, and need to be prompted to think in terms of transferring their talents and skills to other contexts in which they would be appropriate.

Resources

> The plan of the town may change but the location of its wells remains.
> The water in the well never disappears ….
> *I Ching: Hexagram #48 The Well*

Accepting this presupposition suggests that you have the personal power to access within you whatever you need in order to create or achieve what you want. This term 'resource' is usually unspecified in NLP. My vague definition is: a resource is whatever else you need at the time—a positive state, a 'story that works'—that will enable you to take the next step. You act resourcefully when you know that you have the ability to resolve your own problems using your own wisdom.

How do you find resources? First, acknowledge your own abilities, skills, knowledge and creativity. You could metaphorically think of resources as coming from that domain of universal awareness which I refer to as Spirit. Adopting this point of view gives you an overview, so that you can reflect on the issue, what is going on, and have access to your intuition, your memories, your own wisdom. You ask: "What do I need?" and you notice the answer your unconscious mind provides. If you ask someone to 'find a resource', they will do it in their own way, trusting their intuition to come up with just the thing they require at that moment.

When you ask for a resource, it is as though your mind, which is working in your best interests, will produce whatever it wants you to think about consciously. The process of finding such resources which match certain specified criteria, such as 'a time when I was totally present for another person', has been given the grand name of Transderivational Search (often abbreviate to TD Search). Robert Dilts (1990) defines this term as: "The process of searching back through one's stored memories and mental representations to find the reference experience from which a current behaviour or response was derived."

A resource could be something you have already done yourself, or have indirect or second-hand experience of. It is going to something positive, life-enhancing, helping you succeed. Because you already have been in good states, and succeeded in many activities in your life, then those states, that learning is available to you now. A resource could be seen as the essence or learning from experience. You may have coded many such resources—states, qualities or principles—using abstract nouns such as: creativity, confidence, feeling on top of the world, curiosity, the ability to think on your feet—or events such as 'a time when I was ... winning, happy, loving, perspicacious' and so on. You may have a single significant memory, or you may get a cluster of related memories.

If you are seeking a resource, and you cannot come up with anything positive, then it could be useful to think of a similar situation in which you do not have the problem. If you cannot directly connect with a resource from your own experience, you may recognise it as a quality in another person. If you can identify someone who is 'dynamic', 'a go-getter', 'great at negotiating' and so on, then you can copy what they do or try their style on for size. You could even find your qualities of resourcefulness exemplified by animals, birds, or even places in nature. You could have a resource which is the beauty or tranquillity of a special place, which produces a certain state within you.

Although it may seem more appropriate to find resources in your past, there is no reason why you could not have a future resourceful self who has already got what you need. "Imagine that you have already succeeded in this, and notice what you did, so that you can have these things now." This kind of approach is also apparent when you challenge someone who has claimed "I can't do that", by asking them: "So what would happen if you did?" "Just suppose that you do have a choice .... Pretend that you know what to do."

When you work with people, let them find their own resources. The kinds of resources their unconscious mind accesses may surprise you. Their resource could be an abstract concept such as 'strength' or 'confidence' or it could refer to a time or place when they were in a state which it would be appropriate to have again now. Each label acts as a trigger for remembering those times when they had that quality in their life. The desired qualities could be personified in real or fictional characters, such as Mother Teresa or Glinda the Good Witch in *The Wizard of Oz*. They could create a version of themselves which already possesses these resourceful qualities—a kind of personal coach, mentor or guardian angel. A resource could be a physical object with emotional attachments, such as a teddy bear from childhood; a 'magical' object such as a ring or a cloak from their fantasy world; or a place such as a forest or waterfall, which inspires a certain kind of emotion, or that feeling of expansiveness you may get when looking out across the sea to beyond the horizon.

The power of a resource lies in the fact that it puts you in a life-enhancing state which can be activated by a memory, a word, symbol, icon, emblem, or token. A person's resource has meaning for them, although you do not know what that meaning is. The key question is: Does it work for them? If it does, that's fine. You will know it is working because you will see them change as they access its power. Even using the same word for some experience in your own life, you would still not know what it means for anyone else, because every person has their own unique way of making meaning.

Whatever the label they give you ('strength', 'gold', 'Africa'), do not pretend that you know what it means. They are codes for some internal state or memory that the person is now aware of. Honouring their intuitive wisdom is respectful, and maintains rapport. There is little point in offering suggestions to other people about what you think they might need. If you do, they will probably reject them. It's the old "Why don't you …?—Yes, but …" game which Eric Berne defined in *Games People Play* (1964, Chapter 8). People tend to reject such offers.

People are empowered when they realise that they can find positive resources and supporting beliefs when they need them. The Catch-22 is that they are not usually in the right state for accessing resources when they do need them. This is illustrated in Joseph Heller's book as the hero, Yossarian, wonders about the reality of Appleby having flies in his eyes (Heller 1961, Chapter 5):

> "Oh, they're there, alright … although he probably doesn't even know it. That's why he can't see things as they really are."

> "How come he doesn't know it?" inquired Yossarian.

> "Because he's got flies in his eyes," Orr explained with exaggerated patience. "How can he see he's got flies in his eyes if he's got flies in his eyes?"

One way out of this Catch-22 impasse is to first of all change your state. Do anything different, to somehow step away from the issue in order to observe it 'neutrally'. But you need to be able to do this without having to think about it. Therefore plan ahead, set up an automatic response mechanism ahead of time and practise beforehand. Whenever a certain condition is encountered, a 'trigger' fires automatically, which will change your state immediately. However, having the resource is no guarantee that the issue will be resolved. There may be much more to do. However, the way you go about creating your desired outcome will probably be more effective as you are back in the flow rather than feeling stuck.

Whoever has the most flexibility has control of the system

This Presupposition comes from Ross Ashby's work on cybernetic systems (Ashby, 1956: 202–7). In it he posits The Law of Requisite Variety, which states that "the part of the system with the most flexibility will be the controlling or catalytic element in the system."

This metaphor is concerned with "the subject of regulation", which covers "… most of the activities in physiology, sociology, ecology, economics and much of the activities in almost every branch of science and life". However, "Regulation is concerned with *reducing* the variety of outcomes" [my italics], and his law stated briefly is, "only variety can destroy variety". In other words, The Law of Requisite Variety as described by Ashby is actually about returning a mechanical system to stability by reducing the variability within it. If there are many possible things that can happen, then you need to be more flexible in order to deal with them.

Never mind it being the 'wrong' metaphor, in its adapted form it is still a useful guide. It reminds NLP practitioners that they need to take a flexible approach when working with people, and that means having more options than they do, if you are going to come up with new metaphors or interventions that will surprise them into shifting their point of view.

If you always do what you always did … you always get what you always got

This is a plea to 'do something different' because you already 'know' that what you are currently doing, or habitually do, doesn't get you the results you want. We can show the nature of Means and Ends thinking as follows:

Fixed Means and Fixed Ends

Conformity. Following procedures. The programmed behaviour which will guarantee you get the same results every time. This is the direct meaning of the slogan: "If you always do what you always did, you'll always get what you always got."

Fixed Means and Variable Ends

Wishful thinking. This is nothing more than wishful thinking, the delusional hope that 'this time something different will occur'. This is also reflected in the saying, "Insanity is doing the same thing over and over and expecting different results."

Variable Means and Fixed Ends

Flexibility. This is the thinking behind outcome setting (see Chapter Eight). By carefully defining your goal, you then do whatever is in your power to achieve it. This is also the thinking behind setting targets. The problem with that is, that people will do whatever they need to do to achieve them (including fiddling the statistics or the accounts, moving the goalposts, cheating, and so on), even to the detriment of the other services they provide. Caution is needed here. The end does not justify the means.

Variable Means and Variable Ends

Creativity. With no set goal, and no defined methodology, this is more about "Let's see what happens" and "We'll find a way of doing this." This could be the world of the inventor who explores "There has to be a way of doing X" … although it could also be the world of the drifter who 'hangs loose', but who achieves little but their personal pleasure.

Overview of the NLP Presuppositions

In order to function in the world, you have to assume certain things about how it works. These assumptions come in many forms: rules, principles, plans, strategies, value-judgments, obligations, aphorisms and stories. They all provide you with advice and guidance about how to interact with and interpret the reality around you. When these assumptions are made explicit, they provide clues about your underlying philosophy, or about the model of the world of a person or of a system of thought such as NLP.

In examining some of the main NLP Presuppositions we discover something of the underlying philosophical thinking that supports NLP. You may now be getting more curious about the way NLP uses language to describe itself through the metaphors it uses. Metaphors are so pervasive in our language, that we take them for granted. It is when we make the effort to notice them, and explore their ramifications and limitations, that we find "That's not really what I meant to imply", or "Actually, that's not how I understand of the world."

In my explanation of how NLP works, I endeavour to avoid metaphors which assume a Realist model of the world. However, as these metaphors are in constant use, alternatives need to be offered. For example, 'imagination' rather than 'representation'; 'sensory modality' rather than 'representation system'; and instead of 'filters' I prefer 'noticing', 'aware of', 'paying attention to' and so on. However, these are my preferences, and may not reflect your current understanding of your reality, or your use of metaphors. Therefore, one final Presupposition:

Meet the client in their model of the world

As practitioner, coach or therapist, you are charged to take the first step in moving towards the worldview of the other person. You need to know something about how they think and behave, so that you can initially match their way of doing things. This is called getting rapport with the client. If you assume that everyone else thinks like you do, you will soon find that what you are saying is incomprehensible to them, or that you are talking at cross-purposes. You are the one with the behavioural flexibility, with expert knowledge of kinds of realities, so this is where you need to use that expertise to find out about another person's preferences in many different aspects of their life. Once you have rapport in a relationship, it increases the likelihood that you will be understood, you will understand the client, and that the communication between you will be productive. Only then can you begin the task of coaching or teaching them to think in a different way.

However, because of the fixed nature of books, to understand what I have to say about NLP, you will have to adjust to my predominantly Mythic approach. This may not be your preference, but as you have learned something about NLP you will already have experienced this way of thinking as it is essentially about reframing what you already know.

Chapter Six

Rapport

When I wish to find out how wise, or how stupid, or how good, or how wicked is any one, or what are his thoughts at the moment, I fashion the expression of my face, as accurately as possible, in accordance with the expression of his, and then wait to see what thoughts or sentiments arise in my mind or heart, as if to match or correspond with the expression.

Edgar Allan Poe (1844) The Purloined Letter

Getting on with other people

If you are going to help other people change, then in order to intervene appropriately and effectively in their life, you need to know something of how their model of the world is organised at the levels of body, mind and spirit. Edgar Allan Poe suggests that one way to do this is to copy what you can observe of the other person, because by matching certain characteristics (see Figure 6.1), such as adopting their facial expression or way of moving, you can to some extent enter their world and get a sense of who they are. Having a sense of shared reality is called 'being in rapport'; the degree of rapport will depend upon the extent to which you match on a number of levels. Getting rapport with someone is not something you do once and then have thereafter; it is a dynamic quality of the relationship and varies continuously. It can be enhanced by increasing the amount of matching, and by 'pacing' the other person—moving at the same speed. Rapport is neither good nor bad; there are times when you will need rapport in order to communicate, and times when you need to break rapport in order to cease interacting.

People are naturally moving in and out of rapport with each other all the time. They know when they are in harmony with someone else and when they are not, although they are not usually aware of doing anything specific. This will also be apparent to an observer. You can tell when people are in rapport because you see them moving, gesturing, communicating in a similar way, as if they are dancing to the same tune. People in rapport match their natural rhythms of movement and breathing, their energy levels, and generally share their way of being with each other. They feel comfortable in the relationship because they are with others who think and act as they do. They have a sense of being mutually acknowledged, know it is OK to be who they are, and are thus more likely to like those people whom they perceive as being like them.

Once you are aware of the qualities of rapport, you will sometimes notice that you are making similar hand movements, or that you are sitting with your legs crossed in the same way. There is no need to draw anyone's attention to it. Just acknowledge your natural ability, and move on.

Having rapport with someone offers you a greater opportunity for influencing them. Influencing is not the same as 'manipulating'. Manipulation would mean using NLP to get other people to do things you want against their will or best interests. Influencing is about wanting to inform, motivate or lead others so that they may influence and change themselves. Influencing builds relationships. Manipulation ignores the other person's interests, and eventually destroys the relationship. If you abuse the power relationship by using NLP techniques manipulatively, then be prepared for the consequences. As soon as someone realises that they have been manipulated, they will feel resentment. They may then go out of their way to avoid you and suggest others do the same. Be professional and consider the ethical issues involved.

Paying attention to other people

In the initial stages of a relationship you can use the information coming in through your senses to match the other person in terms of what you see, hear, and feel: their physiology, behaviour, use of language, how they speak, and level of energy. You may have to give yourself permission to notice some of these things. Children are often socialised out of observing people closely: "It's rude to stare", and thereafter move around the world with averted eyes. You may gain an intimate knowledge of the pavement or the carpet, but you are ignoring the many non-verbal cues that others continually offer you. An NLP training environment is designed to offer a safe place for getting used to looking at other people again.

Exercise 6.1: Sculpting

This exercise gives you a flavour of what it is like to be someone else. Do this with three other willing explorers.

1. In a group of three or four people, person A becomes the model, and person B the modeler. The others, C and D, are there as 'body sculptors'.

    A chooses a positive state, in which they have a sense of 'going for it' or 'really being myself'. A stands in the appropriate posture, which should feel comfortable for them.

    The others take a moment to observe how A stands, breathes, where they are tense, where they are free, what they are paying attention to, and so on. Observe A in terms of 'what you would need to know in order to copy this person'.

2. B then stands next to A and adopts a similar stance. This is a first approximation. The task of the two sculptors is to make B as much like A as possible, by gathering physiological information about A. They feel A's muscle groups, tension, weight distribution; observe their focus of attention, 'centre', energy level, and so on. C and D communicate this to B both in words and by physically moving B's limbs and adjusting their posture, so that B's physiology increasingly comes to resemble A's.

    It is common for B to feel initial discomfort. After all, they are taking on an unfamiliar posture. But eventually the integrity of this way of being clicks—it works for B as it does for the person being modelled and it becomes easier to maintain. B finds they are able to 'settle into it' and get the sense that this posture is actually worth having. If not, then they need a little more time and to make some slight adjustments, until things 'fall into place'.

3. Once B, C and D are satisfied with the copying and shaping, C asks B, "If you were to move through life like this, what would have to be true for you?"

    B goes inside and notices the qualities, thoughts, feelings, beliefs, and so on that this kind of way of being in the world evokes in them. B may even get some awareness of the content of A's experience!

4. B may want to step out of that experience, and then step in again, and adjust back into that new state. This becomes easier with practice. A may also want to step out and look at B 'doing them'. This is 'interesting information' for A.

It takes time and demands keen observation to do this with sufficient precision and detail so that B ends up with a strong sense of what it is like 'being someone else'.

Getting rapport is about generally moving towards someone else's way of being, rather than trying to become their clone. The interesting thing about matching someone else is that you begin to get a feeling of what it is like being them. The closer you match them on a body or physiological level, the greater your sense of them on the Mind level—what they think and believe, their model of reality.

You might think that if you start matching people deliberately it will be so obvious to them that they will notice and comment. In general, people have little awareness of their own physiology and body-language, let alone what someone else is doing with theirs!

Mirror neurons

There is recent physiological evidence that matching action enables us to understand emotions and simulate others' experience, simply by watching them. Giacomo Rizzollati discovered that there are specific elements of the brain, which he called mirror neurons, that respond to movement information (Ramachandran, 2003). They are activated not only when you engage in an activity, but also when you watch another person moving. This could explain why we enjoy watching sports or dance, because we gain insights into the performer's emotional state. We get 'empathy' and begin to tap our feet. We become part of the action and feel as though that we are also taking part.

Exercise 6.2: " Walk this way ..."

People have idiosyncratic ways of walking. You can probably recognise someone you know at a distance simply by the way they are walking. What could you learn about them by copying their walk? By trying on someone else's style you will experience a changed perception of the world.

In contrast to the previous exercise, which was static and detailed, you could match someone in a 'quick and dirty' way by copying their walk. You could do this in the street or in a shopping mall. If you see someone in front of you walking in a way that strikes you as intriguingly different from how you move, decide to copy them for a brief time. Make sure you have sufficient distance so that you are far enough back to get a general impression of the way they move. Simply start walking as they do. Staying behind them makes it easier to copy them, and ensures that you are not directly visible. If it seems they might become aware of you, resume your usual walk. Remember the salient points of their motion, and try it again later. It only takes a few steps to discover another way of moving through the world. Then let it go; you are only sampling.

Shaking hands

There is the *high official*—the body erect, and a rapid, short shake near the chin. There is the *mortmain*—the flat hand introduced into yours and hardly conscious of its contiguity. The *digital*—one finger held out, much used by the higher clergy .... There is the *shakus rusticus*, where your hand is seized in an iron grasp, betokening rude health, warm heart, and distance from the Metropolis; but producing a strong sense of relief on your part when you find your hand released and your fingers unbroken. The next to this is the *retentive shake*—one which, beginning with vigour, pauses as it were to take breath, but without relinquishing its prey, and before you are aware begins again, till you feel anxious as to the result, and have no shake left in you.

Sydney Smith (1771–1845)

105

People are offering huge amounts of information about themselves during every encounter. In the brief moment of contact when you shake hands you learn something about them from the way they hold your hand: the 'iron grip', the 'wet fish' or whether they belong to a particular organisation. If you have studied any of the oriental martial arts, such as t'ai chi, you may be able to tell a lot more, such as how balanced or centred they are, how far they 'extend down their arm'. Do they 'meet you half way', or is there an imbalance? Do they use a power handshake that lowers your status?

Use the information they give you to copy their personal style. Shake their hand using the same amount of firmness as they do. Take your cue from them—even if you find it uncomfortable. Using someone's name also builds rapport, so ask or listen for their name, and then say it back to them as soon as you can. This acknowledges them, and reinforces your memory. If you sit down, let them take the lead, because once they are sitting it is easier for you to mirror their posture.

Group rapport

People who spend time together tend to adopt group characteristics, share group values, and learn to speak a common language. Behaving in a similar way creates group bonding through shared experience. To belong to a group, you have to conform to some extent to the group norms: "This is the way we do things." Groups have dress codes, jargon, attitudes, rituals and so on. Being like them in some way means you are more likely to be liked by them, and to be seen as 'one of us'.

Exercise 6.3: Group values

Think about the groups you belong to, both at work—the project group, the company; or in your leisure activities—the sports team, the arts group. Make a list and then consider for each group:

What makes us a group? What do we have in common in terms of:
• ways of doing things—rites, rituals, celebrations and ceremonies?

- language and jargon?
- clothing, dress, uniforms?
- values, ethical stance, beliefs?
- what shared experiences have bonded us?

Remember how it was joining a group that was already established.
- What did you have to change or adapt in order to become part of the group?
- What did you have to learn? What rules, conventions, procedures?

If you left a group because you no longer enjoyed being in it:
- What was it that annoyed you? What did you not like about the group?
- How did you choose to be different from them?
- Which values of yours were not honoured by that group?
- How do you think about that group now that you have left?
- What do you imagine they think about you?

Such experiences can be powerful life-changing ones. If you left a group because you no longer felt part of it, then there may still be strong feelings about that on both sides. If you are still in a strong group then you probably feel very defensive when the group is attacked or threatened in some way. This is in the nature of group membership.

Adapt these ideas to how you can gain rapport with one other person. You are, in a sense, learning how to bond with them in a two-person group. The principle is the same: initially you have to adapt to them. In becoming more like them in some way you are subtly acknowledging their lifestyle. The easiest place to start is by adapting your body-posture, gestures and movements to match theirs.

Getting to know you

Being an excellent communicator requires a willingness to do what it takes to get and maintain rapport with others. Your rapport skills can be improved. The following list (Figure 6.1) shows some of the characteristics you can pay attention to and then match in order to more fully enter someone else's model of the world.

Use your sensory acuity to notice or sense, and then match the following qualities of the other person's way of being:

Physiology and State	Notice what they do with their body: the way they move, they move, gesture, distribute their weight, lean, align themselves. Then adopt the same physiology:
	• Match the position and movement of their head, shoulders, spine, arms, hands, torso, and legs and so on.
	• Move in a similar way, adopt their general energy level, animation, and use the same posture and gestures when you speak.
	• When walking side by side, people naturally fall into step—both on the left foot at the same time. If you notice you are out of phase, it is easy to adjust. If their stride is much shorter or longer, and it is uncomfortable for you to match, do what you can without drawing attention to yourself.
	• Assume a similar but more resourceful state than theirs. Do not match an extremely debilitating state, or you will find yourself unable to function!
Breathing	Breathing has the greatest effect on a person's physiology and mood. Note the rate, depth and location of their breathing. Breathing in sync with someone occurs naturally, and getting rapport by matching breathing is easy on a one-to-one basis. How to match someone's breathing:
	• When someone is talking to you, they are breathing out. So when they are talking, you breathe out. When they pause for a breath, you breathe in.
	• People have their own 'style' of breathing: deep/shallow; rapid/slow; free/obstructed. Is the length of the inhalation the same as the length of the exhalation? Are they breathing continuously or do they pause at some point in the cycle?
	• Where are they breathing from: the upper chest, mid chest or abdomen?

- Notice, in peripheral vision, any rising and falling in the chest area. Do not stare! People expand as they inhale and get smaller as they exhale. If you cannot detect movement in their chest area, watch their shoulders: they rise on the in-breath and fall on the out-breath. The movement may be slight, but you will see it from the back as well as from in front. It is easier to see movement in the folds of their clothing.

Language Content	The way people speak provides many clues about them, them, especially whether they are 'one of us' or an outsider, friend or foe.

- Use their actual words: their pronunciation, jargon, pre-ferred terminology, even if you think they are using the 'wrong' word. It is what it means to them that matters. If you paraphrase them, you will be mismatching!

- Use a similar phrase and sentence length—long, medium or short.

- Use a similar tonality: say the words how they say them—rising, on the level, or falling, and with similar emphasis.

- Use similar phatic expressions. These ritual exchanges are for social lubrication and maintaining a comfortable relationship between people. For example, 'Hi', 'Hello', 'How do you do?' or 'How are you?' These do not communicate ideas in the usual sense, nor inquire into someone's state of health. There are many local variants, so that, for example, Australians may say 'G'day' whereas someone from the South West of England would say 'All right?' If you remain silent, this could be interpreted as hostility, distance, alienation, even danger.

- Match their style of language: are they direct and to the point, or slow and rambling? Emotional, or blunt and fac-tual? Do they call a spade a spade, or use a euphe-mism? Do they tell stories and use metaphors?

Model of Reality, Worldview	You will learn to recognise someone's preferred model of reality from a combination of physiological, behavioural, linguistic and cognitive evidence. • What kinds of beliefs do they have about how things happen in the world? There will be clues in the kind of job they do, what they talk about, and the generalities in the way they think: polarities, rules, facts, value judgments, ideas, metaphors and so on.

Figure 6.1 Matching other people

In a conversation people take turns to speak. Only copy someone's gestures or language mannerisms when you are speaking. Waving your arms around at the same time they are will distract their attention. They will wonder what you are doing, and you will lose rapport. When you are listening, put your arms and hands in the same position they assume when they are listening. If you feel you are losing rapport then bring your attention back to what was maintaining that sense of communion—and do more of it.

Matching or mirroring

You can choose whether to match or mirror another person. Matching is copying their physiology exactly. This means that if they do something with their right hand, you also use your right hand and so on. Mirroring means reversing left and right: you use your right hand to mirror their left hand. If you are facing them, this is much easier to do.

Someone's general state tends to change slowly, allowing you to slowly sculpt yourself into their posture, weight distribution, and so on. However, people are constantly shifting, making fleeting gestures and quick movements, so it is worth bearing in mind that if you miss something all you have to do is wait a while and it will come round again. People are creatures of habit.

Cross-over mirroring

It is not always appropriate to directly match the other person's behaviour. Instead you can perform a different behaviour which matches their rhythm and energy in more subtle way. When people are sick, matching their breathing or energy could cause you discomfort or distress. Copying someone who is walking about while you are sitting is tricky. In such cases use *cross-over mirroring*. Pace one aspect of their physiology with a *different* aspect of your physiology. For instance, match their breathing or their pacing up and down with finger movements, head nods, or with your voice rhythm.

Matching someone's voice

It would not be sensible to match every voice characteristic exactly. Suddenly producing a high falsetto with a strong regional accent will get you funny looks rather than rapport! In general, move *towards* the other person's way of speaking, and thus acknowledge them on a subtle level (Figure 6.2).

The impressionist Rory Bremner says that when he wants to imitate someone else's voice, he runs a mental movie of that person speaking in their usual way, and then pretends to be them.

The origin of the voice

You can get a general impression of where in their body someone's voice seems to emanate from. Although ultimately the sound emerges from their mouth, it seems as if it originates

Pitch Range	How high or low the pitch of the voice is. Voices also can vary from a monotone to a constantly changing sing-song.
Tempo	How slowly or fast someone speaks.
Timbre	Qualities of the voice, such as the resonance and the degree of 'strength' or 'presence' of the voice. You might describe this as: nasal, breathy, throaty, rasping, scratchy, wheezy and so on.
Volume	How loudly or softly they speak.
Content Chunks	How much they say between breaths: a few words, or whole paragraphs. Some politicians often talk non-stop and allow few pauses for interruption.
Rhythm	Repeating patterns of phrasing, emphasis, number of syllables.
Matching	It is generally not a good idea to match another person's strong accent deliberately, even if you can do it perfectly. If you naturally move towards someone else's voice then this is probably acceptable, because you are being yourself.

Figure 6.2 Matching voice qualities

elsewhere. Although this particular discrimination may seem unfamiliar, it is easy to learn.

Avoiding overload

If you were to try to match every characteristic you would probably find that you were no longer paying attention to the content of the other person's communication. Therefore you need to assess which of the many aspects are going to be the most salient. Practise your curiosity by finding out what works for you. It may be that matching their overall general qualities is sufficient for creating good rapport. Because you have to start somewhere, this

Exercise 6.4: Exploring the origins

Do this exercise by focusing on the inside of your own body. Imagine the body as having three main zones: Head, Heart and Belly, defined by the bony areas of the skull, ribs and pelvis.

Head   Focus your attention on your Head area, and imagine your voice is coming from the middle of your head, and beamed out through your eyes. How does you voice sound when you speak out loud?

    The voice qualities from the head area are: higher pitch, slightly louder, quicker, clearer, more penetrating, and there is also a quality of lightness.

Heart   Move your focus of attention to the middle of your chest, and have your voice originate there. Imagine it radiating from your heart. How does it sound now?

    Typical voice qualities from the heart area are: warmer, more resonant, middle frequency, slightly slower, and more inclusive.

Belly   Finally move your focus of attention down into your belly, just below your navel, and imagine your voice taking on a gutsy quality as it emanates from there. And notice how that sounds.

    Typical voice qualities from the belly area are: low pitch, slower pace, larger with an airy quality of space to it—more roundness, and more internal.

You can have your voice originate in any part of your body simply by imagining it. How would it sound if your big toe were to speak? Which part of your body would give you the warmest feelings ... the sharpest focus and precision ... be the most laid back?

Politicians and others in public life often deliberately change the origin and tonality of their voice to become more 'acceptable'. They gain credibility by lowering the voice, to speak 'from the heart', or gain power by speaking from low down, from their belly.

Exercise 6.5: Moving from a Centre

You can apply the same kind of thinking to how someone moves. Become familiar with having a centre of energy or impulse in different parts of your body.

Head   First, imagine that your head is in charge of moving you about. Your head and especially your eyes are going to be leading your body around the world. Notice how you make contact with the world moving in this way. What do you notice, and what do you not pay attention to? It may feel as if your body is being dragged along in the wake of your active, exploring head.

Heart   Now shift your focus of impulse to the middle of your chest, your heart area, and begin to move through the world with this kind of energy. As you open your arms, you open your heart. Notice how this feels, how you respond to other people, and to the world in general.

Belly   Shift your centre down into your belly area. If you have done yoga or t'ai chi you may be familiar with the 'one point', *hara* or *dan tien*, described as the 'power centre' of your body. Focus your attention on this spot inside you a hand-width below your navel, and move from there.

Notice what happens when you move your centre of impulse around your body. Play with the idea of having this centre of impulse anywhere in your body. What would life be like if you were moving from your knees? From your right ear? From the tip of your nose? An acting tip I learned was that if you want to pretend to be drunk on stage, put your centre several inches above your head, and have it slowly rotating in a circle ....

When you observe how other people move, locate where in their body the impulse to move seems to originate. Try it out yourself by imagining the impulse to move comes from that place in your body. Thinking in terms of centres makes copying someone's walk exercise easier to do.

is good news for when you meet strangers, or when cold calling. Rapport builds over time, and as you get to know individuals better, you will be able to adjust your behaviour and thus build rapport and long-term relationships. As you continue to communicate, let your attention to body-language slip into the background.

You will never get to know everything about another person. How could you? You don't even have all the information about yourself yet, because you are still in the process of understanding who you are. NLP has provided a number of extremely useful ways of analysing what people do and think in terms of general patterns of behaviour and thought. These patterns are thus more universally applicable. For example, some people tend to think in terms of small-chunk nitty-gritty details, while others go for big-chunk global generalities. This could be a 'personality trait'— something they do consistently over time.

Books on personality—scientific and psychological studies, as well as popular treatments—describe a multitude of charac-teristics. Each system of analysis is based on a different frame for understanding the variations—and it is always possible to find new ways of describing people. This suggests that you can never know someone else's world completely, but you can still communicate meaningfully—on a good day!

Breaking rapport

You do not want to be in rapport all the time. You can choose whether to match or mismatch other people. It is not a good idea to match someone who is ill or is having difficulty breathing due to asthma or emphysema. There are definitely times when you need to break rapport. For example, if you have another appoint-ment, want to get on with your work, or get away from someone who is taking up your time! When it is time to leave, start mis-matching the other person to whatever degree is necessary. Stand up if you have both been sitting. If they don't 'get the message' simply say "I have to go now" and subtly push with both hands, palm down, to indicate "This is how we will leave it. You stay here", and walk away. A good reason for holding meetings in the other person's office is that it is easier for you to leave! When selling, it is recommended that you break rapport just before the other person signs a binding contract, because you want them to be committed to the contract, rather than to you. Make an excuse to leave the room, "I just have to make a phone call", so that they are signing it on their own. This temporary mismatch can actually build long-term rapport by removing the risk of buyer's remorse later.

"But ..."

At other times you may break rapport inadvertently, for example, by looking at your watch, or yawning. Using the word 'but' can quickly break rapport: "I totally agree with what you are saying, *but* ...", "I would like to buy your product, *but* ...", "I'd love to go out with you, *but* ...". The 'but' negates what has gone before. The real communication is: "I don't agree with it" or "I don't want to buy it, and here come my objections." There is a voice tonality which indicates: *'but* coming'! Instead of making 'but' statements, reorganise your thinking and sentence structure to say what you need to say without making excuses. Use 'and' instead of 'but'. An 'and' keeps the flow going, maintains continuity and thus rapport with the other person.

Leading

You could match and mirror someone unceasingly ... but never go anywhere. This is fine if all you want is to have a good time hanging out together. However, if there is a client in front of you, or a business deal to complete, then you need to move on if you are going to achieve your purpose.

One feature of rapport is that it works both ways. You pace them and they pace you. To test the strength of this bond, make a movement the other person does not usually do, and watch to see if they come with you. If they follow, then you achieve your outcome by leading them somewhere new. If they do not follow, go back to matching. Remember that your intention is to influence them in some way: to buy what you are selling, or to change their point of view so that they may become unstuck. When you have good rapport, lead them towards your usual way of doing things—get them to match you. This happens quite naturally and they will begin to get a sense of what it is like to be you—essentially curious and flexible of thought. They will follow your lead and come with you, because they want to maintain rapport with you. Then they will be in a state where change is possible.

Rapport is natural, and you will find yourself automatically copying many of these aspects without thinking about it. It is when rapport is not happening, perhaps the other person appears awkward or uncomfortable, or behaves in an unusual way, or very different from you, that you need to pay attention to how you can get closer to them. Matching what you can see is obviously the easiest way of doing this. However, matching on a holistic level enables you to get rapport at a deeper level.

Chapter Seven

Rapport and the Four Realities

Truth arises from disagreements amongst friends.

David Hume

Matching preferred reality mode

People use different ways of thinking and perceiving to deal with the range of experiences life offers. However, they will tend to home in on one particular way of doing things. The Four Realities model is a useful way of beginning to understand someone's worldview. Each reality mode presents a different style of engaging with everyday life. Although Unitary mode lays particular emphasis on Rules and Principles, each reality mode has its own style and ways of working. To gain rapport with someone in a different reality, you need to understand the rules and generalisations that they are operating with.

You are matching someone at a big-chunk level. The four reality modes are general, abstract descriptions, and there are a great many variations on the basic theme. This book contains numerous examples of how to recognise these four reality modes in practice, and how you can understand each mode of thinking and perception. Each reality mode will have its own 'style' of rapport. First, you need to recognise which mode the person prefers, and then match that preference by thinking that way, and paying attention to what that reality mode is concerned with. However, you may recognise that the person's reality mode is your least-preferred one, and it may be quite challenging for you to match it. On the other hand, if you are completely unaware of where they are coming from, which mode they are in, then you may find yourself in conflict, without a clear understanding of why that is.

Rules to live by

Safety is the final danger.
Jalaludin Rumi (Sufi Mystic)

We live in rule-based societies and groups. Having rules allows individuals, groups, teams, organisations, and societies to function: "I know what to do in this situation. And I know what to expect of other people." The downside is the tendency towards conformity. Most societies employ people whose specific job is to enforce the rules, and to punish those who break them. In the early years, parents and teachers spend quite some time instilling rules in their children. If they did not do that, the children would create their own rules—which is what happens within their own peer groups. As children grow up they move from thinking of the rules in black-and-white terms to realising that rules are arbitrary, made up by other people, and are therefore capable of being 'bent' to a degree. Although people are not taught explicitly how every aspect of society is organised, they tend to comply with rules of etiquette, dress code, and behaviour so as to fit in with others, or not stand out in a crowd. You notice those who are not conforming, though you may choose to do nothing about it.

At various stages you were instructed about formal rules, such as obeying traffic lights and road-signs; behaving appropriately (in terms of movement, interaction, level of noise, and so on) in public places such as schools, churches, libraries, restaurants, and cinemas. You probably obey 'No Smoking', 'No Entry' and 'Keep off the grass' signs. However, simply obeying prohibition rules could make you less alert (and inhibit your curiosity). For example, jaywalking is not permitted in some countries, but is tolerated in the UK. This has the effect that British jaywalkers are less likely to be involved in accidents because they have developed the quick-witted ability to dodge traffic.

You will have picked up other rules informally. For example, when you are in a lift, you stand facing the door and watch the numbers rather than engage with the other passengers. In cities you probably avoid conversation with strangers on public transport; in rural areas you may be expected to talk to or at least greet strangers. People walking in town tend to walk on the right of the pavement, and overtake on the left. This provides a better traffic flow. If you are unaware of this tendency, it could explain why you keep bumping into people!

Technological innovations such as mobile phones require people to develop new rules and etiquette for use. For example, using them is prohibited in various contexts, such as aircraft, hospitals, training courses and theatre performances. In other public places, such as trains, special areas are set aside for this purpose, although this is not universally accepted or applied. The rules are still emerging.

[U] Matching Unitary Reality: Principles and Policies, Creeds and Doctrine

> What the rulebook says
> will change. In time all ink is
> disappearing ink.
> *William Warriner: 101 Corporate Haiku #91*

People want to live in a defined and predictable universe. The extreme Unitary personality may be unwilling to live in one which appears random or chaotic. They prefer their world to have firm rules and regulations which constrain the behaviour of its occupants. They are constantly testing compliance with the laws, and whether new information is consistent with the 'truth'. Principles are to be upheld regardless of any moral judgments, and anything not complying is rejected. They focus on doing the work, getting the job done. Change happens by following agreed procedures that get 'guaranteed' results. New ways of doing things arise from re-interpreting the principles. The Unitary person may work in a job with a strong conformist and rule-based tradition such as legal work, mathematics, or in a strong religious movement. Many business leaders have a strong Unitary streak, in that they get things done their way.

Unitary reality is concerned with truth. Life in Unitary mode is about knowing and obeying the rules, and keeping people in line.

In a Unitary culture, group, society or organisation, you need to know what the rules are, because deviating from them will be punished. Its members need discipline and commitment to get things done. The assumption is that there is one right way, and that what matters is that people conform. Those who don't are initially cajoled into compliance, and if that does not work, sanctions are applied or the individual (often labelled a 'heretic') is excluded.

NLP in Unitary mode has a number of working principles or presuppositions, which were covered in Chapter Five. It also has a set of working practices (see Appendix B). When you are learning to do an NLP exercise in Practitioner training, you will probably be told to "follow the instructions", because in this way it will work. Later, when you understand the underpinning paradigm, you will be able to create your own variations or new techniques.

Rapport with Unitary

To gain rapport you need to know what the rules are, the principles they subscribe to. You need to know both the explicit formal rules (legal statutes, standard business practices, and so on), and the informal rules (how they actually work), because these will tell you what is open to change and what isn't. You must comply with these rules, so that you are perceived as trustworthy, and not going to upset the system and cause instability. In an organisation, adopt their dress code, way of speaking, use of jargon and abbreviations. The Unitary person may come across as powerful if they have the characteristics (and charisma) of a leader. Otherwise they may seem pedantic or rather cold or distant, lacking in human warmth. The down-side of Unitary types is that they blame others or come across as having been programmed with a set of unshakeable beliefs rather than human sentiments.

[Se] Matching Sensory Reality: Facts, Data, Experience, Scientific Laws

> A mind all logic is like a knife all blade. It makes the hand bleed that uses it.
>
> *Rabindranath Tagore, Stray Birds #193*

The Sensory person lives in an objective world of facts, objects, and things, gathering information through the senses, observing, comparing, and analysing how one thing leads to another. Information is 'neutral' in that there are no feelings associated, nor moral judgments to be made. This is the world of process, of cause and effect linkages through time. Change is seen as deterministic or evolutionary, not subject to the petty whims of the human need for control. The Sensory people are likely to be analytical or procedurally minded, and enjoy working as accountants, engineers, technologists, or scientists who investigate particle physics, or genetics and evolution. These people need to know the details, and want to refine the processes that get results.

Sensory-mode people live in the hard-nosed, scientific world of facts and evidence. In order to make sense to them you have to communicate that kind of information. Anything 'touchy-feely' is immediately suspect. You need to talk to them in factual, logical terms, the 'bottom line'. Sensory mode requires rationality and logical proof: "What's the evidence? Can you prove it? Has any research been done on this? Give me the figures." The biologist Richard Dawkins is a strong Sensory person; a fictional example would be *Star Trek*'s Mr Spock.

In developing their theories, Sensory types use their imagination. There is a strong link between Sensory and Mythic realities as both involve divergent thinking. Many scientists are creative in a similar way to the artist, although the end result will probably be more practical, solving technical problems and creating solutions in physical terms.

NLP in Sensory mode is concerned with sensory acuity and gathering evidence using the five senses. It has developed techniques that explore submodalities, cause-and-effect models and evidence-based procedures. The rules of this reality are built upon observation and facts, and involve prediction based on explicit theories and models of change.

Rapport with Sensory

Match Sensory mode using the list in Figure 6.1. You also need to be able to talk their language, and to some extent, think logically in the way they do. This means actually having knowledge and understanding of the content, often in some detail, of their domain, what they are doing. To them the world seems obvious and logical, and they will deride your lack of rational thought— especially if they perceive you as being impractical—an artistic type or a mystical dreamer—or part of the more emotional world of Social reality mode. You could adopt a lower status and assume a position of ignorance, but it would be better to do your homework—thus enabling you to engage in rational discussion.

[So] Matching Social Reality: Values, Ethics, Motivation

> If it wasn't for the human beings, the world would be an engineer's paradise.
>
> *Kurt Vonnegut*

The Social-mode person lives in a web of connections to other people. For them, the group or society is important, and they endeavour to promote the group's values, to act responsibly and ethically, and improve the well-being of all. Many Social-mode types will be found working in the caring and helping professions, in social work, in organisational change, union activity, and negotiation, or working towards the betterment of humanity.

They tend to make comparisons and value-judgments about others, and may feel that their first duty is to serve others rather than to meet their own (selfish) needs. They are heedful of what others think about them (or mind-read what other people will think important). They operate within the limits of the group's wishes. Choosing what to do involves comparing alternatives and setting priorities; reaching decisions comes ideally through consensus, which takes into account everyone's concerns, feelings and wants.

Social types will find it important to prioritise their goals, and sort out their personal value systems, priorities and needs. People become motivated about emotional issues; it is the emotional that acts as the driving force behind their intentions to change. They take action once they have decided some goal is important enough, when there is sufficient feeling that something ought to change because it is worth achieving.

NLP enters Social reality when eliciting values, motivation, and in selecting outcomes: "What do you want? Why is that important?" Intentions, goals, aims have to matter to the person, otherwise they will not want to achieve them. NLP Coaching has an interest in this way of thinking. A great deal of Management theory has been devoted to finding out how best to motivate other people, and discovering what drives them. Social reality is about prioritising and using resources effectively for the benefit of all.

People with a preference for Social-mode thinking will evaluate alternatives, check their own and others' feelings, make value judgments about themselves: their lifestyle, their decisions, way of being; and about the social world they are part of, its morality, and debating whether the perceived consequences of decisions being made will be for the common good. The down-side is that they may compare themselves unfavourably with everyone else, and think themselves unworthy.

If you approach Social mode from Sensory mode, even though you think you are simply providing neutral information, they may see this as a personal judgment about them, and have a strong emotional response. If the information you offer is 'negative' then this may be interpreted as a personal attack. For example: "I feel insulted and rejected because you feel the need to

125

correct my grammatical errors." "You don't like my car/house/ tie/dress/meals ... so you don't really love me!" "I'm a failure. You're telling me I've wasted 20 years of my life trying to make this work!"

Matching values

To match someone else's values, find out what matters to them. You may have divined some of their values by observing what they do, how they present themselves in terms of what they wear, where they live, the kind of car they drive. You will also pick up what is important to them from the way they speak, their intonation, which words they put more emphasis upon or use more frequently. Their tone of voice will also indicate their likes and dislikes, their prejudices and preferences. Otherwise, ask "What's important to you about X?"

Status transactions

Another essential aspect of getting on with other people is your perceived relative status. Whenever people meet, they instantly and unconsciously assess whether they are higher or lower status than the other person. You carry with you your own estimate of your self-worth or comparative status level. This partly depends on your current self-image, and partly on how you assess a particular relationship. Perhaps you see yourself as 'the boss' or 'top dog'; or you feel intimidated and feel 'a doormat' or 'socially inferior'. You have spent your life learning to accurately judge status and social class, based on a combination of factors. If you are British, this information is vitally important socially. British people are class-conscious and perceive the key qualities of general demeanour and accent. Dress sense helps, but spotting designer labels may no longer be a reliable guide.

Perhaps the most important Social-mode aspect of establishing rapport is matching status—or rather, not quite matching the status of the other person. Start off just a little bit lower than they are, by thinking, "They are the expert. I'm here to learn." In this lower status role you will initially be taking the lead from them, be inquiring rather than interrogating, be demonstrating ignorance rather than arrogance. You are asking questions not from a position of trying to catch them out, but from really wanting to know about them, about their opinions, their knowledge. If you come across as someone who already knows it all, then why would you be asking questions, unless you had some ulterior motive?

It is also possible to adjust your status in order to improve rapport and the effectiveness of your communication. In getting rapport and having other people follow your lead, you have to decide whether to play relatively higher or lower status. If you want to be perceived as having authority you can pressure the other person into complying with your wishes—but you will not have rapport with them. Matching someone else means playing *slightly* lower status because you are relatively ignorant. You want to learn about their model of the world and so initially you follow their lead. Once you have rapport you raise your status in order to lead the other person. In a balanced relationship relative status fluctuates as you take turns to lead and follow.

Adjusting your status

For a full treatment of status transactions I recommend reading the *Status* chapter in Keith Johnstone's *Impro* (1979) and *Impro for Storytellers* (1999: 219–231). As this is not normally covered in NLP training courses, here is a brief summary of how to modify your status. You lower your status by adopting a slumped posture, making fast, jerky movements, putting a hand to your face, and prefacing your remarks with "er ..." and "um ...". You raise your status by standing upright, touching other people's heads, moving slowly and smoothly and using a long "errrr" as a holding-off ploy, which means "I'm thinking, so don't interrupt". A status level cannot be imposed upon you if you choose not to accept it, and status does not depend upon an assigned or official role—a tramp can play high status to a king. For example, there is a dramatic status reversal towards the end of *The Wizard of Oz* when Dorothy returns to Oz and realises that he is a sham.

You can adjust your status up or down in the same way that you can shift your centre to any part of your body. To move from a different centre, all you have to do is to pay attention to a specific part of your body, put your attention there, and act *as if* you are moving from that place. In the same way, you can notice the balance in relation to the person in front of you, imagine shifting your status higher or lower than the other person's, and act as if this is true. Or you can imagine someone who has higher status and pretend to be them. When you do this deliberately you will have more control, a greater chance of leading the other person to where you want to go. If you are training others, start high status and gradually lower your status as the trainees become more empowered.

Although you may like to think you live in an egalitarian culture, this is not how life is. Nor does it seem to be appropriate for smooth functioning. Status is a measure of relative power, and varies according to what you are doing. The best way of gathering information is to adopt a lower status and treat the other person as an expert. There are times when you need to be part of the group, and seen as 'one of us'. And there are times when you need to be assertive and take firm action. So think yourself taller, adopt a leadership style that suits you and get things moving. Part of being an excellent communicator means that you can be flexible in adapting your status to the needs of others.

[M] Matching Mythic Reality: Ideas, Metaphors, Creations, Inspirations

It was spring. There was no mistaking it. The air had become like cotton candy, spun not from sugar but the sex glands of meadowlarks and dry white wine.

Tom Robbins (2000: 192)

The Mythic-mode person perceives the world somewhat ironically: "... irony involves sufficient mental flexibility to recognise how inadequately flexible are our minds, and the languages we use, to the world we try to represent in them" (Egan, 1997: 155). They have a different take on life. They make surprising connections, create poetic metaphors, and find humour in the everyday. They seem to live in a unique reality which they have created, and for which they take total responsibility. This is the world of the ideas-person, the inventor, the novelist, the creative artist, for whom the world is their plaything. People could be 'figments of their imagination' or characters in a book. They probably delight in using language inventively and in telling stories. Whenever they 'change their mind' the universe is created anew. Willing something to be different, it becomes so. Everything is possible. Nothing is testable in 'reality' as it is all made up—just part of an unbounded playful universe.

Mythic mode assumes the ability to create your own cascading universe of ideas, imaginings, and dreams. Information is a trigger for new thoughts, associations and ramifications. The key attitude is one of acceptance, and of moving on from what *is* to what *might be*. The Mythic thinker finds the world interesting because it leads to more ideas, further associations. Life is play, everything can be revised, nothing is permanent nor uled by the past. However, this also means that the individual takes credit for, and is totally responsible for *everything* that happens!

NLP in Mythic mode entertains the 'magic' metaphor. It uses ironic thinking in that it presupposes that no version of reality is ultimate or even true. Each person creates their own reality, and can change it in a moment. Because the individual has got themselves into their current stuckness, they also have the power to change their perception, and rewrite the story they have made up that 'explains' why they are as they are. Everyone has the ability to create their model of the world afresh, or revise it by adding needed resources to heal, review, or rewrite some past event, upset or trauma: "If everything is here now, and is of my creation, then I can re-create it in a way which is more supportive of who I am."

Rapport with Mythic

Match the Mythic mind by adopting a similar attitude towards life. This would mean being curious about what is possible, taking nothing as final or definitive, but only a point of view. It also means accepting offers from other people and from the universe in general. That is, take what you are given, and utilise it in some way. This is very much in the spirit of NLP, as for example:

> The NLP spirit includes adopting Bandler's surprising positive attitude regarding any problem or difficulty: 'This problem is great! What can I use it for? What else would it be good for?' (Hall, 2000: xvi).

Accepting offers

What fascinates the Mythic worldview is the flow of ideas. You keep things flowing by accepting what is being offered to you, because it could lead to something interesting. Whatever the other person suggests, at least consider it, possibly with some enthusiasm, rather than dismissing it out of hand. You will match the other person to the extent that you are interested in what engages them. As this is their reality, in order to stay with them, you will have to improvise, think on your feet, take your cues from them.

Respect and enjoy being with Mythic people by 'going with the flow'. Keith Johnstone (1979: 92–104) describes this concept as *accepting offers*. Whenever someone communicates they are 'making offers'. An offer could be a request, a suggestion, a demand, or a presupposition, which indicates their need or intention. An offer in the form of a direct request could take the form: "Why don't we …?", "Shall we …?" or "Let's …." Each of these begins to open up a realm of possible activity. Accepting their offer means entering that particular story or reality by acknowledging its presuppositions and exploring the consequences. The comedian Paul Merton demonstrates this talent of taking an idea and following it as far as it will go.

Much of the time we make indirect offers. These could be conversational gambits, such as "Whew, it's hot in here" or "It's so embarrassing being found out". The person is telling you some-thing about their world, and hoping that you will understand them. If you respond with "Shall I open the window?" or "So what happened to you?", then you are accepting their offer, and entering into their world. You are simply acknowledging what matters to them right now, so "Why not go with it and see where we get to." If the person's opening remark lacks rationality, or seems bizarre: "I can never look him in the face again" and you think, "That's crazy. Of course you could", then hold back responses which come from other reality modes. What you have been given may be the conclusion of a complex reasoning process, and they have assumed that you have been with them all the time. You have a choice. Either you have to do some backtracking to gather sufficient information for piecing the story together for yourself, or you can jump over this current expression and explore the consequences: "So what would happen if you did?"

To maintain rapport, you will have to stay with them and hold on tight! Take what they give you as a starting point, and gradually gather enough information for understanding the story they are telling. As the Mythic-mode person is responding to possible con-sequences, take an interest in what they have imagined is going to happen. Respect their feelings about what they are telling you. You are not there to scoff. Have the attitude that they are telling you something that will be useful, in an unexpected way. By accepting their offers, you will be acknowledging them, and at the same time entering their reality, getting a feel for how the uni-verse operates for them, and expanding your own sense of what is possible. As you do this you need to maintain a safety line, a level of objectivity, to ensure that you are not getting sucked too deep into their drama.

The art of saying "Yes"

There are people who prefer to say 'Yes', and there are people who prefer to say 'No'. Those who say 'Yes' are rewarded by the adventures they have, and those who say 'No' are rewarded by the safety they attain.

Johnstone (1979: 92)

Many people would benefit by learning to say 'Yes' more frequently. It seems so obvious; surely you know when to say 'Yes' and when to say 'No'? From an early age you were probably taught to say No in all kinds of potentially dangerous situations. If you think you are going to be asked to do something horrible, and feel hesitant or uneasy, the 'safest' course of action is the hedgehog's strategy of shutting down all systems. This may or may not work. If your work includes cold calling, meeting customers, dealing with complaints, or giving presentations, you may get cold feet and become nervous, apprehensive, nauseous or whatever. Even when you know that there is nothing to be afraid of—the worst thing that can happen is that the other person says No—the idea of rejection may still terrify us. Richard Bandler suggests we face the world by saying to ourselves, "Piece of cake!"

Blocking

Saying No, refusing an offer, is called 'blocking'. You reject or ignore what another person, or the world in general, is offering you. Blocking loses rapport, because when you say No, or engage in some equivalent, you are stopping or diverting the flow of ideas, and the interaction goes nowhere. There may be good reasons for blocking if what is happening is unpleasant, undesirable, or dangerous. But you could ask yourself: "Why have I created this in my life now? What are my beliefs about this? What do I need to learn? What is the message for me here?" This is a Mythic way of thinking: having created your reality, you can examine why it is the way it is, what you did that brought about these events.

Keith Johnstone calls blocking a form of aggression. Think of the last argument you had with someone close to you. Were you defending your position by blocking, saying No? What would have happened if you had said Yes instead? Imagine this. Someone is calling you all the names under the sun, and you simply agree with them: "Yes, I'm a lazy, good-for-nothing so-and-so!"—which is true from their (Unitary) point of view. What can the other person do in response? They are looking for a fight, but you give them no reason. If you continue to agree, eventually the other person will give up, and possibly see the funny side of their ludicrous behaviour. If such a surprising course of action is one you have not previously considered, try it in a low risk context. You can find this kind of technique in Assertiveness courses and books.

Which decision you make will depend on your ability to step back and consider your short and long-term outcomes. What do you want to happen *right now?* Do you want the argument and all that arguing entails? (Well, you might feel release, or enjoy making up later!) Or do you want to enjoy the relationship in a more creative way? Would you rather be laughing or crying? It is your choice. If you go with Mythic-mode thinking, you can choose to have fun, instead of getting angry or abusive. It is about playing along with the other reality until it runs out of juice. It only takes a few examples for the other person to realise what you are doing, and foresee the futility of this kind of communication. For example, in the film, *Casablanca* (Michael Curtiz, 1942), Rick's way of responding keeps things moving, and it maintains his higher status:

UGARTE:
> ...Too bad about those two German couriers, wasn't it?

RICK:
> They got a lucky break. Yesterday, they were just two German clerks. Today, they're the honoured dead.

UGARTE:
> You are a very cynical person, Rick, if you forgive me for saying so.

RICK:
> I forgive you.

The art of thinking positively

So what needs to happen for you to say Yes more often to life's offers? The simplest way is just do it. Start by practising in safe situations, and experience what happens. For example, when someone invites you to have coffee, go to a show or film, or out for a walk—if your natural inclination is to decline because you are 'too busy' or 'that's not my thing', then decide to change your response and find out what happens when you say Yes.

Maybe you don't notice when you are saying No to offers because it has become a habit. Saying No is a part of our culture. We have had public campaigns trying to 'persuade' teenagers not to take drugs: "Just say No." It is also implicit in 'stranger danger'— despite the fact that you are more likely to be murdered, raped or abducted by someone you know.

Many TV comedy shows use a style of humour in which characters constantly block the flow of ideas, by being negative, aggressive, or by destroying things or people. It gets *schadenfreude*-ish laughs, but is ultimately unsatisfying. Soaps in particular demonstrate the frustrations and consequences of not saying Yes: non-communication, refusing or failing to listen, going into denial. If the characters were being authentic with each other—being open and honest, rather than evasive or deceitful—the stories would probably lose much of the melodrama that keeps viewers vicariously experiencing life by empathising with the characters. Although such stories concern the consequences of decisions regarding relationships it is only rarely that such examples of the No saying culture change us personally or create social reform. Although we are constantly exposed to many kinds of experiences, only seldom do we step back and reflect on our experiences sufficiently to learn from them.

Real time working

Building rapport in Mythic reality gives you a sense of going somewhere together, even though you have no idea of the final destination. This is how good NLP practitioners work with clients. They trust that they have the necessary skills to deal with whatever comes up. (The Sensory person's programmed sequence can be a hindrance when reality does not fit the plan, and they lose rapport trying to get back on track and following the plan.) Pace the client by accompanying them wherever they go, with the intention of discovering what isn't working for them. Once that is clear, come out of that, and use your own Mythic-mode thinking to help them shift from their way of doing things. The 'magic' is in doing something unexpected. However, remember the client is working on serious matters, so take them seriously. Achieving resolution will produce smiling, laughter, the delight of a job well done, even though it was painful at times.

There are, of course, some compulsive Yes sayers, who being of a more Social nature feel obliged to others. This may lead to disastrous consequences if they say Yes to those who wish to dump their problems on them. They will then find that their load increases because news of such people travels fast! Kenneth Blanchard et al (1990) in *The One Minute Manager Meets the Monkey* develop the metaphor of a problem being a monkey clinging to your back. Someone with the problem arrives with a monkey on their back. If you show any interest, the monkey reaches a hand across. The more you offer to help, the more the monkey moves across. Say, "Leave it with me", and the monkey takes up residence on your back!

Pacing someone is not about saying Yes to everything thrown at you. If you tend to find yourself placating others, beware! You need to maintain your personal ecology: look after yourself, and ensure the situation is safe so that you are able to function well. Accepting offers is essential for working with a customer or client, as long as there are relatively clear boundaries. Whenever you enter someone else's reality you need to retain a lifeline so that you can retreat again if things become uncomfortable. Avoid being manipulated. For example, we can both accept and challenge offers. In *Cold Comfort Farm*, the family is ruled by the manipulative Aunt Ada Doom who has taken to her bed claiming a 'disability' based on "I saw something nasty in the woodshed!" Eventually she is challenged by an outsider, Mr Neck:

> "I saw something in the woodshed!"
> "Did it see you?" asked Mr Neck.
>
> *Stella Gibbons (1932: 199)*

135

This response challenges Aunt Ada's power game: her offer has been accepted rather than ignored or negated, and she has to adopt a new position.

Pacing exercises

If you are made an offer of some kind which you find hard to accept, then treat that as 'information' about something you could change. In the following exercises the point of saying Yes is to break the usual pattern of saying No, for whatever reason. No-saying is often a habit; even if you don't say it out loud, you are thinking it. Pacing is being willing to accept the other person's model of reality, and entering into it. The initial Yes affirms that you are playing the game.

Exercise 7.1: Becoming a 'Yes' Person

Choose to say Yes to whatever offers other people make during a fixed period—a day or a week. This could be offers of meals, trips, helping someone out, or an offer of a job. Whatever. Say 'Yes', and discover what happens. Having this awareness means that when-ever someone makes you an offer—an invitation to have a coffee, or a trip round the world—you notice your own response, which means that you can choose to break the 'No' habit.

Saying Yes is not going to immediately plunge you into danger; you are in the realm of language. If you feel threatened by an offer, because someone appears to be criticising you, you can see it as 'their stuff, not mine' and play along with it by matching their delivery. For example, if that person is blaming you: "You're totally incompe-tent ...!" then agree wholeheartedly with matching tonality and enthu-siasm: "Absolutely!" They won't be expecting this. Continue with, "So what are we going to do about it?"

Doing this playfully keeps the pressure down, and you can stay in control of the situation. You do need to be aware of your internal con-gruence when considering the offer—there will definitely be times when you need to say No to avoid violating you own values.

Exercise 7.2: Saying 'Yes'

Do this exercise in pairs.
B asks a simple question and A simply answers 'Yes'. For example:

- B asks questions along the lines of: "Have you been drinking the bathwater again?" A answers by saying "Yes!" enthusiastically.
  Notice where you want to go next as a result of the Yes. For example: "Nearly as good as the 2002, from the southern slopes. Have to see what we can do to boost the rainfall ..."

- B starts an interview by asking: "Your name is John?" (Not their real name.) "Yes." "And how long have you been a lion-tamer (or whatever)?" Accept each offer, and keep the story going. "So what is the most interesting part of the job?"

When you do this, notice your internal response to each offer. Which ones 'push your buttons'?

Whenever A says Yes, and means it, B notices whether A's body language also says Yes, or whether it contradicts the verbal message.

Yes is No

How you say things, your intonation, makes a vast difference. For example, in how many ways can you say Yes, but actually mean No? How many shades of differentiation can you create? In real life you may do this inadvertently. When you have some kind of internal conflict, then there may be a disconnection between what you think and what you say. Politicians begin to waffle. Others hesitate, "Ye-es ...", or somehow negate the Yes with body language—grimacing, head-shaking—that indicates "No", "Maybe" or "Perhaps". To other people they come across as slightly incongruent.

Mismatching other realities

Not every communication succeeds, and the fertile ground of mis-communication and misunderstanding has much to teach us. When people are arguing at cross purposes, exploring their worldviews is key to understanding their respective ways of per-ceiving reality. Therefore, it would be useful to identify any mis-match of reality modes as that will provide clues to the nature of the conflict. Knowing where the differences lie can suggest what you could do differently in future.

First, notice the everyday examples of mismatching you have encountered, for example, the kinds of arguments or disagree-ments that have you been involved in. What were the essential points of conflict?

- Did the other person respond to what you said in a strange, even hostile way, which you thought was uncalled for, bizarre, over the top or totally inappropriate? *"What?"*

- Did you feel that you were being misrepresented or misinter-preted? "That's not what I mean!"

Use the power of your imagination to pretend that you are that other person. Put yourself in their place, and take on as much of their physiology as you can remember. Now see things from their point of view. How did they understand what you were saying? If there was a conflict over ideas, then argue their corner for a moment.

- Having got a flavour of the other person's reality, step out again, and gather evidence of where they are coming from, their preferred reality mode. What mattered to them? What were they attempting to communicate?

- Now do the same thing for yourself. What frame of mind were you in at the time? Where were you coming from? Compare both impressions. To what extent were you in different modes?

By familiarising yourself with how other people think and act, you can learn to switch to their mode in order to gain rapport. Assuming their posture will definitely help, and may provide insights into their worldview. Matching someone's frame of mind is essential for understanding what they have to say. While matching at this level, you will find that you can agree to disagree in terms of content.

Rapport overview

Figure 7.1 gives a brief overview of some commonly used terms and the various factors that come into play when you want to explore each of the four reality modes.

Mode	Gain rapport by	Lose rapport by
Unitary	Conforming to the rules and cultural norms.	Violating the rules. Crossing the boundaries.
Sensory	Matching or mirroring the other person's physology. Pacing their way of doing things.	Doing the unexpected. Mimicking what the person is doing in order to draw attention to it.
Social	Adjusting your status: a little higher or a little lower.	Adopting a much higher or much lower status. Doing your own thing and violating the group's moral code or values.
Mythic	Accepting offers, Saying Yes, Going with the flow, being interested.	Displaying indifference or boredom. Unable to follow what they are doing. Demanding they explain to your satisfaction what it means.

Figure 7.1 Gaining and losing rapport in the four realities

The first few times you break rapport, the other person or group may forgive you—after all, you're new here, and don't know the way we like to do things, and so on. They may try to regain rapport with you. But if that fails, or if you break rapport persistently or aggressively, what often happens is that you are excluded from the group and further communication becomes extremely difficult.

Chapter Eight

Setting Outcomes

You've got to have a dream,
If you don't have a dream
How you goin' to have a dream come true?

Rodgers & Hammerstein "South Pacific"

"I've always wanted to ..."

Do you have a dream that you would like to come true? Would you be willing to do whatever it takes to make it happen? If so, how are you going to do that in a way which maximises the probability of success?

Many people do get to fulfil their life-long dreams. Once they realise their passion, they become unstoppable. So when, for example, they decide to run a hotel in another country; become an opera-singer or pop-star; or circumnavigate the world using an unusual mode of transport, they just get on and do it, because their passion has reached a point where it has become compelling: "I have to do this! I'll just pack up everything and go!" If their desire seems crazy or irrational to others, that could be because others are not enthused by the impulse to action.

The real purpose of your dream sometimes only becomes clear in its accomplishment. Hindsight is illuminating; you get that "Aha!" feeling that informs you of what your dream was really about. After the event people often say, "If I'd known when I started what I was letting myself in for, I doubt whether I would have started. But now that I have achieved this, I realised that I managed to meet the challenges that arose, and in the process I have learned a great deal, including a lot about myself. And now, looking back, I can appreciate what happened, despite it being tough. It has made me a better person." In *The Wizard of Oz*, Dorothy and the others realise that they have got what they wanted, not from being given it, but as a result of the adventures they have had.

Curiosity in action

If you ask people what they want, they usually tell you about what they are lacking, rather than what they already possess and value highly. You might be curious about why they do not yet have what obviously matters to them, and what needs to happen for them to fulfil their dreams. It could be that their circumstances do restrict their life, but it is also likely that what prevents them from achieving their desires is their beliefs about what is possible, or even the way they use language to frame their wants. Here is an opportunity for being curious about how they are limiting themselves, and how that could be changed.

It is human nature to be curious about what other people are doing, and about how things could be different, especially if the person is stuck, or their current predicament is not to their liking and offers few apparent options for changing. People often need guidance or coaching in finding ways out of the impasse. It is 'thinking outside of the box' that poses the initial obstacle. Having alternatives means they can immediately widen the scope for fulfilling their ambitions.

By observing someone's behaviour you can gain insights into that person's model of the world, understand what motivates them, and predict, to some extent, what they are going to do next. You learn to interpret other people's intentions, wants and desires from their state and behaviour. You can also learn to recognise when they want something from you. If you are expected to meet their needs, you need to know what those needs are. In a business context, you need to ascertain your customer's desires if you are to satisfy them.

Setting outcomes

Clarifying what you or someone else wants is an art. It requires both having good rapport with them, and the careful use of questions. This chapter looks at the kind of guidance NLP provides on how to set outcomes. In the next chapter, we will examine the art of asking appropriate questions, and how these questions influence the kinds of answers you get.

Outcome setting is one of NLP's key processes. Various guidelines—'well-formedness conditions'—have been drafted for use in helping you clarify your ideas about what you want, and for getting you to consider some of the implications of your hoped-for changes. ('Well-formed' is a linguistics term. A well-formed sentence is one that follows the rules of grammar, and is correct for a native speaker. In this context, 'well-formed' means that best practice is being followed, and that a particular outcome has a higher probability of being attained.) It seems reasonable to assume that you are more likely to achieve your goals if you can imagine in some detail how you want your future to be. A rich vision is compelling. You will be more motivated to achieve your outcome if you know it is worth having and fits your lifestyle. It also guides you when the going gets tough. Should you become distracted or diverted from your path—which is almost inevitable —your inspirational vision will remind you where you are heading, and put you back on track.

To achieve a goal you have to constantly monitor what happens. To know how effective your interventions are, you must decide ahead of time what kind of evidence will let you know that you have a result, that what you planned is actually manifesting, and which events are irrelevant and can be ignored. It is also sensible to have contingency plans and alternative means for fulfilling your vision. As changes occur, the world will be different, and key relationships will also adjust as other people learn to relate to the new you. There will be ramifications and consequences that you will not have foreseen, which lead you to choose further outcomes.

Kinds of outcomes

There are many different *kinds* of outcomes that people say they want. For example: states of being, things, qualities, skills, abilities, relationships, status, knowledge, understanding and so on. So let us look at these in more detail.

States

People express desires for particular *states of being* they would enjoy being in. These can be verbalised using *abstract nouns* such as 'happiness', 'peace of mind' or 'harmony'; or using non-specific *verbs*: to be happy; to feel more confident; to increase self-esteem.

The remarkable thing about wanting to *be* a certain way is you can just be it. A state is not a time-dependent process. As you imagine (or remember), so shall you be. This was commented on by the psychologist William James, who suggested (1950: 474) that "we can produce not remembrances of the old grief or rapture, but new griefs and raptures, by summoning up a lively thought of their exciting cause." Therefore, to be in a desired state, all you have to do is to think yourself into it by remembering a time when you were feeling that way. Whatever your desire, you will be in that state again, at least to some degree. This is possible because your body-mind remembers that state. For example, you may find yourself blushing or shuddering when you recall that incident which was so embarrassing …!

Because people can 'access' (remember and be in once more) any state they have ever experienced, NLP uses this technique frequently. (See, for example, the Circle of Excellence technique in Chapter Ten.) When you want someone to be in a particular state, such as 'feeling resourceful', 'confident' or 'eager to buy', all you have to do is to suggest to them that they "Remember a time when you were feeling resourceful …" and so on, and their mind automatically summons up the appropriate memories, and they are in that state once more.

144

It may seem surprising that you can have *happiness* or *peace of mind* 'just like that'. But if the term has a meaning for you, then it acts as an anchor for creating the associated state. Think of the word 'happy' and you begin to feel happy. It helps to adopt the appropriate posture. It is hard to be happy by bending your neck forward so that you are looking down at the floor. You can alter your state at will, though you may first need to adjust your thinking and change the focus of your attention. For example, if you want to have peace of mind, think peaceful thoughts, and be at peace within yourself. Stop paying attention to the misfortunes and miseries in your life and count your blessings, as they say. There is an NLP quip that "One day you'll look back on this and laugh. So why wait?" Humour is a great state-changer. However, if you are in a strongly negative state, such as depression or grief, you may encounter internal resistance, as though your mind is saying "You need to be in this state for a while longer." If someone says they want a certain state, you could help them re-access it by having them recall those times when they were in that state before. "Remember a time when you were X" triggers the appropriate memories.

Note that states, such as confidence and happiness, often arise more as by-products of doing things which engage you more fully in life. These abstractions—'confidence', 'happiness'—are not directly achievable ends in themselves. When you know more about yourself, do work that you enjoy, follow your passions, then you are more likely to feel confident and happy. Therefore, don't take someone's wish-list at face value. You will need to notice the kinds of words they use, to ensure that what they say they want is actualisable, rather than a phantom generated by their linguistic habits.

Things

When you ask "*What* do you want?" the assumed answer is often in terms of a *thing* to be acquired. Things are usually defined in terms of *common nouns*, for example: a yacht, a holiday in the sun, a top of the range car, and so on. In the business world, it could be increased profits, the latest technology, or a bigger office. People

145

also want 'money'—but money is merely a means of acquiring something else—material goods, or a feeling of security. You need to find out: "So if you had more money, what would that enable you to do?"

A 'thing' answer may be exactly what someone needs, especially if they are missing a vital part of a piece of equipment. But that probably will not tell you about "what happens then?" Things tend to have a greater perceived value when you don't have them. After you have acquired them they lose some of their specialness, and become taken for granted. In other words, things in themselves are neutral; people give a value to them, and this value will vary over time.

Exploring consequences

As someone who is intensely curious about people, you will want to know "How will having this alter things?", "How will you personally be affected by having this?" Therefore, you need to find out the *intention* behind the desire, what having it will enable them to *do*, how it would enable them to behave differently and expand their possibilities for action. Ask: "What would having that do for you? What would it qualify you to do, that you can't do now?"

NLP refers to this kind of questioning as 'chunking up'—you are expanding the frame of their awareness by asking for something more general and over-arching. If you continue to chunk up, you arrive at a point where people say they want a particular state such as peace of mind (see above). In that case, you will need to find out "What is stopping you from having that right now?"

Exploring the consequences is a Mythic-mode activity, and this line of questioning gets people to investigate the larger context in which the specific outcome will be occurring. If outcomes are stated in terms of things, or 'milestones'—terms which indicate the completion of a specific change process, such as organising a conference, or completing a training programme—then it is a good idea to have them extend their thinking beyond that point, and consider the longer-term benefits, both to themselves and to others. Ask:

"So if you had that [thing], what would that do for you?"

Keep asking this question until you reach some kind of 'ultimate' state, a key value, or a state such as 'contentment'. "If I did that I'd be happy. I'd feel confident."

Milestones

> History books begin and end, but the events they describe do not.
> R G Collingwood (1978: 98) An Autobiography

The completion of an activity can also be a desired outcome. Part of making meaning of life comes from dividing it into 'episodes' or 'events' which have a sense of unity, and are bounded by specific beginnings and ends. They are marked out because they have some kind of emotional impact. For example, getting the book you have written published, marrying the love of your life, qualifying as an NLP practitioner, and so on. Although these milestone events—the publication, the wedding, the qualification—provide you with a sense of closure, they are in a sense arbitrary cut-off points. Life doesn't stop at that point, but that event marks a neat ending for that particular story. Setting milestone outcomes can motivate you into action, but you also need to consider "What happens next?" or "Having reached that point, achieved that goal, what then becomes possible?"

Failure to think things through can lead to unforeseen, even disastrous consequences. It is all too easy to have a wish come true in too literal a way, or find that you have been careless in specifying what you want, as when King Midas turning everything he touched to gold. Your first impulse might not give you what you really want at all.

Also, have them consider the personal ongoing consequences and effects on the system of achieving their stated goal:

- "So if you got that, what would be the impact on any other people involved?"
- "If you had *x* what would that enable you to do (that you can't do now)?"
- "How will the world be different if you achieve this outcome?"

Qualities

People also want to exhibit certain qualities, usually put in terms of *adjectives*. Apart from wanting personal qualities, such as being 'kind', 'generous', 'confident' or 'famous', people often state their desired qualities as *comparisons*—'more ...', 'better ...' and so on. Being social creatures, people compare themselves to their friends, neighbours, and so on, in order to maintain their relative status, because they wish to remain in their social groups, or be perceived as conforming to the latest fashion, whatever that is. For example, they want to be better dressed, better educated, richer, happier, wealthier and so on. In order to clarify a want which is expressed as a comparison, you need to know both sides: who or what is being compared to who or what else? Comparing your current self to your earlier self may be a more valid comparison to make. Comparing yourself to other people could be a cause of continual dissatisfaction, and this could be a limiting condition in your life.

A comparison needs some kind of assessment or measurement of 'how much more or less'? For example, being richer could mean having a few more pennies or cents, or several million pounds, euros or dollars; being slimmer could be defined in terms of shifting clothing sizes, of how many kilos the person wants to lose over a set period of time; if they want to 'lose weight' you need to have some indication of their final desired weight or else they could shrink to nothing!

Relationships

Human beings are social creatures and need the companionship of others. Most of us start within an existing social unit, the family, and then spend the rest of our lives moving from one social group to another, acquiring circles of friends, colleagues, buddies and acquaintances. We need emotional attachments. We need to know that we are accepted for who we are, that we are liked, feel that we belong. When you find yourself among people who do not know you, then a primary goal is to be accepted by them, so that you become part of that social grouping.

Most people desire enduring partner relationships. Sometimes, in moments of singledom, when the desire for a relationship becomes paramount, the unattached person draws up a detailed 'person specification' for their 'perfect partner'. Consider the consequences of actually getting what you specified and no more. That relationship would probably turn out to be rather limiting and ultimately boring, as there would be few surprises—which is one of the factors of a good relationship. Relationships need to grow and evolve—and it is these 'what happens next' factors which we find hard to specify.

Knowledge

Some people like to know things, and acquire information, facts, data, and so on. They always want more information, to know the latest about what is going on in the world, or in their immediate neighbourhood. They want to understand how the universe works, or how other people are able to achieve what they do. The solution is to go and find out. Libraries provide historical knowledge in all fields. The Internet has become a great tool for locating and finding information. However, it is not perfect, and you will still need to do some research by trawling through documents, by asking people or finding an expert who can give you what you want to know, or show you where to look. If what you want to know is not available, you may have to do the research yourself.

Skills

People, businesses, organisations say they want 'skills'. A vital part of personal growth comes in developing abilities, learning new skills and behaviours, and becoming more competent. For example: knowing how to sell, how to play the piano, how to spell better, how to communicate effectively to various kinds of people or how to relate well to other people. One aim of NLP is to find people who achieve excellence in such activities, and model the essential features of skilled performance. But when we consider what a 'skill' is, we run into a language problem. Are skills things you have? The educationist Robert F Dearden (1984: 78) says that "There may indeed be features in common to all skilled perform-ances by virtue of which we call them skilled, but it does not follow that it is the same skill which is present in each case; in the skater, the juggler, the flautist, the chess player, and the linguist."

One way out of this impasse is to change abstract nouns such as 'skill' or 'excellence' into other formats, because of the difficulty of knowing precisely what they mean. In NLP such words are referred to as *nominalisations*. Instead of the abstract noun 'skill', consider the adverb 'skilfully' as applied to some *action*. This shift of viewpoint suggests that it is more meaningful to treat 'skilled' as a description of a level of performance. You evaluate how well something is done, and base this judgment on a comparison. For example, it may mean 'better than the last time they did it', 'better than someone else does it', or 'world-class'.

Learning to do something skilfully requires practice and time. Are you willing to do what it takes to reach a high level of compe-tence? To assist your learning you will possibly need some form of instruction. Written information is useful, but at some point it is essential to have some appropriate role models to copy and teach-ers or mentors with whom you can check your progress. Finding role models is relatively easy. You don't need to know them per-sonally. All that matters is that they exist in your mind, based upon your experience of them in public life, in books or on the tel-evision. Notice something that they do which you would like to do, and copy them. Take whatever would improve your capabili-ties. Children are surrounded by role models (for good or for bad) whom they copy; this is how they learn to speak, play, grow up, argue, negotiate, manipulate their parents and so on. It would seem that many skills need to be acquired in childhood, and then maintained throughout adulthood in order to become 'expert'; there is some truth in the slogan "Use it or lose it".

Alternatively, treat 'skill' as a code for something you don't understand, and move on to "So if you had that skill, what would you then be able to do?"

Understanding

On a personal level people want to make sense of their lives, and find greater understanding of themselves—to know who they are, what they are meant to be doing. By reflecting on their own life, preferences, way of thinking and so on, they enrich their sense of identity, purpose or personal mission. Understanding comes through the creation of stories which explain the way your model of the world functions. Further understanding and self-knowledge come from intervening in the world and noticing what happens. Lack of understanding is one of the driving forces of curiosity. First ask a question. Then notice that the universe provides feedback or answers—so long as you pay attention to what happens and messages that may surprise you.

"If only …"

Many people find it hard to accept change, and have a strong avoidance fantasy which leads them to say "I want it all to go back to how it was before", to pretend that the current state of affairs didn't happen. Logically, this is absurd because if you reinstated all the previous conditions, they would lead once again to the present situation, and you would be no better off.

People sometimes claim that one special thing, state or resource will be the magic ingredient in their life, which will enable them to do whatever. They say, "All I need is x, and then I'll be all right" or "If only I had y I could …", "I just want someone to wave a magic wand." The implication being that all life's problems will be solved, and then "I can live happily ever after." This is fantasy. You need to notice these kinds of wishes and point them out. There are no magic wands, fairy godmothers, or genies in lamps. Most of the time you have to work in order to achieve your desires. Here, you need to explore the realms that open up once the desired ingredient has been obtained: "So if you had that, what would you then be able to do?" and find out how else that could be achieved.

Visions

Having a vision is like creating an alternative universe (Mythic-mode thinking) in which things happen more to your liking. A vision is likely to have a richness of detail, and will have accounted for several likely scenarios and their probable consequences. In practical terms, imagine your alternative reality, and let it run for a while to see what happens. Make sure this is long enough to get a sense of whether the consequences are really what you want. Does it meet your criteria, fulfil your need or values, is it sufficiently interesting and worth continuing with? (a variation of NLP's *future pacing*). Having developed your vision, check it out with other people in Social mode. What is their emotional response? Does it grab them? Are they motivated by it? How would they prioritise elements of the vision? You need to ensure that it is sufficiently appealing to expend your (or the organisation's) resources, time and effort on implementing it.

No regrets

> "Cheshire Puss," she began, rather timidly, as she did not at all know whether it would like the name: however, it only grinned a little wider. "Come, it's pleased so far." thought Alice, and she went on. "Would you tell me, please, which way I ought to go from here?"
> "That depends a good deal on where you want to get to," said the Cat.
> "I don't much care where—" said Alice.
> "Then it doesn't matter which way you go," said the Cat.
> "—so long as I get *somewhere*," Alice added as an explanation.
> "Oh, you're sure to do that," said the Cat, "if you only walk long enough."
>
> *Alice in Wonderland*, Chapter 6

Setting well-formed outcomes is not compulsory! If you don't care what happens, if you just want things to be different, then everything can become fun or interesting, a challenge or an opportunity. Whatever happens, the world will be different. Whatever you do, you get 'results'. You cannot fail, and you get a lot of feedback. If your world becomes very different, as Dorothy found in the Land of Oz, you will quickly have to learn to adapt to the new conditions. That means paying attention to *everything* around you because any detail could be important for your survival. One benefit of not organising your goals is that it is impossible to get sidetracked, as every path is as interesting as any other.

Well-Formed Outcomes

Setting an outcome is a deliberate activity in which people intend change by imagining how their lives could be different, and then devise ways of achieving their desired goals. NLP has formalised a set of well-formedness conditions to be considered in the process of setting outcomes. The following list (Figure 8.1) summarises the key points. Addressing all of these conditions should ensure that sufficient thought is being given to realising your outcome.

The NLP well-formedness conditions for outcome setting

1. Stated positively (towards what you want)

2. Described in sensory-based language (see, hear, feel)

3. Started and maintained by you

4. Appropriately contextualised in terms of time, place, people

5. Maintains the current positive by-products, the secondary gains

6. Considers the ecology of the change in terms of cost, time, sense of self and effect on the system.

Figure 8.1 NLP well-formedness conditions

1. Stated positively

You are more likely to realise an outcome which is stated in terms of what you *do* want, rather than what you *don't* want. In other words, specify something which you want to move towards, rather than something you do not like which you would want to avoid. The world provides ample opportunities for being frustrated, and people often state what they want to avoid. A powerful motivator is fear, particularly the fear of losing status. Thus they want to avoid making mistakes of every kind, such as forgetting names or anniversaries, or being caught out by scams, and so on. Personal dissatisfaction leads them to wanting to give up smoking, or losing weight.

The problem with negatively stated outcomes is that first you have to imagine a positive image, and then somehow change the polarity. Try this: "Don't think of a zebra." What are you thinking of? A zebra! You may also be trying to get rid of that image somehow, by crossing it out, replacing the stripes with spots or changing it into another animal, but this can only happen *after* you have first invoked what you are not supposed to be thinking about. You cannot *not* think of something you are not supposed to be thinking about without first thinking about it!

There are good reasons for stating outcomes positively. Thinking about what you *don't* want actually reinforces that negative idea, which then increases the chances that you will end up with exactly the thing you don't want! For example: "I want to stop smoking" gets you thinking about smoking and the benefits it currently provides. Imagining 'stopping smoking' is hard. Choosing to live healthily or "I want to enjoy doing physical exercise" are more achievable as you can actually imagine doing them.

Everyday life is full of prohibitions notices such as "Don't drink and drive" or "Don't walk on the grass." Remember the warning given on TV by trained people doing dangerous stunts: "Don't try this at home!" What are you supposed to be thinking? Even if you weren't thinking about such activities before, you are now. As adults we have learned to process these kinds of injunctions, but young children may not have. Tell them "Don't touch!" and what do they do?! Being asked to conceptualise *not* doing something is hard.

People also use many negative instructions in everyday conversations. For example, telling people "Don't worry about it" or "You can't miss it" when giving them directions. You cannot be sure what such statements make them think of—they may be temporarily confused, or wondering why you should be drawing attention to these things for them: "Why are they telling me not to worry? Perhaps there is something important I ought to know." Or they follow the instructions and miss the turning. Therefore, it is probably more effective to state things positively. You do that by first noticing your own negatively framed language. Instead of beating yourself up for this, choose to phrase things the other way round. It can be quite challenging, but with practice you will succeed.

In a negative, blaming and 'away from' culture, people often tell you what they don't want. If you are working with someone who is clear about what they do not want, or want to get away from, then pace their unwanted outcome by saying, "OK, so that's what you don't want ...", and sensitively switch the polarity from negative to positive, by asking: "What would you rather have?", "What do you want instead?", "What would you prefer to be doing?" or "So if you didn't have that, what would you then be able to do?" Get them to think positively, otherwise you are merely reinforcing the limiting aspects of their desires and they end up with even more of what they don't want! This is like mentally turning and looking in the opposite direction. Have them stand up and look at the 'mess' they want to get away from, and then have them physically "turn to face another way" so that they are looking in a direction which is uncluttered and expansive ... . They may enjoy doing some blue-sky thinking.

2. Described in sensory-based language

It was originally suggested that you imagine your outcome in sensory-based terms—what you would see, hear, and feel when it was achieved. This is linked to the notion of evidence:

- "How will you know when you've got your outcome?"
- "What will you be seeing/hearing/feeling when you've got it?"
- "How will other people be aware that you have got it?"

This is vital if, for example, you are specifying a planting design for your garden or producing an advertising brochure for your business, and want to receive materials which are accurate, as you designed it and in the correct quantity. Having the direct evidence of your senses will inform you that you have achieved your outcome. For example, if you are planning a conference, you will know when you are ready because you will have the venue and catering sorted, a confirmed list of speakers, sufficient numbers attending, and the programmes printed.

How rich is the vision of your imagined future outcome? Is it sufficiently robust that other people can visualise it, 'step into it'? If not, then are you sure you have got it clear? Ensure that an outcome is sufficiently realisable by basing it on the evidence of your senses. Describe in terms of what you see, hear, feel, taste and smell, so that others can use those building blocks to create their own understanding closer to how you perceive it.

This sensory-based notion is falling out of favour, because such superficial aspects may be insufficient or inappropriate for many types of outcomes. People often have vague outcomes: a worthwhile job, a good relationship, being able to make a contribution to society or to fulfil their personal mission. They are OK about the 'variable means' because they are able to recognise when they are on track, are willing to accept what life offers them, and know that even though it may be surprising, they will still achieve their desire in some form. Therefore, outcomes should be specified at the appropriate level. For example, in planning a garden you may need a detailed description of every plant and its location, but this checklist approach may be inappropriate for specifying a good working relationship with the garden design team or winning a prize at Chelsea.

Worthwhile goals are often abstract or ongoing processes. A basic paradigm is: "I want to do x in order that y will do/have z." For example, "I want people to find appropriate ways of using these new paradigms in their own practice of NLP so that they advance its development." You may envisage this, in sensory terms, by imagining practitioners and clients sitting and talking, or exploring metaphors physically by moving around the room together, but these may not fully represent what such an outcome is really about.

General action/process goals cover: "I want to find a way of ...", "I want to know how to do...", whatever it is. This is the challenge of the inventor, designer, creative type and so on. For example, you might want to be better at communicating, improve your health, or increase sales and so on. General or divergent goals are useful when you are open to change, and for inspiring others who will then find their own solutions.

If you ask others (perhaps in a role as manager or team leader) to fulfil your general outcomes, then you should expect variation and innovation. When outcomes are vague—'raised standards', 'increased output'—different people will interpret them in their own way. Politicians often propose fine sounding objectives (wiping out terrorism, cutting drug use, reducing global warming), but how to achieve them is unspecified and may be impossible. Therefore, it is useful to have some specific markers that let you know when you have reached your goal. Vaguely hoping that "I'll just know when I am there", could mean that you won't know when to stop, and you'll keep on going! This happens to people who want more money. They continue to work hard, or keep on gambling .... There never comes a time when they have 'enough'. It's actually the activity that motivates them; the rewards are less important.

There is also the danger in over-specifying an outcome. If you are specifying trees, shrubs or flowers, then you need to state their Latin names, varieties, and also their age, size and condition. But in terms of everyday desires, you need to stay open to the surprise of the unexpected. Perhaps you have had that experience of getting exactly what you asked for, maybe a birthday present you coveted. When you actually got it, was that a good experience, or did it leave you somewhat deflated? Think about your own life and career. It is highly unlikely that it worked out exactly as you planned it. Did you enjoy the process of living with some uncertainty, or would you have preferred to know exactly what lay ahead of you?

3. Started and maintained by you

Can you personally take the first step, then keep going and eventually attain your outcome?

In the early days of NLP, this condition was included as a specific prompt for therapy clients who found it difficult to see themselves as agents of change. For the general population this is not usually a limiting factor. However, there are certain situations where this could be relevant. For example, in a dispute, you insist that the other party has to take the first step: "He has to apologise before I will consider it", "I'll only give up my weapons if you do." When people insist on such conditions, they could be in for a long wait. If both sides are making such claims, stalemate occurs. There is little point in demanding that others must change first, and blaming them when they don't. Would you rather be right or would you rather get your desired outcome? One way would be to get each party to chunk up to the overarching goal they are seeking—peace, harmony and so on, and then find ways for them to achieve this while still holding to their own values. By seeing issues in terms of the bigger picture, and by taking responsibility for your own life, you are more likely to achieve your goals.

Many projects require several people for their completion, and it is important that you can gather around you the team you need for the purpose. In a management or leadership context, you may need the collaboration of a team in order to begin. It may be appropriate to ask:

- "Can you be sure that others will come on board?"
- "How can you influence them to do this?"

Finding resources
Do you have the resources you need to achieve this? If not, what else do you need? You are not starting from nothing; you already have many resources that will assist you. If you are aware

of anything lacking, such as practical skills, specific know-how or further knowledge, then acquiring them becomes a sub-goal. For example, to set up a bed and breakfast, it would help to get some experience in the hospitality industry, or at least visit several B&Bs to do some research on what that lifestyle is like from the proprietor's point of view. To give a presentation, you will need to know how to organise your material, probably how to use computer technology, and the practical skills of projecting your voice, utilising space and engaging with a variety of audiences. With no direct experience, the goal is in fantasy-land. Backtrack and identify a more immediate outcome which involves gaining the relevant know-how.

4. Appropriately contextualised

It is unlikely that you want something all of the time—24/7—in every context, and with everyone you meet. Therefore you need to define some boundaries:

- "When, where and with whom do I want it?"
- "When, where and with whom do I not want it?"

For example, having boundless energy can be extremely beneficial, but not when you want to relax or get to sleep. So where do you draw the line?

Outcomes may also have a 'best-before' date, or a deadline after which they would be no longer required. So ask:

- "When do I want this by?"
- "For how long?"

It seems we each have a preferred rate of change in our lives. Some people live fast; others have a more relaxed approach. (It is useful to notice this when you are getting rapport with them.) Most people need time to adjust to changes. 'Instant' upheaval may be a shock to the system. Consider:

- "How rapid a transition do I want?"

- "How fast do we want to move?"
- "How can we match our rate of change to external conditions?"

5. Maintaining current positive by-products

Change rarely means making a complete 'clean sweep'. Wherever you go, your personal history goes with you. Actually, most of what you currently do is worth keeping, at least in terms of generalities or 'transferable skills'.

"What do you get out of your present behaviour, that you wish to preserve?"

Some people may find that the existing positives far outweigh any unknown future benefits. This might apply with smoking, for example. People smoke for good reasons—being sociable, being part of a certain culture and so on. The cigarette is a powerful token of group membership. Consider these factors before you decide to change that behaviour. If you were to change it, what replacement activities could achieve similar benefits?

6. Ecology

Think about the costs—the monetary cost and the opportunity costs (what else you could be using that time and energy for), how it affects your sense of self, and the possible effect on the system.

Consider the consequences of attaining this outcome:

- "What will be the benefits of having achieved this outcome?"
- "What will be the costs of *not* achieving it?"
- "Is it worth the cost to you?"
- "Is it worth the time it's going to take?"

Compare the likely outcome with the present state. Is it still worthwhile in terms of:

- "Is this outcome in keeping with your sense of self?"
- "How will this change be representative of who you are and who you want to become?"
- "How will achieving this outcome enhance your sense of who you are?"
- "What will be the consequences for yourself and for others?"
- "Is your outcome ethical? Is it supported by your values?"
- "Is this outcome in accord with the principles you hold about the way things should be?"
- "Is this interesting enough to want to continue with? Is it fun?"

Helping other people set outcomes

Outcome setting is a change process. Instead of focusing on the present stuck state, the person is invited to consider some alternative realities in which they are beyond the impasse, with a choice of solutions, doing what they would rather be doing. Changing their state of mind in this way enables them to come up with options. Specifying what they want to be different presupposes that it appears feasible to them, and that the means of achieving it is within their power. Instead of perceiving themselves as stuck or as a 'victim of circumstance', they are now using their imagination to find alternative ways of reaching their goal, and contemplating some of the possible ramifications of their change scenarios.

If you just ask someone, "What do you want?" they are often struck dumb in a kind of Unitary reality, trying to sort through a mass of information about their lives, in which they are too involved. Then you often get a "Don't know" response. You can make it easier for the person by setting a frame for thinking in. Help them get some mental distance by having them think about themselves as composed of parts or roles within their own personal system. Having a part with a specific function somehow seems more manageable. "Think of a part with a specific intention for you." "Imagine you have a part which would be excellent at performing a specific function that you do not currently have. What would that be?" Or you could specify a context and then find what the need or want is: "In this context, what is missing, or isn't working too well?" Bandler and Grinder explore this tactic in *Reframing* (1982: 78).

Metaprogram biases

Although the list in Figure 8.1 offers useful guidelines for clarifying what someone wants, it is biased towards certain kinds of outcomes which NLP values highly, which is an aspect of the preferred worldview of NLP. As such, certain people are classified as 'expert outcome achievers' because they demonstrate a certain flair for achieving their stated goals, share a certain way of thinking. Nevertheless, people are achieving outcomes all the time, and there are many ways of doing it. How people set and achieve their outcomes could match their 'personality' or their general behavioural preferences. NLP outcome setting also has preferred metaprogram biases, particularly towards, detailed and small-chunk, self and so on (Treasure, 2002). However, this does not mean that everyone has to think this way. For example, people who protest about genetically modified foods would fit a different set of biases: away from, big chunk, other-orientation.

It is commonly assumed that an outcome is something you actively go out and seek. So just consider for a moment what it would be like if you were to think of attracting an outcome to you (Faulkner, 2003). This could be seen as an Active/Passive polarity. We find a similar distinction in our metaphors for time: are you moving along a path through time, or do you remain static, and time washes over you as with an ever-rolling stream. There is the expression that some people attract good luck. So could you attract what you want?

Consider the metaphor of the shop. You decide what you want to sell, set up attractive premises, and wait for the customers to come in through the door. Sometimes, when you are busy serving one customer, others appear. The danger is that if you do not acknowledge them, they may simply walk out again. You never know which customers are going to be the big spenders, and you really cannot afford to ignore any of them. It doesn't take long to assess what most of them are there for.

What don't *you want?*

The range of human desire is enormous. One way of beginning to sort them would be to consider some polarities. We have already seen that NLP prefers positively stated outcomes, but this is a choice. People who choose negative outcomes also get changes. Those who prefer to think convergently may want greater certainty or security, or to make sure their investments are safe, or to know some guaranteed ways of making a profit, building their business, discovering the truth. On the other hand, divergent thinkers might want more of a free hand in exploring options, finding out what opportunities have to offer in terms of furthering their interests and finding other ways of understanding their world. This is where knowing exactly what you *don't* want scores, because that then opens up a vast array of alternatives.

What do you really *want?*

People often start by giving safe answers because expressing a lack could indicate personal failure, and lead to a loss of status, appear weak or deficient, and so on. If you notice this pattern, and you want to find out what they *really* want, then adopt a relaxed, intimate tonality yourself, and speaking from the heart ask them, "And what do you *really* want? What would really turn you on, so that you just have to have this outcome …?" Tread softly, because you want them to open up, to reveal aspects of their dreams that they may never have told anyone else about before. Take what they say seriously, and find a way of sharing their passion for exploring what lies deeper.

Whenever people talk about their wants, check their body language, level of excitement, aliveness and so on to ensure that they are sufficiently motivated. Don't accept a suggested outcome if they appear incongruent—"part of me wants this, but another part of me doesn't ..." If they talk about their goal in a flat, dreary, or bored voice, you could repeat this back to them in an even more boring voice, until you get a laughter response. Or tell them how they sound, and suggest that you don't believe they really want this at all. If you have not witnessed any enthusiasm, you can be sure that not much will happen.

The Self–Other polarity

> Ask not what your country can do for you; ask what you can do for your country.
>
> *J F Kennedy*

The NLP outcome process is oriented towards Self, and takes little account of what Others are going to get out of the changes you propose to make. However, some people are motivated primarily because their interventions are intended to affect other people, or because they will be doing things with other people. They want inclusive outcomes, and gain satisfaction from working in a team or by providing some service or benefit for their clients or customers.

Follow through the thinking on your own goals by considering the benefits to others of what you are proposing to do:

- If you achieved your outcome, what would that do for other people?
- How would it affect some of your key relationships?
- How would other people respond to you, or to the changes in you?

"Both sides now"

Setting an Other-oriented outcome means that you need to consider their needs or the potential benefits to them. For example, when drawing up a 'person-specification' for your ideal employee, colleague, partner or mate, remember to look at things from that other person's point of view. A relationship is a two-way process. Consider:

- "What would the other person appreciate in me? What am I bringing to the relationship? In what way would that benefit our relationship?"
- "What does my company offer a potential employee? Why would they want to work for us?"

In other words, why should they want to be with you?! Remember that no one owes you friendship (just as no one owes you a living). You have to work at relationships, which, once established, need to be nurtured.

Ownership

Another aspect of this concerns the ownership of the outcome. Sometimes people are trying to please or placate someone else, rather than wanting the outcome for themselves. Check:

- "Is this *your* outcome? Do you actually want this, or are you doing this because someone else wants you to?"
- "Do you feel you *ought* or *should* be doing this for whatever reason?"

If you are under pressure to do things for other people, or feel obligated to them for whatever reason, then you might be less motivated or less committed to seeing them through. However, you do not have to do anything about these issues unless you want to. At the moment you are just flagging these issues up, gathering information about what you do, and your preferences.

Permission

Unitary types have to obey certain sets of rules or principles. There may be strong ethical concerns about violating the rules, and that means that certain outcomes are not allowed. If you identify this mode of thinking, it would be wise to check personal outcomes: "Do you have permission to do this?" or "You're not going to get punished by doing this, are you?" Similarly, Social types may feel that in doing things for themselves, they need approval from certain significant others within the relevant social group. Therefore, it is important to check that their own wishes are in accord with group values: "Would it be OK for you to do this?" "What would the others say if they knew you were going to do this?"

Outcome planning

Some people like to plan what they are going to do in great detail. They hope to identify and reduce the risks they might encounter, and take sensible precautions to ensure that their time, money, effort are not going to be wasted (whatever that means for them). Although doing some planning is a good idea, trying to plan every last detail could mean that you never get started.

With any kind of stated reservation, you need to ascertain whether they are whole-heartedly committed to this particular change. It could be that their first stated outcome is a smoke-screen, and you need to find out what they *really* want. Check the non-verbal communication, the degree to which you get a congruent answer. If the person claims, "I'm waiting for the right moment", that could be an excuse for avoiding the possible consequences, or might suggest that they have not yet thought things through properly. Using caution, you could accept their 'offer' and respond by stating the obvious: "Well, that's not going to happen then!" and wait to see if there is a tacit agreement, or outraged protest. If the latter, ask for specifics: "OK, so what are you going to do first?" There is rarely an ideal time to begin as there are always going to be mitigating factors, and conditions that have not yet been met to their satisfaction. If they do not want to start now, ask them what conditions would need to be met for them to begin. "So what else needs to happen, or be true, in order for you to begin?" Question the criteria they come up with by asking: "So if you *did* have that, would you then be ready to start?"

You could suggest to them that in working through this outcome-setting process they are clarifying the issues, and that things are now underway! Making them commit to a deadline does focus the mind, and would be a way of reaching better understanding of the real issues.

Managing a change project

Until you start taking action, an outcome is only a dream. Some dreams can be so huge and all encompassing that it is difficult to know where to start. It's like the old riddle: How do you eat an elephant? Answer: one bite at a time. Perhaps acquiring proper project management skills would be the most appropriate outcome to attend to next!

- Break down big outcomes into relatively short-term manageable sub-goals. Ensure that each step is manageable and achievable, and then you will have a series of small successes along the way, which should be acknowledged and celebrated! This maintains motivation.

- Think in terms of what you are going to be *doing*, and for *how long* you will be doing it. The psychologist Douglas Hofstadter (1985: 47) proposed his Hofstadter's Law: "It always takes longer than you think it will take, even if you take into account Hofstadter's Law!"

- If you are planning a long-term project which involves a team of people, then expect that some of them will leave during the project and that any replacements may need training.

- Establish a feedback system that lets you know you're on track, that you are getting what you want. Build in flexibility: have contingency plans, alternatives for getting to your goal.

- Define an exit procedure which specifies the evidence that tells you when to stop, when you have enough. Set a deadline, after which this outcome becomes obsolete. You may also need an exit procedure for abandoning the project if it goes wildly off course or if external conditions change greatly. That may mean cutting your losses. Although you will lose what you have already done, you will not be wasting further resources. However, you will have gained experience, and there may also be other benefits or learning in the future.

Although the future is unpredictable, uncertain, or risky, it is not the case that anything could happen. There are patterns and regularities in the way the world changes, which we perceive as flow, development, growth, unfolding or evolution—depending upon your choice of metaphor. Any future planning should take such 'natural' change processes into account. As you plan your future, assess the degree to which your outcomes are:

Appropriate (it is in keeping with your personality, ethics, and lifestyle)
Ensure that what you want is in keeping with your personal values, your moral and ethical beliefs. It is pointless achieving outcomes that you would not want to live with, are 'not really me', or do not align with the identity of the organisation.

Achievable (it is possible to do this)
Specify the level of performance required. Some outcomes need only be 'good enough'. Excellence or perfection—such as zero defects—comes at a price.

Limit the number of goals for any particular team or group. In general, people are not good at multi-tasking (although women are allegedly better at it than men). Anything more than one goal at a time could potentially cause internal conflict, because each goal could be vying for attention, or unresolved goals are nagging away at the back of the mind and are distracting.

Worthwhile (it adds value to human existence)

A goal should benefit all of mankind, or, as the medical profession suggests, "at least do no harm". Think 'bigger' and choose outcomes that enhance humanity, rather than just you and your immediate customers.

Is this project something you can really commit to? (Be honest!) Check any objections that arise. They need to be cleared before going ahead.

Interesting (there is more to be explored)

Choose goals that create options, rather than close down choices. Life becomes more interesting when you have more possibilities for the future. A transformative change project should be interesting of itself, not hyped up. People should want to own the vision, be part of it.

Durable (it will be appropriate for some time)

The longer the duration of the project, the more the world's political and economic environment will change. Your original goal may become obsolete. World events are unpredictable; it is unwise to assume that conditions will persist for long periods. Consider, for example, the effects of environmental change, tourism, pollution, transport, crime, oil prices, labour costs, and so on.

Collaborative (it takes into account what others are doing)

Your goals need to mesh with other people's projects, goals, outcomes. If you do not know what others are up to, you could be duplicating effort, rather than sharing expertise. Here is another opportunity for finding allies and supporters. It is easier to maintain a change programme when you are with like-minded people with whom you are sharing the experience.

Revise your original plans as you think through all of these points. Check your revised or amended outcome to ensure it is ecologically sound—that is, would you feel comfortable if this were to actually happen?

Ready?

And finally, having been through this outcome editing process, consider: "Are you ready?" If you have a strong feeling that you are ready now, and that nothing is going to get in your way, then go right ahead. On the other hand, if you have a niggling "Yes, but ..." feeling from some part of you, (or some part of your team) then you need to explore further. If the outcome is worth going for, is it worth going for *right now?* Notice your internal response: is it a strong, congruent "Yes!"—or do you detect any hesitation? "Yeah, well, er, sort of ..." means "No". If you find any resistance, check what else you need to do. That could be your next outcome to work on. If not now, why is that? What is the benefit in delaying putting this into action?

The Journey or the Goal?

Have Ithaka always in your mind.
Your arrival there is what you are destined for.
But don't in the least hurry the journey.
Better it last for years,
so that when you reach the island you are old,
rich with all you have gained on the way,
not expecting Ithaka to give you wealth.

From C P Cavafy: Ithaka

The NLP outcome setting process is designed to shift someone's point of view, and the way they perceive their desired future. Instead of concentrating on the past or the present, it gets them thinking about the future. Rather than simply being a checklist, outcome setting is more of a mental discipline. The process encourages people to think through the consequences of their desire to change the world, their intentions and actions. Defining an outcome is about setting the wheels in motion, getting clear about where you are, what you would like to change, and how you might achieve it. Many of our desires are fantasies; by running them through this checklist you can eliminate those which are unrealistic and refine what is achievable so that it is worth going for.

It could also be that the process of getting an outcome is more important than arriving somewhere else. For example, in *The Wizard of Oz*, the four main characters have clearly defined outcomes, which motivate them to visit the Wizard. This is what gets them to make the journey. However, they find the Wizard is a sham and unable to do anything. But in the process, their wishes have come true. It is the journey that matters. People often find that what they get is nothing like how they imagined it, but far better!

Chapter Nine

Asking Questions

I keep six honest serving men
(They taught me all I knew);
Their names are What and Why and When
And How and Where and Who.

Rudyard Kipling (1902) Just-So Stories

The art of asking the right question

Much of the business of 'doing NLP' involves asking questions, because you want to understand why that person who has sought your help is stuck and how best to intervene. The primary use of questions is to gather information. As you elicit information, you may need to ask the person to provide more details, to fill in the context, explain any jargon they use, and generally clarify what they mean. It may help to know what happened previously and what they expect to happen next.

Go beyond the first responses. Often the first answers you get are the safe ones. People are naturally cautious at the beginning of a relationship of this kind, and want to protect themselves. What they say at first is more about testing the waters: Is it OK to tell you this? After all, they may be unsure what you are going to be doing, or what they can safely reveal. As you build rapport, you will find your questions can become more searching. Only when you have a sufficiently clear idea of the nature of the person's problem or issue, and some understanding of their preferred reality model, can you plan how to intervene in order to lead the person to a more resourceful place.

Intervention questions only have the potential for creating change if they are 'right' for that person at that time. There is an art in asking the kind of question that will change the person's perception of reality. It will probably be a perspicacious question that they have not asked themselves, and will therefore get them to reflect on their own experience in a different way. The questions you ask shift their point of view and expand their frame of reference so that they are thinking more flexibly and acting positively.

In a learning or therapy context, the questioning process is itself an intervention. Provoking thinking by asking questions may be more important than getting answers—although the learner or client may benefit from the answers they arrive at. For example, with outcome setting, the key question "What do you want?" is designed to shift someone's thinking away from the present situation into an imagined future, in which they can explore that which is not yet the case, but could be. (NLP and coaching incline towards the future. Other forms of therapy, such as counselling or psychoanalysis, concentrate primarily on the past, believing that people need to understand their past in order to move on. NLP does not subscribe to this belief, and considers "what do you want?" as far more salient.) The question challenges you to think about what you would like to experience instead of your current situation, and then to plan ways of achieving it. The belief is that by imagining a rich vision of how your future could be, it is more likely to come true. Whether this is a valid principle or not is not the point. What does matter is that people who have positive expectations will be more motivated to achieve them.

It is important to gather the information about the person's situation *before* using any technique. You can only intervene effectively once you have identified the issue that concerns them, have some idea of how they are stuck, and know something about how they want things to be different. The way they describe the issue may provide clues about the particular reality mode they are in (Figure 9.1).

Mode	Typical Expression	Reason
[U]	"I'm stuck." "There is nothing to be done."	They believe their model of reality is a true representation of the way the world is.
[Se]	"There is no way of doing X." "It doesn't work." "I don't know how it works."	They are missing a skill, or they have an ineffective strategy or methodology.
[So]	"I can't decide." "I know I shouldn't, but ..." "I don't see the point of ..." "Why are we doing this?"	They have not evaluated or prioritised the options, there is internal conflict around their value-system, or they are not sufficiently motivated by any of the current options.
[M]	"I don't understand." "I have no idea what to do." "I'm lost." "I can't see the wood for the trees."	Everything is open, and they have no way of achieving closure. They have no guiding principles to keep them focused. They may use metaphorical terms to describe their plight.

Figure 9.1 Stuckness in the Four Realities

Sometimes when people start telling you why they have sought your help—"There is this person at work who ..."—you are not sure what the issue for them is. At the earliest opportunity you need to inquire: "So how is this a problem or an issue for you?" Eliciting the 'real' problem may take a while, because the person may not be clear themselves, or they fail to differentiate between the trivial and the relatively important. You need to know what they want to change: "What does this stop you doing?" Then elicit their outcomes: "What do you want to do instead?" and to have them prioritise their needs: "So which is the most important of these, such that if you changed that, all the others would have to change as well?"

Because everyone's model of the world is unique, there are going to be significant differences between your worldview and every-one else's. If the person says, "I just don't think in that way", there is no point in imposing your model of the world onto them. You need to find out how theirs works. Ask questions until you have gathered sufficient information for understanding their worldview: what makes them tick, what led to them getting stuck, what are their needs, wants and desires, what is important to them? Then, as you explore their world in your imagination, you will be able to find things to question: limiting beliefs, anything that does not make sense to you, eccentric logic, inconsistent values, violations of their moral code, or language and analogies which describe their experience in unresourceful ways. Based on this information, you can find an intervention strategy to help them change appropriately. Part of this will be in constructing well-formed outcomes.

There are always opportunities for misunderstanding other people, either because they are not expressing themselves clearly or because you do not have sufficient experience to comprehend what they are talking about. You are lacking the appropriate set of closures and therefore cannot make meaning of the jargon or technical terms they are using. In such a case, it would be possible for you to ask questions and acquire the appropriate knowledge. However, when you are discussing subjective experience, there may be no common vocabulary as the frames for understanding are not clear. For example, in a modeling context, you want to discover what someone does to achieve their goals consistently. Getting useful answers is not as straightforward as you might think. Experts often do not have conscious understanding of what they do, and they provide vague answers: "You know ... Well, I just sort of ... get properly tuned in, and then it just happens ...." Constructing your model of their reality can be a frustrating and time-consuming process.

People respond to being asked questions in different ways, influenced by their personal experience. Some relish the inquiry, because they feel acknowledged, and they happily explore possibilities and gain insights into their own functioning. Most people want others to take their problems and issues seriously, and they are willing to answer questions because they appreciate someone else's undivided attention. Even filling in questionnaires can provide a sense that your views and opinions are important. In general, people want to know more about themselves, and a significant proportion of the population eagerly fill in magazine quizzes, perhaps as a way of acknowledging their own special qualities or ideas. A willingness to examine your shortcomings could be seen as a sign of emotional maturity—both for individuals and for organisations.

Evasive replies

There will be some people who give evasive answers. They do not want to reveal much about themselves because it might make them look stupid or lose status. They may associate being questioned with personal guilt, being found out or shown to be ignorant. Others will give you answers that they think will please you, rather than address their own needs. Before they reply, they select an 'acceptable' answer, rather than what they really want to say. People may also think that their answers have to be creative, clever or original, because anything mundane or conventional will be derided. Even if the question is 'unanswerable' they may feel they have to make some response. Therefore maintain your awareness of the non-verbal responses you are also getting, and challenge them appropriately if you think you are being fobbed off.

Some people are experts at not actually answering the question put to them—and it is not just politicians! You will probably recognise responses that are deliberately avoiding the issues, as their answers never quite connect with what you really want to know. You might draw their attention to this: "I notice that you seem to be avoiding answering my questions directly." Some people may be anticipating the question they think you are going to ask and then answer that—and try to frustrate your strategy of asking unfamiliar questions. Others may be quite explicit: "I don't want to go there ... talk about that ... want you to know is this." There is little point in forcing anyone to reveal what they wish to keep secret. Respect the person's wish, but still flag this up as their decision not to explore this area—for now. Suggest that there may be a time when they need to make this more explicit. "At the moment, this is something you would prefer not to talk about. So let me know when you are ready." This will put some subtle pressure on them to be ready. If you are dealing with an organisation, then are people there willing to make public what has previously been hidden? An immature company may prefer to sweep things under the carpet; a mature one will use this opportunity to learn about themselves and to grow by committing to change.

The NLP Logical Levels

Because of the importance of asking questions, Kipling's 'six serving men' have been used systematically in NLP since the early days. Robert Dilts, a major developer of NLP, devised a schema based on these questions which he calls the 'Logical Levels' (also 'neuro-logical levels'). This has given rise to a whole range of processes which aim to help people to become 'more aligned'—in other words, to perceive any situation from several points of view and then integrate them. The Logical Levels model is basic to NLP practitioner courses, and is described in many NLP books (such as Dilts, 1990: 1-2). Although the particular labels have varied over time, essentially, the questions are arranged in the following structure:

Question Form:	Level:
Who else?	Spiritual/Beyond …
Who?	Identity
Why?	Beliefs and Values
How?	Capability
What?	Behaviour
When? Where?	Environment

Figure 9.2 Robert Dilts' Logical Levels Schema

The model assumes an upward progression, each level offering greater generality. For example, asking *How* someone did something, presupposes *What* they did, and *When* and *Where* they did it. It is also assumed that the effects of changes at a 'high' level will trickle down. So if, for example, you change your beliefs about what is possible, that could easily affect your behaviour and the environment, as you decide to get rid of that which is obsolete, and engage in different activities. In this sense, this list can be seen as hierarchical. But there is some dispute about whether Dilts' model actually constitutes a hierarchy. Given the precise meaning of 'logical levels' in Logic and Mathematics, the term is clearly a misnomer, because a higher level has to 'include and transcend' what is on the level below. Wyatt Woodsmall (1999: 53) comments that, "If the model was simply labelled 'some important elements to consider in any change context', then I would not have a problem with it." But then NLP has frequently borrowed terms from other disciplines, which it then uses in its own imprecise or indiscriminate way. However, while the definitions are in dispute, the applicability of the schema is not.

As Kipling suggests, these questions are extremely useful for gathering and analysing information; they cover the range of any topic quite thoroughly. For example, you could apply this schema to structure and organisation of information. If you are confronted by a mass of data, this offers one way of beginning to sort it and find patterns. When you are designing projects and presentations, the schema ensures you cover all aspects of a topic as you address each question form. It is also useful as a diagnostic tool for identifying where someone is stuck. The question which gets a feeble response could be an appropriate place to intervene.

Making changes at different Logical Levels

When you want to make changes in your life, or within an organisation, consider which level would be the most appropriate for intervening at. For example:

- *Environment:* Adjust the temperature. Change the time at which people arrive or leave, or have breaks; rearrange the furniture; adopt a new dress code and so on.

- *Behaviour:* Instigate new procedures and processes.

- *Capability:* Send people on trainings to learn new skills, or Continuing Professional Development (CPD).

- *Beliefs/Values:* Find out what the prevailing value system is (this is not usually made explicit) and get group consensus on any improvements that people would be willing to adopt. Clarify the beliefs that people hold about the organisation, and provide appropriate experiences in order that they may reconsider them.

- *Identity:* Produce a new logo, a new image for the organisation. You may want to devise a company mission statement about 'who we are'.

Perceptual frames

In the 1995 movie *Jumanji*, the Robin Williams character, Alan Parrish, is resurrected 26 years after having been sucked into a boardgame. Parrish encounters Colin, who is now a cop driving a police car. He asks, "What year is it?" Colin answers, "It's brand new."

Questions are not 'neutral'; they arise from your own personal and inevitably 'biased' frame of perception. You frame your question according to your current perception and expectations about what might happen. The frame metaphor suggests that you only pay attention to certain information and ignore everything else, in the way that a picture frame directs the focus of your attention to a specific area. Paying attention to what is in the frame will affect how you behave and the way you respond to others. The various paradigms being considered all provide perceptual frames. This book has the intention of enabling you to perceive the world in terms of the Four Realities frame.

In the story above, Robin Williams has adopted an information gathering frame, whilst the policeman's frame is about protecting his status. When a question comes out of the blue, the person may not recognise where you are coming from, because of the mismatch between your respective worldviews. At the moment of realisation, each can understand the other's perceptual frame and respond appropriately.

Your perceptual frame will be related to your intention. If you want to elicit a client's history, then your focus will be on the story of their life. Using an outcome frame means you will be oriented towards the future, and be curious about outcomes, directions and purposes. NLP encourages a curiosity frame, which directs your attention to exploring different models of reality. For example, you could be curious about how the person perceives their world in terms of noticing similarities and differences, because this relates to the way they make meaning of it. Do they tend to compare two experiences and notice what is dissimilar and perceive what has changed, or do they prefer to make connections and find analogies and metaphors for interpreting new experiences?

So how did you respond to the Robin Williams story? If you didn't see the joke at first, how did you respond to it? What happened so that it suddenly 'clicked'? What does that say about you?

Convergent and Divergent questions

A question sets a frame which directs the person towards certain general kinds of answers: convergent responses narrow down the options, move towards closure; divergent responses widen the range of possibilities, move towards openness. Before you ask your question, decide which kind of answer would be more appropriate. When you are gathering information, you usually want convergent responses: specific details of things and processes, unambiguous descriptions, evidence of well-formedness. You need to know their outcomes, the intended results. On the other hand, when you want the person to have more choice, you want wide-ranging and divergent answers: general plans, strategies that open up options and possibilities, or 'what if …' thinking that suggests areas to explore, alternative ways of moving beyond the present constraints and so on.

Actually, unless they 'just know' the answer, people first think divergently, and then evaluate and select one answer from all they have considered. However, just having the final result of their deliberations may not be what you want. When people are stuck, enlightenment may come from exploring their thinking processes. Sometimes it is more important to examine *how* they find answers, rather than the answer itself. In so doing, you can elicit their values and criteria for decision-making, so that they become clear about the basis upon which they are choosing.

The question forms themselves exert a subtle influence on the kinds of answers that people give. This often goes unnoticed. People tend to match their answer to the type of question form they have been presented with. For example, when you were asked above, "How did you respond to the *Jumanji* story?" you may have been inclined to think in terms of actions: you laughed, smiled, frowned, looked puzzled and so on. On the other hand, answering "What was your response …?", your answer might have been a noun: laughter, bewilderment or an adjective: amused, baffled and so on. Again, when you thought about "What does that say about you?" you probably came up with a description. This may seem obvious, but asking a 'what' question does predispose people to finding convergent or definitional answers in terms of *content*. If you want people to think about the *process* they used to reach their conclusion, asking *How* questions is probably going to be more effective. But it really comes back to your intention in asking.

Looking at the question forms in the Logical Levels list, most of them request specific or convergent answers. You want the person to come up with precise information, to make definite decisions, to be clear about their current knowledge of their reality.

Whether the question forms act in a convergent or divergent direction depends on your intention, and on the way you ask. For example, adding 'specifically' 'precisely' or 'exactly' to any of the question forms suggests that you want a definite answer. On the other hand, you could speak in a musing kind of way, and use *hedges*—the 'sort of', 'kind of' words which suggest fuzziness or imprecision. "When you think about doing X, what sort of ideas do you come up with?"

Continuing this line of thought, the basic NLP outcome frame question "What do you want?" is quite convergent in what it presupposes, and many people's initial answers will be in terms of things (although they may choose to treat this as a 'general inquiry' and supply a less specific desire response). The *What* question engages the mind in a massive search through their experiences, memories and imagination. Apart from the superficial (a nice car, more money) this is not an easy question to answer, because the answer has to come from deep inside. If you knew it already, you would already have it or be working towards it. Expect "I don't know" responses and suggest that perhaps what they want first is to find out what they want, or how to answer these kinds of questions.

What questions

The answers to *What* questions are likely to be nouns and adjectives, things and qualities, events and milestones. The *What* tends to influence people into thinking in terms of *things* they want, rather than the *process* of getting them. It is probably easier to define an outcome as an event or milestone, the end result of the change process, leaving the actual process of getting there open in some way, allowing room for adjustments. After all, the world is going to be changing even as you move towards your goals. Focusing on the essential *What* you may miss the larger picture. For example, people buying property may concentrate only on the house, and forget that they have to live there all year round, get on with the neighbours, go shopping, take the kids to school and so on. Finding your dream home may temporarily blind you to the reality of living in a new location.

How questions

Because *What* is so common, asking *How* questions can be 'surprising' and flip your mind out of its familiar groove. It is the unexpected nature of *How* that can shift your focus to a place where it can reflect on your wider experience. *How* questions lead you on a more divergent quest which takes you into an alternative reality where ideas and information need to be assembled, where you contemplate hypothetical ways of responding to events, and so on. However, asked with another tonality, the *How* question can also pin you down, define your plan of action, the exact sequence of events needed to achieve a specific goal.

Why questions

Kipling completes his poem about questions with:

> One million Hows, two million Wheres,
> And seven million Whys!

Our society abounds with *Why* questions. Journalists want to know why things happened (and who is to blame), and people in authority are routinely asked to justify their behaviour or intentions. But *Why* does not usually shift anyone's thinking out of its routine programming.

In the early days of NLP, Bandler and Grinder decided to break people of this habit, because it did not produce change, by 'forbidding' NLP practitioners from using *Why* questions. (For an account of this see Hall, 2002). This injunction was not about banning *Why* questions altogether, but to get practitioners to use more effective questions—in particular, *How*—for producing change, and for thinking in more Sensory-mode terms.

Consider what happens when you ask a *Why* question. Pay attention to your mental state and your internal landscape as you seek an answer to "Why did you choose to study NLP?" Notice what happens both in your physiology and in your imagination. Did your head move backwards a little? You will probably find that you are no longer in the here and now, but in a somewhat distant, reflective mode. Did you engage in an extensive scan of your personal history to construct your answer? It will probably be based on a story about part of your life, and explain, subjectively, either what happened, or what you expected to happen.

Why can produce a response from each of the four reality modes (Figure 9.3). Essentially, you get either a justification or a story. In convergent Unitary and Social-mode thinking, the person will tell you which principles or values are being honoured. This could be a statement of their beliefs about the way the world is, or about what they consider sufficiently important to justify a particular course of action.

Why in divergent Sensory and Mythic-mode thinking takes you into story-mode in two possible directions: the past or the future. A story about the past usually explains the logical steps which led to your deciding to do what you did. A future story or scenario will outline what you expect to happen, the perceived con-sequences of your action. In practice, though, you are more likely to get a mixture of explanations. Maybe your story tries to justify your actions by stating your hoped-for outcomes, and your expectations about the perceived benefits of taking such a course.

[U] The Truth. The principles being obeyed.	[Se] The Past. Historical sequence of events that led to the present situation.
[M] The Future. Intention. Expectations and Consequences.	[So] The Motivation. Judgment. The Values being honoured.

Figure 9.3 The Four Realities of Why

These answers can provide insights into your reality-mode prefer-ences, your decision-making process, your values and criteria, and so on. For example, what kind of reasons did you give for choosing to study NLP? Did you do it because someone told you to (for whatever reason), or for sound economic reasons—to fit in with your career progression? Did you want to have more precision in your methodology for producing change? Were you influenced by other people (your friends or colleagues were doing NLP and you didn't want to be left out); or did you choose to do it because you were curious (having met a practitioner, or having heard or read something about NLP) and wanted to know more about it? Whatever the reason, it is only when you are asked that you create a 'rational' story to explain your decision. As with all storytelling, it is your natural ability to organise information that creates a 'convincing' story. If the story satisfies, its job has been done.

Asking a *Why* question can easily produce changes in state, especially if you use a tonality that suggests an ulterior motive. For example, "Why are you studying NLP?" said with narrowing eyes …. If people feel they are being 'interrogated' or made to justify their straightforward actions or intentions, they may become unresourceful and resist further questioning, and you are unlikely to receive a rational answer. If the questioner adopts a position of authority (believing they are justified in asking), and asks, "Why did you do that?", one effect is to undermine the decision someone has made, or even to challenge their right to have made such a decision. However, using a different tonality, one of supportive curiosity, you can help the person explore their model of the world in terms of its values and criteria, and the belief system that holds it together.

What if questions

Another useful question is *What if*. Contemplating "What would happen if …?" takes you into Mythic-mode thinking, which is divergent and open-ended. *What if* is a door into the imagination, through which you get to explore the likely (and unlikely) consequences and ramifications flowing out of the present situation. This is the basis of the NLP concept of 'future pacing', and of the management tool of Scenario Planning (for example, Schwartz, 1991). You imagine how you will be, feel, act in the future, given that you make some change now. Because you imagine this 'future' you can alter or revised it, until it is sufficiently attractive and motivating that you set out on this new course of action. People are generally adept at imagining futures, though they may limit how far into any particular future they will go. By deliberately following through some of the *What if* possibilities, you will enhance your flexibility in thinking through ideas and be somewhat more prepared for what will actually happen.

"As if" Frame

The As if Frame encourages people to explore possibilities by imagining that they are not stuck, or by pretending to be someone who has a different model of the world. This enables them to jump over any immediate obstacles, so that they can investigate their imaginary world and benefit from this alternative point of view. The following phrases are useful for getting the person into the appropriate state of mind (Figure 9.4).

Apart from that …	Pretend you could do whatever you want …
Just suppose …	Pretend that you can do this. What happens?
Have you ever wondered about …?	If you were to suspend reality for a moment …
Hypothetically speaking …	If you could dream …
How would it be if …	If you were to wave a magic wand …
Imagine the alternatives	Take a flight of fancy …
What would happen if …	How would X deal with this?

Figure 9.4 "As if" prompts

The 4MAT Model

The four questions—*What, How, Why, What If*—have been assembled into a practical schema for presenting information to others. The 4MAT System was devised by Bernice McCarthy in 1980, and is currently used in many American educational institutions. McCarthy says that the purpose of the model is to "raise teacher awareness as to why some things work with some learners and other things do not" (McCarthy & Morris, 1994: 7). It is a simple yet effective way of organising material for teaching to a group of learners, presenting to the members of the board, or writing an article, brochure or report. McCarthy found that when introducing new ideas, the order in which you deliver certain kinds of information was critical. Although most people have a strong preference for one particular mode, when you have a mixed group, you need to follow the pattern: *Why, What, How* and *What if*. This sequence is psychologically comfortable for most people.

Sequencing these questions

Why

Start by answering a *Why* question, because the audience wants to know that what is coming is important and worth staying around for. If it doesn't motivate them or concern them, they have probably got better things to do. Tell them why the information is worth knowing, or why the activity is worth doing. Members of your audience will be thinking "What's in it for me?" so outline the benefits for them.

What

Then tell them the *What*, the facts, the basic information, what you want them to know.

Learners need some content, so that they can do something with it, either mentally, or in doing something far more practical.

How

Suggest *How* they could use this information for making changes, achieving their outcomes, and so on. If you are doing an exercise, this is where those who prefer doing, or having 'hands-on' experience will find their preference satisfied.

What if

Finish with some *What ifs*, the probable results of doing whatever. Because every action has consequences, it is wise to think about them beforehand. Every activity opens up further possibilities, and offers opportunities for further exploration. "What would happen if I were to ...?" "How is the world likely to be different ...?"

Connecting the Four Reality modes and the Logical Level questions

The preceding ways of using questions appear to be stand-alone processes. Given that one of the aims of this book is to find a paradigm which integrates the disparate pieces of NLP, the next challenge is to find out if it is possible to integrate the Logical Levels model and the 4MAT schema into a more general model. If we can find similarities at a basic paradigm level, then we can extend our understanding, and find other applications.

I once gave a talk on the Four Realities model at an NLP Psychotherapy conference and demonstrated the Metamirror process (see Chapter Twelve). At a later session the presenter used the Logical Levels frame for her demonstration. As I watched her doing an exercise, I suddenly realised that she was using a similar process to mine, though with more stages. I suddenly connected the Logical Levels with the Four Realities: the superficial details had been obscuring the underlying paradigm. Condensing the Logical Levels into four boxes means some of the question forms have to share the same box. However, it does seem to fit reasonably well. Maybe, before reading on, you could use your understanding of these models to map the NLP Logical Levels questions onto the Four Realities schema.

The Four Realities paradigm gets its power and its wide applicability from being very general. There are many ways of finding specific exemplars. You do not have to invent anything; the four parts already exist, and we usually have names for them. Like the other mappings I refer to, it could seem like 'making it fit', especially with regard to Mythic mode. There appear to be relatively fewer words in English for Mythic concepts, though when you know what you are looking for, you will find an appropriate Mythic version. The test is: Does it work? The Four Realities questions model (Figure 9.5) provides a useful understanding of the interventions you could make, and enables you to extend the range of applications. You could use the Four Realities frame to determine which aspect of an issue needs to be addressed—that is, which aspect is under-represented, or is not usually considered—because it is the non-preferred mode of thinking.

As with the Logical Levels schema, it is better to see all modes as applying simultaneously and systemically, rather than using them in a strict sequence or as a hierarchy. Each is important, though in certain contexts, some are going to be more worthy of attention.

Unitary:	**Sensory:**
Content, Definition:	Process, Sequencing:
What? Where? When? (Who?)	How? How it happens
[Environment + Behaviour]	*[Capability]*
Mythic:	**Social:**
Meaning, Metaphors, Making Connections:	Deciding, Judging, Evaluating:
What if ...? What else ...? (Who?)	Why ...? What's important about ...?
[Identity]	*[Values]*

Figure 9.5 The Four Realities questions model

[U] **Unitary** mode defines the current truth of the situation in terms of the content and context. The foreground focus is on the *what*—the **behaviour** (and *who* is performing it); the background context is on the *where* and *when*—the context or **environment**. Both of these are vital for knowing what *is*.

[Se] **Sensory** mode moves into alternatives: the structures, processes, cause & effect models that demonstrate *how* things happen. *How* is recounted in terms of strategies, plans, and **capabilities**—the ability to act flexibly, the alternative ways in which goals may be achieved and intentions fulfilled.

[So] **Social** mode is about **values**, what matters to us, *why* we do what we do, based on our personal judgments and assessments.

Beliefs has been excluded from this model, because the term 'belief' is so wide-ranging that it can apply to more or less any description of someone's model of reality. There are beliefs which apply to each of the four reality modes, although beliefs are predominantly convergent: Unitary beliefs may take the form of rules or principles; Social beliefs can be in the form of morals or ethics. Sensory beliefs are based on science and logic; Mythic beliefs explore the creative and imaginative ideas we have about ourselves, and the metaphors we use for comprehending ideas.

[M] **Mythic** mode can be interpreted as being about the self *who* is making meaning of the universe, or making connections. We connect and understand what disparate experiences have in common through the use of metaphors. A metaphor draws attention to that which is similar or what is different. There is no single question form for this, although we do ask, "What is this like?" or "What would be a metaphor for that?"

The connection between Mythic mode and Identity involves the way we construct the world around us, how we make meaning of it, and how we perform the 'magic' of change.

Mythic mode also explores: What is possible? Where does this lead, what opens up? Instead of asking "What do you

want?" when outcome setting, use a Mythic-mode suggestion such as: "Think of a story that you would like to come
true."

Note that in this explanation, *Who* appears twice, as it has both
objective and subjective meanings: "who is present" and "who I
am".

In order to accommodate the Levels of Body and Spirit we need to
extend this model; other interpretations of the *Environmental* and
Spiritual dimensions are covered in Chapter Eleven.

How to ask questions

Before you start asking questions, you need to gain rapport with
the other person. When you ask a question, it is a good idea to
look at them while you are speaking. Their initial non-verbal
response may happen extremely quickly, and if you are looking at
your note-pad, you may miss it.

Be clear of your own intentions for intervening in someone else's
reality. Use a framework, such as the Four Realities, Logical
Levels or 4MAT models, so that you can work in a way which
tends to match the person's line of thought (or at least, will make
sense to them). Part of your task as a questioner is to identify
where you have leverage. That is to say, choose questions which
interrupt at least one of their patterns and which therefore have
the potential to shift the person's perception of their situation by
getting them to do what they usually do not do. Reflecting on
their own experience alters their understanding.

Managing your state is important. For gathering information you
need to be genuinely curious, fully present and to pay exquisite
attention to the person you are with. If you are not being authentic, perhaps wishing that you were elsewhere, or wondering how
you could hurry them up ... then they will pick up on this. If you
notice you are 'switching off' because you are getting bored, then
point this out to them. "You know, as you tell me this, I am feeling
really bored. I'm wondering how it is for you." It gives them

the opportunity to check in with their own feelings—they may actually be boring themselves, especially if they have told the same story so many times that it has become a habit.

What is obvious?

When you regard the person in front of you, notice what is obvious about them. The question "What is obvious here?" comes from Gestalt Therapy. Do not ignore information about another person which could be indicative of their general way of being. How are they presenting themselves, in terms of their clothing, their jewellery, make-up, piercings, tattoos and so on. Do they conform to current fashions, or do they seem to prefer to do their own thing? Is their clothing neutral greys and blacks, or do they wear bright colours? Their outward appearance can make it easy for you! This is how the person chooses to communicate something important about themselves. This could be valuable information, but you won't know what it means or whether it is significant until you have checked it out. There is no point in guessing, when you can simply state the obvious, and get their response.

If deciding how to present yourself is a conscious choice, then consider: What does that say about them? For example, is someone who wears several mismatching bright colours going to be a 'colourful' person who tends to 'clash' with other people? This kind of obvious metaphorical connection can provide a short-cut to understanding more about the person, as it saves a great deal of questioning. It could be that they are not consciously aware of how they come across because it has become customary or they do it unthinkingly. When you draw the person's attention to their appearance, that could produce a shift in their understanding. They could also dismiss your observation as irrelevant, your literal interpretation as nonsense, because there is no symbolic meaning in what they do! However, by focusing on what is obvious, you are providing them with an opportunity to make connections and give meaning to their physical appearance.

Dealing with silence

> Silence is a mirror. So faithful, and yet so unexpected, is the reflection it can throw back at men that they will go to almost any length to avoid seeing themselves in it ....
>
> *Tom Robbins (2000: 324)*

As the person gives you an answer to your question, give them your undivided attention. Look at them, because it may be that the non-verbals reveal more than the words themselves. Observe their body-language, especially their facial expression and eye-movements, as it is these small changes that give clues to their thinking patterns. Listen to what they say, but do not delude yourself that you know 'exactly what they mean'. You don't, even though the words seem familiar. It is far safer to assume that the words they use are secret codes for their experience, which only they know about. So extend your inquiry beyond that by asking, "So if you had X, what would that do for you?"

Allow the person time to respond. If they are silent, avoid jumping in to rescue them. If you feel uncomfortable with silence and fill it with another question, you may be inadvertently giving them an excuse for avoiding the real issue. Key information often emerges when the person feels they have to fill an awkward silence. Reflection takes time, so welcome these reflective moments, even though they seem to stretch out .... Allow a pause to continue just as long as they are engaged in thought.

Neither is there a need for you to do their work for them. For example, a client who came for coaching said, "I thought you were going to suggest some ideas for me." Some possible responses would be: "About ...?", "Such as ...?" or "So if I were to suggest an idea, what kind of idea would that be?" Remember who owns the problem, and beware of those transiting monkeys!

If you pay attention you will often notice that thoughts are being 'censored'—that is, the person comes up with an answer, then thinks about it, and then decides not to say it. If someone is taking 'too long' to answer the question, suggest they simply say the first thing that comes to mind, whatever it is. "It may not make sense, but just say it anyway." Don't expect 'perfect' answers instantly. When you ask someone to restructure the contents of their mind, it could take some time to reorganise it, and then to construct a story to explain it.

Notice what the person does *not* say, or seems to be avoiding or ignoring, as this information could hold the key to moving out of stuckness. For example, some people do not use 'I' but 'they' or 'one' instead. Check whether such preferences or omissions are relevant. Be open about this: "I notice that you do not mention …. Is there any reason for this?" Check that their body-language aligns with the content of what they are saying—that they are congruent in their replies. Again, you might want to point out any incongruence, to find out what else is going on for them.

People probably do not want to linger with what is uncomfortable for them, so they rush on to the next safe topic. If difficult questions are perceived as stressful, they seek an easy way out by coming out with a pat answer, one they don't have to think about too much. However, by not allowing them to indulge in such habitual responses, they have to spend time with the stuckness. Your questions should urge them to get curious about their own behaviour, explore alternative views, and then reorganise and restructure their ideas in such a way that brings out new understanding. As their model of the world changes, they will then have more options available. What they actually say as the answer to your question can be irrelevant—the work has already been done, or is ongoing.

Four ways of avoiding the question

Blaming

Some people are unwilling to take personal responsibility for their own lives, for getting stuck. Instead, they will blame other people for their present state. They may see change as the responsibility of others, and will say things such as: "If only *they* got their act together …" or "All I want is other people to change, and then I'll be all right!" One approach to this is to exaggerate their claim, make other people responsible for everything in their life, and suggest that really they are just a puppet for them. The extreme nature of this suggestion should produce some kind of denial!

Remaining detached

Other people may take a detached or fatalistic view of their lives, and see everything that happens as a result of forces they cannot control or affect. They may have a frantic or resigned attitude to this, either trying against the odds to change the world, reminiscent of the hero of Franz Kafka's *The Trial*, Joseph K, who tries in vain to find out what he has been accused of and how he can affect the power of his unseen controllers. They give up the struggle as they realise the pointlessness in trying to change the Unitary mindset and its accompanying Sensory Bureaucracy. Other people will attribute their current stuckness to their genes, or their birth sign, or any other excuse that allows them to not be in charge of their own life, such as Fate, Kismet or Karma.

Doing it for someone else

Have you ever had someone say to you "I shouldn't be doing this!" or "I ought not to tell you this, but ..." and you wonder, "Who is in control here?"? Is there some other person or group who decides what happens in this person's life?

Some habits are tough to break. The person may not want to break them, even though they are limiting or debilitating, because of what they represent—maybe a significant relationship with a parent, carer, or teacher which dates back to when they actually were dependent upon someone else. To do their own thing would be breaking that connection, and they would feel bad about doing it. So they still check in with what that other person would want, rather than doing what they really want to do. You could get the person to update their perception of this relationship by asking

"So if this person were here now, what do you think they would want for you? What would they consider would be in your best interests?"

It could be that our emotional feelings are the final arbiters on our behaviour. For example, another avoidance strategy is to seek a sympathetic response. The person says, "I'm depressed", "I'm useless" or "I've got a terrible memory". A challenging response that doesn't give them a way out is to simply say "Oh". To encourage them to continue, to say more, all you need to use are some prompt words, such as "And ...?", "Because ...?"or "Really?" with a rising, questioning inflection. You could play-fully suggest, "Just pretend you have an excellent memory!" Or you may stay in the silence, and perhaps raise an eyebrow ... Alternatively, you can use a *How* question, such as, "*How* do you make yourself depressed?" The person has to think about them-selves from another viewpoint before they can answer. Act as a mirror. If the person says things which you do not understand, or what seem to be bald statements such as "I was feeling sad", and no more, then repeat, "You were feeling sad ..." with an open-ended questioning tonality.

Telling stories

Many people avoid the possibility of thinking deeply about them-selves by recounting ready-made and often well-rehearsed stories. To familiar questions they have pat answers which ensure that nothing changes. As you listen, you may get the impression that what you are hearing is not new, that they have told this story before, perhaps on many occasions. Most people have their own collection of stories—based on what happened to them, or to the car, or the neighbours, or to old school-friends—which they tell to available audiences on social occasions. You may have honed your own stories to perfection. And as you tell that particular story about the time you did X ... one more time, you realise that it has lost its lustre, it is no longer lively or amusing. A quick check of your audience will reveal eyes glazing over, or people itching to get away.

If you notice that a person has gone into 'story-mode' and appears to be reciting rather than reflecting, then you need to bring them back to the present. If a provocative style is OK for you, then one way of interrupting would be to start yawning, or pretend to fall asleep! Otherwise wait politely for a pause in the flow, and then intervene by raising your hand and saying "Stop!" You could then straight-forwardly check your perception: "I think that you may have told this story before. Am I right?" Or you could ask a specific question about what they have said. Your intention is to get them to see things afresh, find a different angle, rather than give them a chance to explain or justify. So ask them: "What was the most unusual part of this?", "What did you learn from this?" or "So what does this story say about you?" You might inquire about what is important or relevant about the story. Or ask: "And the point of this is ...?" People only have ready-made answers to predictable questions. Therefore, your strategy will be surprising.

Sometimes people tend to beat about the bush and not commit themselves to a definite or Yes/No answers. In that case, you could force a decision upon them by suggesting, "I'll take that as a Yes/No!" This will get them to consider the options now presented. You may have stated the answer they would have eventually reached, or the answer presents them with immediate conflict. Either way, they have collapsed the probabilities and you both have a clearer idea of where to go next. They may want to justify that choice, but this is unnecessary from your point of view. You simply want them to accept the choice they have made and consider its consequences.

Curiosity leads you to explore where people don't usually go. Questions intended to create change have the effect of metaphorically getting the person to stand back from their limiting situation, so that they can expand their vision, and explore what lies beyond their current limitations. Taking the wider view, other possibilities then become available to them. Once they are curious, thinking outside the box, their universe expands accordingly. However, that in turn will become another larger box with its own set of limitations. Whatever your current perceptual frame, you can also think bigger .... There are no ultimate or complete realities—just ways of perceiving in the moment, each of which will in its turn become obsolete. Asking questions means thinking one step beyond the present question. And beyond that .... But one step at a time.

"If this is the answer ... what was the question?"

It is often the case that it is your language, and especially your metaphors, that have got you to a place of limitation and restricted choice. And all you have to do then is to ask a "How can I ...?" question and notice the answers you get. When you ask questions, the mind delivers answers. However, they may be answers within a different frame, and you do not immediately recognise them. If you adopt the frame of expecting the unexpected, then you are more likely to notice what you actually get, rather than dismissing it as random noise. You then need to make the connection between the answer and your original question: "How does this answer help me?" It could be the process of making the connection that shifts your perception, your frame of mind.

My t'ai chi teacher used to say: "If you want to know how you're doing, look around ..." What is the world telling you about where you are right now? Is your world bright, and fun to be in? Do you wake every morning raring to get on and enjoy life even more?

You could play with this idea by assuming that at some time in the past you asked a question and that in an unexpected way the universe has produced an answer. As it is not immediately clear what that answer is, you need to read between the lines, as you consider, "What is this about?", "What is the message for me?" What was it that you wanted to have, or to know how to do? How does this present state meet your needs? You may need to interpret the evidence in a symbolic or metaphorical way. And if you are not happy with this answer, then you know what to do.

Chapter Ten

Working with Parts and Roles

All the world's a stage,
And all the men and women merely players;
They have their exits and their entrances;
And one man in his time plays many parts,
His acts being seven ages.

Jaques in As You Like It, Act II Sc 7

From One to Many

Looking at the world—at yourself, at other people, and all the myriad of things that you can discriminate—gives you a strong sense that "This is how it is". The world has a sense of completeness, it appears to be full of definite things, and this suggests a high degree of permanence and stability. You experience yourself as an *individual*—'that which cannot be divided'; as 'me'—an enduring identity; and as living in a world which has substance, continuity, and tangible reality. This illusion of reality is extremely powerful because it admits of no others. The trick is to remember that in one sense you are choosing this point of view. Such a monolithic experience of the world is a Unitary perception: what you see is what you get, and that is it. There are no alternatives. Although it certainly makes living in the world easier most of the time, it can also rob you of the power to change anything. No wonder it is easy to sometimes imagine that you are stuck!

Remember that the truth of Unitary mode is not absolute, but only a truth in that context. You can perceive reality from other points of view. If you assume, for example, that you are constructing reality from your own experience, knowledge and understanding, then you will be less easily 'taken in' by your senses, and you can enjoy the complex illusions your mind creates.

You do not always perceive yourself as an individual, but as consisting of a number of aspects or sub-personalities. For example, the various characters in the *Wizard of Oz* could be seen as representing aspects or 'parts' such as *heart, intelligence, courage, intuition*, and so on. Thinking of yourself as being 'divided' will be familiar when you consider the experience of being undecided, untogether, being of two minds, or of being pulled in different directions. You might describe this state using a 'parts' metaphor: "Part of me wants to go to the party, but another part of me would like a quiet evening at home." "I'd like to be famous, but I wouldn't want to have my privacy intruded upon." Have you ever thought that you were 'going to pieces', or felt you were 'beside yourself' or 'all over the place'? Were you told to 'pull yourself together'? If you were to do that, would the sum of the parts add up to a 'whole' or would there be gaps or spaces in your life?

You probably consider that you have some unacceptable or 'unwanted' behaviours, or you do things that you wish you didn't do (referred to metaphorically by the psychologist C G Jung as 'the shadow self'). Maybe you engage in activities which 'aren't really you'. You may become aware of such internal conflicts when you are hesitant or resist doing certain actions, or when you do things and feel bad afterwards. You might think of this as having some kind of battle raging within you, which is either inhibiting your behaviour, or somehow giving you pause for thought. One way of making sense of this experience is to see yourself as composed of parts, each with its own intention. If you are not honouring all the needs of the various parts, there is bound to be disharmony.

NLP uses this parts metaphor for creating ways of moving out of stuckness. If you perceive yourself as a monolithic being, it is hard to find alternatives. However, if you assume you comprise a number of parts, you can use that metaphor to your advantage. For example, the NLP Six Step Reframing technique (see below) presupposes parts with specific functions: the creative part, 'the resource part' or 'the part which organises the other parts'. By entering into dialogue with these parts, you can ask them to come to some agreement amongst themselves—assuming of course that your parts will have your best interests in mind. You can also use your imagination to adopt different points of view or Perceptual Positions (see Chapter Eleven) and mentally relocate your locus of vision by moving back to observe yourself, by stepping into someone else's shoes, or seeing things from a fly-on-the-wall position. This ability to separate, move and expand your awareness is vital to the change process.

The Sensory realm of parts

Operating in Sensory mode enables you to analyse, break things down into parts, steps, sequences, building blocks, aspects, and so on, to provide an alternative way of seeing how your reality has been put together. What appeared to be monolithic is now seen as having a composite structure, built from elements or parts. Instead of being faced with a single block, the edifice can be dismantled brick by brick, timber by timber, until it is reduced to its components. You begin to see how the elements were combined logically, hierarchically, and sequentially into that experience which you would wish to change. Then it becomes much easier to rearrange, reorder, delete or substitute those elements. By changing the way things happen—the programming—you can move on, revise your model of the world.

What makes NLP special is its emphasis on analysing how you have created a particular perception, and in ways of re-creating them in order to enhance your life. For example, the NLP concept of submodalities focuses the person's attention on the qualities of the *content* of their perception, in terms of size, distance, brightness, colour, orientation, and so on—the kinds of qualities that a designer would be interested in. By redesigning your perceptions, you change their meaning. For example, when Dorothy goes from the sepia world of Kansas to the Technicolor world of Oz, you may experience an emotional jolt. Your experience also involves *process*: the sequence of events that happened, the strategies you use to fulfil your needs, the stories you create to understand your life. Changing the sequence and elements of your strategies to match those which your skilled role models demonstrated is a way of creating personal excellence. Running a memory or story backwards, in the way that you can fast rewind a video-tape, will definitely change your emotional response to that event.

The headache cure

A separation process can be used for dealing with some kinds of physical ailments such as headaches. Your Unitary understanding says that "I and my headache are one". One approach is to separate 'me' from 'my headache' by imagining moving the headache outside of your body. Put it out in front of you where you can see it. Give it a colour. What colour is it? Bright or dull? What colour and brightness would you like it to be? Does it have a shape? What shape would be better? See it begin to change to that colour and shape. Maybe the headache has a message for you. If it could speak, what would the headache tell you? And so on.

You have changed the reality in which that headache existed. By putting it where you could deal with it, you can adjust its qualities or submodalities, so that it takes a different form, which in turn affects your response to it.

A collection of roles

You can also perceive yourself as being multi-faceted when you consider having or taking on a number of different roles in various contexts, to meet differing needs, or to perform a variety of functions. For example, at any one time you can be a child, student, parent, lover, adviser, carer, breadwinner, team-player and so on.

You can also see yourself as a part of a larger whole or social group, as a member of a family, organisation or professional body, as belonging to various clubs, societies, or teams. Other people may impose other classifications upon you according to your lifestyle, shopping habits, religious beliefs or political views.

Instead of thinking of yourself as being composed of parts, you now see yourself whole, but as a part of some larger entity. From the group's point of view, as a part or member of it, you have a role or function to perform within that group. Consider, as part of that entity, "What is my role? What am I meant to be doing?" Roles are for specific activities to be performed in specific contexts or circumstances only, not for life.

Changing roles

You may physically change your role by putting on a uniform: "These are my gardening clothes", "Do you like my wedding outfit?" Metaphorically, you may see changing your role as trying on various pieces of clothing: "I'm trying this [way of thinking] on for size." You could even adopt a whole personality, and discover what that would be like. When you assess a new role, you move to Social-mode thinking and evaluate that role in terms of its appropriateness for you. How easy is it to take on the role? You try it on for size to discover whether it fits, or whether a proposed or anticipated change is to your liking, will meet your criteria, or produce the outcome you desire.

This is a natural thing for people to do. Young children enjoy dressing up, pretending to be adults, or mimicking their favourite fictional character or real-life sporting hero. Teenagers often adopt roles to try them out, to find out "Who am I?" Many computer games are specifically designed to have the players adopt roles which they then act out in an unconventional, nonhabitual way. Internet chat rooms also provide an opportunity for young people to pretend to be older, wiser or more socially successful. They report that the anonymity of electronic communication makes it easy to take on another personality. If you are shy, then you can explore what it would like to be more outgoing. Then you not only attract attention to yourself, but you can make other people feel good. It also offers the possibility of talking to someone outside of your usual social circle with whom you can discuss matters which relate to your family, to yourself growing up, and so on, because you would feel embarrassed talking about these things to people you know. In my own experience, young people have emailed me as a result of reading my books because they want to communicate with someone who can possibly answer their questions. This is an appropriate activity to engage in during the teenage years, and I always respond to such requests. It is desirable for young people to explore their identity, to have them try out alternative personalities and roles, in order that they can move into adulthood with some idea of who they are and what they are going to be doing.

Adults also adopt different roles according to context, maybe as part of their job: "Right, now I have to go into Sales mode" or "I have to entertain our guests." In an NLP context, you need to take on different roles when doing exercises with other people (Appendix B contains guidelines on the roles for doing NLP exercises), whenever you are establishing rapport with others, and it is the essence of the Sculpting Exercise 6.1, which enabled you to adopt someone else's physiology for a while.

The Mythic realm of realities

Mythic-mode thinking is monistic: you and the reality you have created are as one. But this reality is unlimited and impermanent. As you are the creator of your reality, you have the ability to create any reality you choose. You know that they are all true in their own way, that each has its own validity. It may be temporary, but it offers the opportunity to explore, to learn, as long as it remains interesting. Having this kind of understanding is ironic. You have to believe in the illusion in order to get on with your life, while knowing that it is all made up.

In Mythic mode, you live in a universe of your own creation, take on any role or identity you choose, and 'be' that person. You act *as if* the reality is true. In this mode of thinking, you are still an individual, but different from the one who was stuck. This is a useful ploy: be someone who has already solved this problem, or who demonstrates the skills you deem appropriate, such as Einstein, Henry V, Machiavelli or whoever.

Your internal team

Given all these different ways of perceiving yourself, any one of them could be used in moving out of stuckness, or away from a limiting worldview. Although it is possible to identify specific roles, in the NLP process known as Six Step Reframing you treat your collection of parts with specific roles or functions. In order to understand each part or role, you first get rapport with it, and then explore its purpose for you. Then it becomes possible to understand how they interact, and to negotiate with them to produce a more aligned and harmonious arrangement.

Given that you already have experience of splitting yourself into different roles, remember that you also need to maintain an integrative or leadership role which will manage the rest of your internal team, and maintain a unified purpose. If all your parts, roles and personalities are aligned, you will come across as authentic to those you are working with.

Six Step Reframing

The Six Step Reframing process was an early development by Bandler & Grinder (1979: 160; 1982: 114). It was designed for dealing with unwanted behaviours, but you can also use it for any kind of conflict, stuckness, for dealing with secondary gains, for any issue in which you can imagine you are dealing with several parts with conflicting needs.

This process draws on your ability to work as a mediator with your internal parts and their roles when conflict has arisen. For example, you could imagine that you have a part which has the role of maintaining good health, and another part which wants excitement and takes risks. Because you have a range of desires and interests, it is not always going to be easy or obvious how to make clear decisions about your course of action. One way to resolve this internal conflict is to accept this personification, deal with the parts and roles as you would real people who are engaged in conflict, get them all talking to each other, and find a way of reaching a resolution. Treat each of the parts or warring factions with respect. You need to get in rapport with them, acknowledge that they are doing their best to serve you, and to clarify what their intentions for you are. To do this, you need to trust your mind to provide you with the answers. This is about accepting the messages your unconscious mind sends you, and finding their meaning in the context of a conflict between disputants who are 'part of me'.

Assume that each party in the conflict has its own agenda, needs, intention for the whole. The first step is to establish rapport with each of the parts, and to ask them if they are willing to communicate with you. Once you have cooperation, you need to find out about their specific intentions for you. The direct approach is to ask them. It may seem strange to ask yourself questions, but heed the wisdom of: "If you ask a question, then you will get an answer." Pay attention to the answers which come. Your mind will also give you names, roles for the parts within this particular conflict, such as 'the part that wants to travel' and 'the part that wants to stay home'. Other parts will be introduced as you need them.

Outline of the Six Step Reframing process

1. **Identify an unwanted behaviour, conflict or stuckness.**
   What do you want to change? What is the issue to be resolved? How could you perceive this as a conflict between parts? Which parts might be involved? What would their specific wants or outcomes be?

2. **Establish the positive intention of that unwanted behaviour.**
   Make contact with those parts in turn, acknowledge their existence, and gain rapport with them. Go inside and say "Hello" to the part of you responsible for this unwanted behaviour or one side of the conflict. Notice what happens, what kind of response you get. You may see pictures or words, hear a voice, or have some kind of feeling.

Thank that part for responding, and then ask it: "What is your positive intention for me?"

If you get a negative intention, chunk up by asking: "And what would that do for me?" until you get a positive outcome.

In a conflict, address all the parties involved, and find out each intention in the same way.

3. **Go to the creative part of you.**
   There is no point in assuming that you can resolve this consciously. If you could, you would have already done it! Therefore have a part which has this ability. So go inside again and make contact with that creative part of you. Say to yourself, "I would like to talk to the creative part." Notice what happens. Get rapport with this part. Then have that creative part generate at least three alternative behaviours that are "more acceptable, more immediate, more available, easier, faster than the one you are using now" (Bandler & Grinder 1982: 185), or find a way of mediating in the conflict by finding some possible solutions that will honour the positive intentions and satisfy all parties.

   Tell the creative part to give you a signal when it has done this. Otherwise it could do this and close down, and you would be none the wiser. If you think of this part as cleverer than you, then adopt a lower status, and politely request that it does these things.

4. **Secure agreement for the new behaviours.**
   Now revisit the other parts, and get their agreement that they will try out these new behaviours, or work towards the resolutions that have been generated by the creative part. It is a good idea to put a time frame on this.

5. **Future pace.**
   Test that you have (already) got a change by going into the future and exploring the consequences (this is covered in more detail below). Imagine yourself in a future context, seeing yourself acting confidently without the previous hesitation or stuckness, or with the conflict resolved and harmony reigning

once more. Does this seem real? Notice how you will be behaving differently. Also check whether there are any other changes that need to be made. If so, ask your creative part to deal with this, until the situation feels OK.

6. **Ecology check.**
   Go back inside and ask if there are any other parts of you which are not OK with these new behaviours or decisions. If there are any objections identify the part and its positive intention and repeat the process from step 2.

Dealing with internal conflict

Six Step Reframing is conventionally done as a internal exercise, though there is no reason why you should not have the different parts sitting round a conference table, or whatever. You can manage the internal conflict by having the two parts ('the part of me that wants X' and 'the part of me that wants Y') to physically take up separate locations, so that they can address each other, as well as you. In Gestalt work, this form of dialoguing was known as the Two Chair Technique. By taking each (physical) position in turn, the person engages in a dialogue, which, with coaching or guidance, should lead to a resolution of their issue.

However, conflict resolution is not always easy. Some simple conflicts that can be resolved by getting each party to chunk up their needs to a more general kind of want, until you find common principles and values. Whereupon it becomes a matter of sorting out the specific manifestations of these principles or values that will satisfy both parties. There is a similar technique in which the person can separate the two sides by embodying them in their hands: literally 'on one hand ... and on the other hand...' and then finding a way of bringing them together, and reintegrating them into yourself.

Many kinds of conflict are far more complex than this, and an approach to resolution which is based on Four Reality thinking has been developed by Will McWhinney (McWhinney, 1995). I have written briefly on this in *Change Manager* (Young, 2003: 217–230).

Using spatial separation

One way out of being stuck is to find a way of distancing yourself from that context. You can simply leave by walking away; or mentally or physically step back and move to 'neutral ground' in which you can reflect on what is happening. But remember that this can be a Catch-22 situation: you need to get unstuck in order to stop being stuck, and the moment you can think this way, you are no longer stuck. But when you are stuck, you perceive yourself as not having that option. What do you do? You anticipate certain kinds of problem situations, and set up the escape mechanism beforehand, using an anchor triggering for the state— working on the Body level. You are acquainted with many anchors that produce negative or anxiety states, such as the sound of alarms or explosions, the sight of blood or flames, the smell of burning or of rotting meat, and so on. In the same way that music or perfume can be used to create positive feeling states, you could devise your own triggers that will enable you to be in a resourceful state whenever you choose.

Circle of Excellence

The Circle of Excellence is a key NLP technique that uses the notion of spatial separation. You would use it for enhancing your state for specific contexts or occasions, for example, feeling more at ease when presenting, or more confident attending a job interview. You could think of your Circle of Excellence as a portal to a different space or way of being, your Land of Oz, so to speak, which you can enter whenever you choose. To set this alternative reality up, start by imagining a spot on the floor which you can step onto. You are then going to anchor a number of life-enhancing resources to that movement, so that when you step into your Circle of Excellence you will experience a more positive and supportive way of being. To do this you need to anchor several life-enhancing states—'stack' them—so that at some future time you will be able to access that composite resource state when you want it.

Outside of the Circle is your reflective space for gathering resources—the specific states appropriate for your future event. By remembering a time when you were in a particular state, you experience it once again. You need to combine at least three resources. Each time you think of one, imagine having it now, and then increase its intensity. As it begins to peak, step into your Circle and fully experience that feeling again. As it reaches maximum intensity, anchor that experience using different sensory anchors. Decide on the specific anchors you are going to use beforehand. For example, make your Circle coloured or otherwise memorable (Visual), say a code word (Auditory), and a special touch (Kinesthetic). You could apply pressure to part of your arm or hand which you would not normally do (choose something you can do without drawing attention to yourself). You could shake hands with yourself. When you want to reactivate this particular state of excellence, fire your kinesthetic anchor, say your code word to yourself and imagine stepping into that circle.

Using this combination of anchors will immediately put you into your desired state, such as feeling calm and confident, or fired up and ready to go. When you have stacked your three or more states, test that this is sufficient. Imagine the future situation which would have been stressful, put yourself in it, and fire your anchors. Notice how you feel. If this is what you want, then you are finished. If not, step out again and ask yourself, "What else do I need?" Find a further resource and add it in.

Time metaphors

Testing your work is a vital part of the change process. When you are working with a client, it is important to test your work while they are still there to ensure the intervention has worked and that they know this. One way of doing this is to use a spatial metaphor for time.

Time is often visualised as a line joining past, present and future. For example, history is often represented as a timeline, usually with the past on the left and the future on the right, probably because in our culture we read from left to right. Sensory-mode thinking perceives time as a linear sequence, a single line running from the past towards the future. This metaphor offers a way of analysing an issue into its past, present and future parts by arranging them spatially along a timeline. Physicalising the time-line on the floor makes it much easier to deal with events in your life: you move back or forward along the line until you locate the place which represents a specific event in your past or your future. By stepping into these different locations, you can assume the relevant point of view, and perceive your reality from that perspective.

As with the Circle of Excellence, if you need to reflect on your experience or gather resources, you just need to step off the line to do so. The timeline metaphor also uses the idea of floating or fly-ing above the line—both to get movement through time, and to provide a different perspective: you can look down from a bird's eye view, or be 'above all that'.

If you wish to change a particular behaviour or response which you currently have, then the timeline metaphor allows you to track it back to its origins in your past. When you ask yourself to 'go back to where this all began' then your mind will locate its source somewhere along your timeline. Using a spatial metaphor makes this process easier, and more believable. Often you will not be directly aware of the source memory and you could be sur-prised at what comes to mind. For example, if you locate specific ages along your timeline, and then find that when you reach age eight you get a signal that a particular memory is associated with an event then. You make sense of this by either remembering those events at that age, or you create the story about such-and-such an event occurring at that age, which is the 'cause' of your response now. This story 'explains' how things are right now. However, there is the danger that you confuse the story with the 'reality', which is what happened in many cases of False Memory

Syndrome (see Yapko, 1994), in which some therapists promoted the idea that their clients' stories were true.

There is no point is checking records or diaries to find out if that event 'really' happened. That is not the point; the historical truth is irrelevant. What you need is to be able to intervene in a way which will bring about a desired change now. An effective way of doing this is to change the story you are currently running by rewriting it. It is far easier to revise a work of fiction than to actually travel back in time and change events directly!

Future pacing

You can also use a timeline to find out what is likely to happen in the future. You do not need to consciously create a scenario. Instead, you assume a future self which has already made the change. Visit this future version of you by walking up your time-line just as far as you need to go in order to experience that altered state, step into that you, and experience how it is. Are these consequences what you want? If you have specified the kind of change you want, then you should be satisfied. However, it is possible that you forgot some aspects, and therefore when you 'future pace' yourself you get a message that something else needs to be attended to now.

Future pacing is essentially a Social-mode evaluation of your proposed outcome or change. Ask yourself:

- Is it what I want? Does the change hold? Will it endure for a sufficient length of time?
- Is the change ecological? Does it have unforeseen consequences—on yourself, others, the environment—which now appear less desirable?
- Now that you have this, do you really want it? Ask yourself: "Is this me?", "Is this what I really want?" You may have created an outcome which is not really for you, does not match your values.
- Are there further changes you need to make?

Remember this is imaginary and that you can still make adjustments now in order to improve what is likely to happen. Even then, when the future event does occur, you may find that all the work you did has been 'forgotten' because you have incorporated the changes in your general (updated) way of being, and that what had been an issue in the past is now no big deal.

Working spatially: The Disney Creativity strategy

The working space does not have to be a time metaphor. It could be the set of spaces you need for different roles, as though you were an actual team of people each of whom needs their own space. An example of using spatial separation for separate roles is the Disney Creativity strategy. This is based on something that Walt Disney would do in the creation of his cartoon stories.

Making a feature length cartoon film is a collaborative effort. To give his team a good overview of what he expected, Walt Disney would tell the story by acting out all the roles himself, doing the characterisation, the dialogue and so on.

> ... almost everyone agrees that *Snow White and the Seven Dwarfs* first existed, almost frame by frame, in the mind of Walt Disney. Nobody had to guess at Walt's vision of the film. One evening in 1934 he gathered his artists together in an empty soundstage ... acted out the entire story .... The hours-long performance was the living script the animators turned to again and again as they struggled to complete the film.
>
> *Bennis & Biederman (1997: 41–2)*

By following Disney's example, NLP has developed an effective process for many kinds of creative activity. The essential element is that you separate the roles of the creative process, so that each can do its best work without interference from the others. It then becomes a kind of production line—as in the original animated film-making process.

Walt Disney adopted three roles which he called the Dreamer (the creative role), the Realist (the practical role) and the Spoiler (the role which finds fault and reasons why it won't work). In NLP the Spoiler is called the Critic. These three roles can be located in physical space in front of you, far enough apart to maintain separation, yet close enough to interact. The key to this is that you enter each role in the correct order: first you dream (Unitary–Mythic mode), then you realise the dream in practical terms (Sensory mode) and, finally, you assess the result (Social mode) and make any changes necessary by returning to the Dreamer, and amending the vision. Because many people criticise their own creative efforts too soon, they never get to realise them. Delaying the critical function until after some of the practicalities have been explored makes the process more successful.

Team roles

There are numerous models of that aspect of management which is concerned with leadership and teams. Apart from describing the various styles of leading and managing, there are several well-known models or descriptions of the various roles within teams, such as Belbin's eight-role distinction (Belbin, 2000). This model has roles in all four categories: the two individual roles are the Chair and the Plant; the team roles, Sensory and Social modes, are each differentiated into three functions. No one can perform optimally in every work role activity, so you need to assemble a team of people who combine their talents to achieve their outcomes. Teams comprise a variety of individuals who demonstrate complementary skills and talents, which means that they can achieve what the individual cannot. For example, the three roles demonstrated in the Disney creativity strategy could easily be performed by individuals who have those specific preferences and abilities. Team leaders need to know how best to organise the various members so that they work well together and achieve excellent results.

You are only going to use certain skills at certain stages of the project. You do need to have someone who can act as a critic or explain why things won't work, but you do not need them all the time. It is useful to have such a 'polarity responder' who will flag up potential problems, indicate what is unlikely to work and thus save time and effort, but as with the Critic in the Disney strategy, there is a time and a place for this function, and you need to ensure you get its benefits at the appropriate moment. If you have someone who feels it their duty to carry out this role regardless, then you need to find a way of keeping them in check. One way would be to begin seeing things from their point of view.

If you are using any kind of model which has parts or roles, you may find you can work more effectively if you physically adopt those different positions, as you are separating out what is usually lumped together. For example, de Bono's *Six Thinking Hats* and *Six Action Shoes* models (de Bono, 1991) suggest that you imagine wearing a hat or shoes of a different type and colour for engaging in different kinds of thinking and activity.

In the next chapter, we will explore this notion of parts and functions in terms of what NLP refers to as Perceptual Positions, and in the final chapter, we will put all of the ideas in the book together and explore an 'archetypal' NLP exercise, the four position, four-role Metamirror technique. This can be seen as an embodiment of the Four Realities in action, and functions as the paradigm for many an NLP change process.

Chapter Eleven

Perceptual Positions

You don't see something until you have the right metaphor to let
you perceive it.

Robert Shaw, quoted in James Gleick "Chaos", p. 262

Frames of perception

There is a limit to how much you can pay attention to at one time.
What you perceive depends upon your current intention and
your perceptual frame—what you expect to be there, what you
assume is relevant to your needs. You 'ignore' everything else
until you encounter something which does not match your expectations. Then your perceptual frame changes and you become
aware of an alternative interpretation or way of creating closure of
your reality. Each closure comes from your existing knowledge
and understanding acquired through previous experience. You
know what tables and chairs are because you have grown up with
them, so there is usually no problem identifying further tables
and chairs, even though they may be made of unusual materials
or of a novel design. However, when you encounter new concepts
which are unfamiliar, such as the term 'nominalisation' in NLP,
you have to learn what they mean by making connections to
things you are already familiar with: "It is a kind of abstract noun
(such as 'relationship') referring to an ongoing process (such as
'relating')", and so on. Otherwise you will not be able to understand what other people who use those particular perceptual
frames for interpreting the world and who refer to those concepts
are talking about.

Another example: some people use their hands to illustrate what
they are talking about, and literally point out aspects of their
models of the world. If you are unaware of the significance of this,
you will attach little or no importance to their hand-movements.

You will not see the meaning of their gestures until someone knowledgeable about *spatial marking* and *anchoring* explains what is happening. NLP has introduced a number of new ways of perceiving the world, in terms of noticing body-language, eye-movements, incongruence, limiting metaphors and linguistic utterances that you were probably unaware of before you read an NLP book or attended a course. Were those things there before? For you, no.

Much of NLP focuses on the way people perceive and describe their reality. As NLP has grown, those ways were codified, extended, formalised, and stated as generalised patterns. This chapter explores another generalisation, the NLP Perceptual Positions model, which probably originated during the mid-1980s. However, this model often gives rise to misunderstanding and confusion because it has lacked a complete and consistent paradigm. This chapter shows how it is possible to understand Perceptual Positions by fitting them into the Four Realities model together with the three Levels. For this to make sense, you need to reframe what you know about the NLP Perceptual Positions into a more coherent, streamlined model. This will improve your understanding of how to use this concept in your own practice.

Throughout this book I have been promoting the idea that change comes from shifting your point of view. As Richard Bandler points out (1985: 38), a point of view can be anywhere, anytime, any one. It is possible to adopt any point of view that you can imagine. This includes past and future, other people, animals, inanimate objects, imaginary people: "What would the Wizard of Oz have to say about this?" or "If you made this change, how would you see yourself differently?" (Bandler 1985: 137). There are many common phrases in English which indicate an ability to shift your point of view. For example:

> From a historical perspective …
> The customers' view on this …
> The legal thinking is that …
> If I were you, then I would tell him to …
> As a teenager, I used to think that …
> I guess that your client would see this somewhat differently.
> One day you'll look back on this and laugh.

Having such an enormous variety of points of view can be entertaining and enlightening. However, it would also be extremely useful to find generalities or patterns within this range of possibilities. The questions to ask are: Are these points of view all 'just different' or is there a way of organising them into categories which would simplify our understanding? If so, what kind of distinctions do we need to make?

Associated and Dissociated

One point of view distinction is between being *associated* or being *dissociated* in your perception. Associated means that you are fully engaged with the world. Your awareness is located, as it were, within your head, as though you are looking out through your eyes. This is a familiar point of view, inside your head, a bit back behind your eyes.

On the other hand, it is possible to have a point of view located anywhere else. For example, you could imagine what the world would look like from the dissociated positions of a bird flying above a scene—a bird's eye view; from the point of view of a fly on the wall or from a TV surveillance camera; or even from a worm's eye view, how things would appear from ground level. The difference here is that in such images it would be possible for you to see yourself, your physical body from the outside.

There is also another point of view which you take when you are thinking about your experience, past, present or future, in which you take the role of an observer. You are separate from the experience, as though you are watching a movie in the cinema, or the multiple screens in the control room of the TV studio, able to see or switch to any point of view you choose. You also have the ability to manipulate the image: zoom in or out, change the speed, pause, or reverse the events unfolding, and so see beneath the surface, beyond the direct evidence of your senses, to see themes or patterns which organise the events for you. In fact, exactly what you have been doing while reading this book.

Bandler (1985: 40) defines them thus: "*Associated* means … seeing it from your own eyes. You see exactly what you saw when you were actually there." On the other hand, "*Dissociated* means looking … from any point of view other than from your own eyes." This difference between an associated and a dissociated point of view is a key piece in the NLP Fast Phobia cure. People with phobias are fully associated and experience overpowering feelings. Those who overcome phobias are able to create a mental separation so that they can observe themselves having the phobic response 'over there' without being overwhelmed by those feelings. This ability to distance yourself allows them to observe and reflect on what was happening in a rational way. Ex-phobics reached a point where they finally decided they had had enough. They saw what they were doing as ludicrous or boring, and chose to stop doing it. When you are able to look at yourself at a distance engaging in unwanted behaviour, it is easier to think about making a change.

The distinction about whether you are looking out of your own eyes is probably not as clear cut as it may at first appear. For example, it does not take into account that you could be looking through your own eyes but at a distance, as if you were looking through the eye-holes in a mask. You might want to check whether you are looking out through the centre of your own eyes, or through the centre of the eye-holes in the mask, and to adjust the way you are looking to discover what difference it makes being off-centre, or peeping through, and so on.

Another way of making this distinction is to recall a memory, and then consider whether you were 'in the experience' or whether you can see yourself in that image. If you see yourself (your imagined self) in the picture, from the outside, then you are dissociated. This distinction between paying attention to the outside world, and thinking about things inside has a number of names. It could be perceiving, 'looking directly at the world, seeing what is *really* there', compared to imagining or hallucinating, 'seeing in your mind's eye'. You may be 'lost in thought' rather than engaging directly with the world around you. In some forms of therapy work, the distinction is between *uptime* and *downtime*. Bandler & Grinder (1979: 55–6) say: "… we put ourselves into what we call 'uptime', in which we're completely in sensory experience and have no consciousness at all. We aren't aware of our internal feelings, pictures, voices, or anything internal." When you are in *uptime*, you are able to give full attention to your client, hear what they are saying, see what they are doing, and so on. You are sharing an experience. However, in *downtime*, you are temporarily unavailable, as you are engaged in internal processing, making sense of your experience, thinking about what to do next, and so on.

You can also have this downtime sense of switching off or disengagement when you are bored or not interested in what is happening around you. You might experience this when you are watching a movie and not enjoying the story, so you start wondering how they did the special effects, which other movies you have seen the actors in, how the story has been adapted for the screen, and so on. The opposite—suspending your disbelief so that you enter the fictional world of the movie—means you are totally entranced and completely caught up in the drama.

History of Perceptual Positions

An extension of this idea gave rise to the concept of Perceptual Positions. The NLP concept of Perceptual Positions emerged out of the work of Judith DeLozier and John Grinder (1987) during the period when they were working on New Code NLP. In *Turtles All The Way Down* they draw upon Carlos Castaneda's books about a Yaqui shaman or *brujo* called Don Juan. During the 1960s and 70s Castaneda wrote a series of books about his encounters with Don Juan and the shamanic knowledge he acquired as his apprentice. He tells tales of altered states of consciousness, his ability to 'become' different animals and birds, and is introduced to the notion of First and Second *Attention* (DeLozier & Grinder, 1987: 185, 191). First Attention is the way we pay attention to and assemble the ordered nature of our everyday world. Second Attention is more an awareness of the possibility of order, which is the whole universe of possibility which contains every possible way of perceiving things. This would appear to be similar to Hilary Lawson's concept of *openness* (Lawson, 2001a).

In early NLP three Perceptual Positions were identified, namely, First, Second and Third positions. Essentially, these relate to whether you are adopting the point of view of Self, Other or Observer (Figure 11.1). These are similar to the roles undertaken during NLP exercises (see Appendix B). Moving from one position to another is sometimes referred to as 'shifting referential index'. The notion of a 'triple description' meant that you had information from all three points of view about a particular event, which thus gave you more choice in interpretation and options for intervention. The Observer position was equated to being 'outside the loop' of the interaction between Self and Other, or the Practitioner and the Client. Third position was thought of as being 'neutral'.

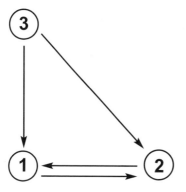

Figure 11.1 First, Second, Third positions

In the late 1980s, Robert Dilts created a technique which he called the Metamirror (see Chapter Twelve) in which a fourth Perceptual Position was added. The use of this Fourth position in the exercise is quite clear, although his later re-definition creates some confusion. Dilts says that "[Fourth position] is essential for effective leadership, team building and the development of group spirit. As the term implies, fourth position presupposes and encompasses the other three perceptual positions. People who are not able to achieve fourth position have difficulty experiencing themselves as a member of a group or community." (Dilts 1998). This would suggest the thinking of someone with a Social-mode preference.

Therefore, we need to clarify the purpose and function of each Perceptual Position. Think of Perceptual Positions as points of view used for a specific *purpose*. Each has a particular focus or frame for paying attention to the world in a unique way, and provides a different way of intervening in the world. It should come as no surprise to find that this interpretation of the Perceptual Positions maps onto the Four Realities. By extending this connection to include the three Levels of Body, Mind and Spirit, we arrive at a Six Perceptual Positions model. (Six is the upper limit, because of the limitations of our perceptual capabilities—we cannot go beyond Spirit and stand outside of the system.) This model eliminates the confusion by focusing on the different *functions*. However, before we look at the implications of this model, we first need to look at how Perceptual Positions have been described in the NLP literature.

First position

This is you being yourself in the centre of your own space, engaging with the world in a direct and associated way. You are being fully yourself, acting in real time, in the moment, to meet your own 'selfish' needs. You are thinking on your feet, fulfilling your intentions, doing things for your own benefit. At the extreme you are oblivious to other people's needs or feelings.

Second position

In Second position, you are thinking and acting as if you are someone other than your everyday self. You could see this as taking on a role, rather as an actor becomes the character in the play or film that they are engaged in. An actor who is good at their job will be skilled at hiding their technique. For example, Michael Caine (2003) says of his role in *The Quiet American*:

> What I always try to do in acting, in movie acting, is to try and make the wheels disappear, and you only see the person. ... You can't see me there; you just see Thomas Fowler.

For most of us, one way of experiencing a non-habitual point of view is to pretend to be someone else, to imitate their way of speaking or walking, which is what you were doing in Exercise 6.1. There is an example of doing this in the film version of *The Wizard of Oz*. The three friends wishing to rescue Dorothy from the Witch's prison pretend to be guards and march in at the end of the column using the same movement characteristics as the other guards, and thus remain undetected.

Second position is about putting yourself in someone else's frame of mind and body, 'being them' by stepping into their shoes, 'walking a mile in their moccasins'. DeLozier and Grinder also explored the notion of how it was possible to take on different personalities, to shift your habitual way of being, and exhibit the characteristics of another person or personality. This came to be known as 'second positioning' someone or something. It has also the meaning of thinking yourself into someone else's place by considering their cognitive stance: how they would see things from their particular worldview. For example, this would be useful for anticipating how your opponent in a game or conflict would be likely to behave. It is often told that certain military leaders would have a portrait of their 'enemy' on the wall so that every morning they were reminded to consider that alternative point of view, in order to out-think them.

If you fail to take account of other people in a relationship, you will probably end up being frustrated. If you were to set an outcome for finding the perfect partner, and engage in all the steps outlined in Chapter Eight, you are likely to be thwarted unless you expand the frame and remember that you are dealing with two people, not just yourself, and therefore need to consider both sides of that relationship, both points of view. This, for many people, is an interesting challenge. Not only do you specify what the other person has to be like, but you also need to consider "What is in it for them?" "What is it that *I* have to offer that other person? Why would *they* want to spend time with *me*?" To find this out, you could imagine yourself in their position, and take a good look at yourself from their point of view! That might suggest how you could change yourself! Without this second-positioning you may be continually disappointed.

A similar situation arises when you are thinking about what a relative or friend would like as a present, such as for their birthday. If like most people you give them what you like, then they may or may not be totally delighted. (It would be a good opportunity for checking their congruence upon opening the present!) On the other hand, wondering what they would enjoy, given your knowledge of their likes and dislikes, would be a far better strategy for producing satisfaction. This is also a good strategy for understanding those people who are not able to articulate their needs very well—such as babies, young children, and those with learning disabilities. You have to imagine what the world would be like for them, and then ascertain the probable needs they have at this time.

In a therapeutic context, getting someone to pretend that they are no longer stuck, by putting themselves in the future (having them move along their timeline) or by bringing in the resource of being someone else, then you are also exploiting the opportunities of second positioning a limiting state. In other words, moving to second position is a way of creating choice—either by adopting other personalities, or by stretching yourself over time. This is another aspect of Sensory mode.

When you are in Second position, you are still associated and speaking from the point of view of "I"—even though the *I* in question happens to have an identity dissimilar from your usual one. In this sense, Second position is similar to First position. It's just that you are being someone else, and imagining what it would be like looking out through their eyes, given their model of the world, their biases, preferences, and so on. This should be a very different experience from being yourself. If not, then you are not really in Second position. You could practise this ability by watching a character in a movie (which gives you repeated opportunities for observing what they are doing) and consider: "What do I need to do, to think about, in order to achieve a similar result? How do I need to use my body? What do I need to think? What is my intention? What do I want to achieve? What is my worldview?" The better your ability to imitate them, the more you will get a sense of what is driving them in that role.

Third position

Third position is usually defined as a position from which you can observe what is going on from outside of the action. You have the sense of not being directly engaged and have stepped back from the you in First position, and now notice yourself 'over there', as though you are watching a movie of yourself.

There are several terms used in NLP for this kind of thinking, and sometimes the terminology is confusing. We have already considered the difference between being associated and being dissociated. This is where the 'looking out through your own eyes' definition falters. When you are standing outside of the action, you are still looking out through your own eyes. However, seeing yourself in the action would suggest that you are dissociated or in Third position. The distinction about looking out through your own eyes is more to draw attention to whether you are directing your attention externally or internally.

Observer or Witness position

Developing the ideas about the practice of doing NLP exercises in threes, third position is also identified with the Observer position. Andreas & Andreas (1989: 85–88) introduce the three terms: Self—Other—Observer. Observers are supposed to be neutral, unbiased, paying attention to the facts of the event. This is similar to the Witness position. In Robert Heinlein's science fiction novel, *Stranger in a Strange Land*, the society employs Fair Witnesses in legal matters. For example (Heinlein 1961, Chapter 11):

> Jubal called out, "That house on the hilltop—can you see what colour they've painted it?"
> Anne looked, then answered, "It's white on this side."

In other words, a Fair Witness does not make inferences about what they cannot detect using their senses.

Voyeur position

Western society has become increasingly devoted to reality TV programmes in recent years. These put the viewer in a kind of voyeuristic position. You observe, but you cannot influence what happens. Although the technology may offer the illusion of 'interactivity', this does not mean you can intervene and change the events in real time, but only that you can access the output of different cameras, or vote collectively. Surveillance cameras are commonly used in public places such as shops, shopping malls, streets and in many business locations as well. The belief is that this is a way of increasing safety and security. However, it also means that someone somewhere is able to watch what you are doing, and make decisions about the meaning of your behaviour, without you being aware of them. Programmes such as *Big Brother* promote the idea that this is OK, and that there is entertainment value in watching other people for long periods and in quite intimate detail. This notion was explored in Peter Weir's movie, *The Truman Show* (1998), in which the hero, Truman Burbank (Jim Carrey), discovers that he is the star of a 24-hour soap opera watched by millions.

This kind of intrusion into other people's private world has been growing since the advent of mobile television cameras. It has become a television cliché that you break up a talking-head sequence using cutaways. At sporting events, award ceremonies, and social events where the public and celebrities attend, it is acceptable for the camera to turn to look at the audience or the crowd, without them being part of the action, or aware that they are being observed.

What is the fascination in doing this? How do you respond to seeing other people behaving ordinarily or emotionally in public? To what extent do you feel a emotional bond with them, an empathy for their state? It could be that we do this naturally, as part of being human. But what is the attraction of watching other people unobserved? Is there a 'peeping Tom part' in each of us? Perhaps in the case of TV programmes such as *Big Brother* we want to think of ourselves as better than them: more intelligent, having higher status and greater flexibility in behaviour. Or perhaps you are seeking vicarious life experiences: "What would I do in that situation?" You want to be a celebrity, a hero or a role model for others, and this is one way of doing it in your imagination. In this way you get to explore some of your own fantasies and learn about the consequences of certain behaviours.

Meta-position

The prefix 'meta' is used rather loosely in NLP terminology. Robert Dilts and Judith DeLozier add confusion by suggesting that "Meta position is a point of view outside the communication loop with knowledge of the beliefs and assumptions from only one's own first position. Observer position is a point of view outside of the communication loop in which the observer purposefully suspends any beliefs and assumptions about first and second positions" Dilts and DeLozier (2000: 941).

The meaning of 'meta' outside of NLP is more precise. Watzlawick (1974: 95): explains that "… any opinion (or view, attribution of meaning, and the like) is *meta* to the object of this opinion or view, and therefore of the next higher logical level." This meaning of 'logical level' is different from that used in NLP. The term originally came from group theory. A category or general class description (such as *Transport*) is said to be at a higher logical level than the members of that class (*Cars, Boats, Planes, Bicycles,* and so on). Gregory Bateson used the notion of 'logical types' to develop his ideas about change.

Einstein said that, "You can't solve a problem with the same thinking that created it." This means that you need to think on a higher level. The essential nature of change and problem solving is that you have to be able to perceive events at a higher level in order to see how else they could be organised. Just observing an event by stepping back does not mean that you are 'meta' to it. The common phrase 'thinking outside the box' does not necessarily indicate going meta either. You are only meta when you can see a particular event in the context of a class of other similar events. For example, being familiar with various genres of film would enable you to classify the kind of movie *The Wizard of Oz* is.

You could describe it as a fantasy, as a musical, as an example of The Hero's Journey, and so on. By considering it within the bigger frame you can identify themes and patterns, find commonalities, and make connections and generalisations.

We can make more sense of these terms by relating them to the basic paradigms. I would suggest that there is no consistent or clear distinction between the Observer and Meta-positions as currently used in NLP. The term 'Meta-position' is merely a shorthand jargon term used for describing the ability to mentally stand back and reflect on one's experience. 'Going meta' is used to refer to the action of stepping off your timeline, or out of your Circle of Excellence. You 'go meta' in order to change your state, gather resources, before reentering the associated active state of being yourself engaged in activity.

Third position and Social mode

John McWhirter (2002: 52) inadvertently provides a clue to understanding this when he says that it is only when you "think about what [you are] trying to do by evaluating and where this might lead; is it relevant and useful?" that you are in a 'meta' position. Actually, this is not a meta-position either, but it does suggest a link to the Four Realities model. The two activities he describes: evaluating and exploring the consequences are precisely what you do in Social and Mythic modes respectively. In Social mode you evaluate and make judgments about what is happening in First (and possibly Second) position. You 'see yourself over there' and make some kind of assessment about what is happening. Remember that evaluating is convergent thinking. You are choosing, narrowing down options as you seek to define a course of action or level of performance. You do this by assessing the whole range and then assigning a particular value to the performance in question. Once you are clear about the value of an activity, you may be motivated to do something different (such as deciding to stop having a phobic response), or decide that you like what you see and are motivated to do more of it.

The ability to evaluate what you are doing is useful when you are performing in public—as a presenter, trainer or after-dinner speaker. How are you coming across? You may practise by watching yourself in the mirror or on video beforehand, but when you are in front of an audience, you will have to put yourself in the audience's position or at the back of the hall and assess the kind of impression you are making. This Third position Observer role enables you to judge how well you are doing. Many actors claim to monitor their own performance by watching themselves from the back of the auditorium. This ability provides valuable information about any necessary adjustments you need to make.

Seeing the Perceptual Positions as aspects of the Four Realities model informs you about the kinds of activity that are appropriate. In First position you are defining the world. You look around at your reality, your universe. It appears real and integrated. It is what it is. Second position acknowledges multiple perceptions of reality. You know that each person has their own version of reality. In Second position, using Sensory-mode thinking, you are able to analyse that seamless reality into separate parts and roles, and to see things from different points of view. In Third position you are able to stand back and evaluate those perceptions. You have feelings about them, realise that you have preferences, and that your values are influencing what you perceive. That leads to the question: how does Fourth position relate to Mythic-mode thinking?

Fourth position and Mythic mode

Fourth position has always been there and has formed a vital part of the development of NLP. However, lacking a paradigm, it remained disconnected. The function of the Fourth position was already recognised (as is usually the case with missing parts of four-part models), but when the notion of Perceptual Positions was introduced later, it was not perceived in those terms. It is only when you look back in the light of the *functions* of each of the Four Reality modes, that you can see the connection. This is an example of what Edward de Bono refers to in his Lateral Thinking—the need for "moving sideways across the patterns instead of moving along them as in normal thinking" (de Bono 1992: 15). He goes on to say that "... we can also see why every valuable creative idea must always be logical in hindsight".

The Four Realities model enables us to re-perceive the Fourth position in hindsight. There are two main roles of an Observer in an NLP exercise. Both roles have the intention of giving feedback, but in different ways. There is the process of evaluation, which assesses how well the operator is doing in terms of working with the client. And there is the role of exploring the consequences and devising alternatives, to consider what else the operator could do in order to help the client change. At the end of an exercise the Observer will adopt Social-mode/Third position and offer feedback on what worked and what didn't. They will also go into Mythic-mode/Fourth position and offer alternative ways of doing the exercise: "One thing that you could do differently in future is ....."

We need to look at Mythic mode again in terms of the function of this perceptual position. The Mythic-mode thinker entertains the notion that reality is all made up, and that they are the creator of the universe. However, any particular version of reality is just a way of perceiving it; any other version is equally valid, and can be created at will. Mythic mode is monistic in that there is one creator, but it offers the facility of creating multiple understandings, parallel universes, different meanings. The Mythic person has the ironic sense that even though no particular reality is a 'universal truth' (because they are all figments of the imagination, and of language), they still need to exist in a physical universe, and therefore for the purposes of living they have to take some aspects of reality seriously and act as though they are true.

You are already familiar with the Mythic approach to change. In the early days of NLP it was referred to as 'magical' and in the early NLP books was called 'reframing'. For example, see Chapter 1 of Bandler & Grinder's *Reframing* (1982). This is Mythic-mode thinking in action. It is about the ability to see options in what things mean in someone else's model of reality and to come up with a pattern interrupt—a surprise—that will shift the meaning for them. For example, if somebody says that they are confused you could reframe that by explaining that confusion is a necessary stage in the process of dealing with new information, and indicates that they are in the process of learning.

Reframing is not a new idea. The psychotherapist Paul Watzlawick and his colleagues provide a brief history of reframing in *Change: Principles of Problem Formation and Problem Resolution* (Watzlawick et al, 1974: 92–115). They find many examples of reframing throughout history, in reality and in works of fiction, though it was probably never called by that name. Bandler and Grinder acknowledge Watzlawick's work and refer to it in *Reframing* (1982: 2).

Robert Dilts' Fourth position

Robert Dilts introduced a different understanding of Fourth position, describing it in terms of 'we'. He says (1998) that it "... involves being associated in the whole system or 'field' relating to a particular interaction. It involves experiencing a situation with the best interest of the entire system in mind." However, in this explanation Dilts offers no rationale, but just expresses a need to have the view of the group, or the system, rather than just of the individual. Other NLP practitioners (Ardui and Wrycza, 1994) have followed this version because when they are consulting within organisations, they find it useful to make their clients aware of the larger perception of the system they are within. For example, you might find it useful to ask: "What would your group think about this proposed change project?"

Perceiving yourself as part of a social group is actually another aspect of Social reality-mode thinking. The group may perceive itself in terms of 'we' and 'us' but there is no essential difference in *function* between the individual and the group *evaluating* their experience. Although it may be useful to become aware of what 'they' think about what is happening or what the organisation has as its values or moral position, these viewpoints all demonstrate a similar kind of thinking. It could even be that for individuals to observe from a group point of view, they need to second-position them! That would provide a glimpse of reality as seen through the blended perceptions of a group of individuals.

That's fine. It's possible. It would actually be useful when using the Metamirror technique for dealing with your feelings about a group rather than an individual.

What matters here is that it is not the *location* or *range* of the Perceptual Position or point of view that matters, but the *function* —the intention and ways of intervening in the world. In Third position you focus on the values, the feelings, the emotional state of the event and assess or judge an event from outside. Judging requires evaluating different aspects of experience; this influences your decision-making and suggests what action to take. In Fourth position you hold alternative realities in your mind and make connections between them. Exploring the probable consequences and ramifications of an intervention is one aspect of future pacing. Adopting an alternative reality reframes your experience and changes its meaning.

A possible basis for this version of Fourth position

The model which seems to underpin the model used by Dilts and others to explore Perceptual Positions is based on the two continua of Self—Other, which is similar but not identical to One—Many; and Associated—Dissociated (which is rather different from Determinism—Free Will). When you combine these two metaprograms into a conceptual space (Figure 11.2), you get:

	Self	*Other*
Associated	Associated Self (First)	Associated Other (Second)
Dissociated	Dissociated Self (Third)	Dissociated Other (*Not in the Model*)

Figure 11.2 Dilts' Perceptual Positions model (with thanks to Mike Treasure for this explanation)

This kind of two-dimensional model is useful for exploring four positions. You choose whatever dimensions you like and then combine them. Some combinations are going to be more meaningful than others. Compare this with the Four Realities model (Figure 11.3) and notice the key differences. For example, Third position in Social mode is plural, connected to the group. However, in Figure 11.2, Third position is seen as the singular Self which observes and evaluates. Perhaps a 'Dissociated Other'position would mean thinking in terms of "What would your mother say about this?" but this would have a similar function to Third position.

	One	*Many*
Deterministic	Unitary (First)	Sensory (Second)
Free Will	Mythic (Fourth)	Social (Third)

Figure 11.3 The Perceptual Positions in the Four Realities model

In Figure 11.3, on the left-hand side of the Four Realities model, *One*, there is only one universe. You create it yourself and other people are 'figments of your imagination'. For Unitary, there is only one true reality. The Mythic is the solitary creator, living in a multiple universe, accepting any number of different models of reality, with the freedom to choose any version of reality they please. With that goes an awareness of the infinite variety in which change can be conceived and implemented.

Reframing and Fourth position

A point of view is just a point of view. The meaning you make of your experience is dependent upon how you currently understand your experience. It can neither be absolute nor correct; it is just how you are making sense of your experience at the time.

When you shift your point of view, your point of reference, then the meaning of your perception of reality changes. In practical terms Fourth position is about making changes to the way you make meaning of your experience. You can follow through actions to explore the consequences, the implications. Additionally, you can make connections between disparate experiences and notice similarities, that X is like Y in some abstract or not immediately apparent way. In the process, you generate metaphors.

A third aspect of Fourth position is the ability to entertain different meanings for the same experience. Reframing is the process of shifting someone's point of view to deliberately alter their interpretation of their experience. For example, a book is something you read, but it could also be something for propping open the door, or handy for lighting a fire. This multiple meaning perception is the basis of many visual illusions. What is interesting about these is that the visual system is unable to hold both views simultaneously.

Holding several alternative meanings as true simultaneously can be unsettling, paradoxical, or entertaining. You may enjoy exploring the nature of a non-Unitary universe in which contradictory truths exist, such as the quantum world of Schrödinger's Cat, which is both alive and dead at the same time. In the parallel worlds of Robert Heinlein's *The Number of the Beast* (1980) the Land of Oz has equal validity with other universes. Philip Pullman's *His Dark Materials* trilogy involves traveling between parallel universes. Peter Howitt's movie *Sliding Doors* (1997) and Tom Tykwer's *Run, Lola, Run* (1998) both explore alternative versions of reality. The classic Japanese film *Rashomon* tells a story from four different points of view, and so on. Switching meaning is the basis of jokes and puns. Reframing is the basis of much humour. Frames of reference are easily changed. Your awareness suddenly flips from one worldview to another, and the incongruity results in laughter.

So this accounts for four Perceptual Positions. However, a fifth position has also been proposed.

Fifth position

> The most beautiful and deepest experiences a man can have is the
> sense of the mysterious. It is the underlying principle of religion
> as well as all serious endeavour in art and science. He who never
> had this experience seems to me, if not dead, at least blind. To
> sense that behind everything that can be explained there is a
> something that our mind cannot grasp and whose beauty and
> sublimity reaches us only indirectly and as a feeble reflection, this
> is religiousness. In this sense, I am religious. To me, it suffices to
> wonder at these secrets and to attempt humbly to grasp within
> my mind a mere image of the lofty structure of all there is.
> *Einstein—from "My Credo"—an address given at the German League*
> *of Human Rights in Berlin in autumn 1932*

From those who have thought about such a concept, there seems
to be general agreement that a Fifth position would involve
adopting a universal perspective (Bodenhamer & Hall, 1999: 56).
This point of view would actually be a meta-position to the first
four, being on a higher logical level and above all of the cognitive
activity on Level II. This is what I have been calling Level III or
Spirit.

You could imagine metaphorically entering this domain as you
scale the boundaries between the four modes in the process of
change. Being (temporarily) on a meta-level enables you to
change your thinking. This is where you go when you change
your mind. It is difficult to describe; you just know that you have
done it, but have no knowledge of what you actually did. This
limitation to awareness implies that having any further position
beyond the Fifth is neither possible nor meaningful. There is no
way of conceptualising such a position. Gregory Bateson (1972) in
his discussion on Levels of Learning (similar to logical levels—
each level being meta to the level below) suggests that "Learning
IV would be change in Learning III, but probably does not occur
in any living adult organism on this earth."

You could think of Level III/Fifth position as being where
resources come from—the world beyond the familiar world,
where your mind is part of universal consciousness. There are
inevitably difficulties and ambiguities in using words to describe

this Level III position, because the realm of Spirit is beyond language. Even so, throughout history many have attempted to describe the indescribable—the numinous, the state of grace, and so on. In the process they have given us many rich examples of language, and fine art of many kinds (see Lawson 2001a, Chapter 16). Even though we are dealing with what is essentially unknowable, if we act as if we are in this state, through meditation or whatever, then this can bring an enlightening perspective to our everyday lives.

Zeroth position

To balance the model, we need to include a lower level of functioning that incorporates the Level of Body. For this we need to conceptualise a Perceptual Position which is also non-linguistic, noncognitive. Again, this is something we are already familiar with—it is just that we have not perceived it in this particular frame before. Such a position is not going to involve thinking as such, but what we do at the level of context or environment. This is the domain of physiology, changing states, anchoring, gaining rapport through body-matching and mirroring, and so on. I call this the Zeroth position, because in one sense you do it without thinking, and it also completes the pattern without requiring a renumbering of the other positions. Much of NLP works by utilising this Zeroth position because it is often easier to change someone's cognition by switching to working with the Body, their physiology, or by physicalising spatial metaphors, and so on.

There is physiological evidence that perception is possible without conscious awareness. Some people who have suffered brain damage suffer from an extraordinary neurological syndrome called blindsight. This was discovered by Larry Weiscrantz and Alan Cowey at Oxford (Ramachandran, 2003). Even though they have no knowledge of what they are seeing they are still able to accurately point to things in front of them, even though they have no conscious awareness of this. This should not be too surprising. Most drivers have the experience of trancing out while driving along a monotonous stretch of road, and suddenly realise that they have no awareness of driving during those last few minutes. This other vision pathway in the brain (which runs through the brain stem and superior colliculus) is 'looking out for us'. We also know that if anything unexpected happens, then we immediately flip back into conscious attention, and deal with that event.

The Six Perceptual Positions model

Thus we end up with the Six Perceptual Positions model (Figure 11.4) in which the six positions are arranged in the following pattern:

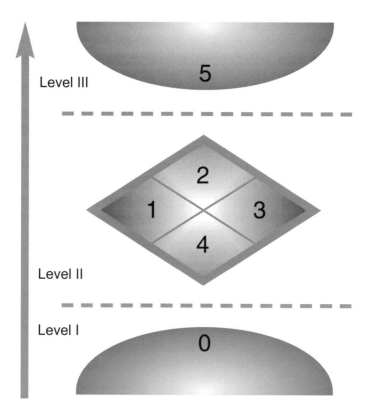

Figure 11.4 Six Perceptual Positions

This model combines the Three Levels with the Four Realities composing Level II. You may pause to consider the implication of this model, which is that although many of NLP change processes are designed to work on Level II (the Linguistic Level), change often comes from utilising the other levels of being which are non-linguistic. This means that understanding how we change is not open to conscious examination. NLP is successful because of its emphasis on nonverbal intervention, and because it uses processes which bypass the conscious mind—such as the physiological effects of exercise, movement, anchoring, and so on, and in using hypnosis and other ways of going beyond conscious awareness using trance states. NLP techniques often involve a mixture of all three levels, and thus its techniques will surprise us into change. The NLP Presupposition that all change happens at an unconscious level points in that direction.

The functions of the Six Perceptual Positions

The functions or actions represented by each Perceptual Position can be neatly encapsulated as follows (Figure 11.5):

0	Zeroth	Responding, Reacting
1	First	Defining, Discriminating, Knowing
2	Second	Sequencing, Analysing, Finding Alternatives and Options
3	Third	Evaluating, Judging, Deciding
4	Fourth	Associating, Connecting, Creating Metaphors
5	Fifth	Accepting

Figure 11.5 The Functions of the Six Perceptual Positions

The elements of this schema are all familiar. What is new is the way they are integrated into a single paradigm, and the meaning and implications of this.

Satir Categories

There already exists with the domain of NLP a model which describes the dysfunctional side of these positions. Known as the *Satir Categories*, it comes from the work of the family therapist Virginia Satir, who was one of the models of excellence studied by Bandler and Grinder in the 1970s. The Satir Categories, if they are included in NLP trainings, are often perceived as interesting but somehow disconnected from the rest of NLP, presumably because there has been no way of making a connection with it. The Six Perceptual Positions model now enables us to do that.

Bandler and Grinder worked with Virginia Satir in order to find out the models she was using and the factors which led to her success when working with dysfunctional families. This information was published in *Changing with Families* (1976). Virginia Satir "... identified four communication categories or stances which people adopt under stress. Each of these Satir Categories is characterised by a particular body posture, set of gestures, accompanying body sensations, and syntax. Each is a caricature" (Bandler, Grinder & Satir, 1976: 59) (Figure 11.6).

At that time, the concept of the Perceptual Position had not been created. Instead, Bandler and Grinder linked these ideas to what they were currently exploring, the different senses: Visual, Kinesthetic, and Auditory. They managed to connect three of Satir's Categories with ways of processing (Bandler & Grinder, 1976: 69).

Satir Category	Caricature of	Focus of attention	Primary Sense
Blamer	Service	Other	Kinesthetic
Placater	Power	Self	Visual
Super-reasonable (Computer)	Intellect	Context	Auditory*
Irrelevant (Distracter)	Spontaneity	None of the above	—

* At that time no distinction was made between *Auditory* and *Auditory internal dialogue*.

Figure 11.6 Aspects of Satir Categories (based on Bandler, Grinder & Satir, 1976: 60, and Bandler & Grinder, 1976: 69)

They claimed that this approach was especially useful for identifying the kinds of relationships their clients demonstrated in their family setting. This is important because they had a new frame for interpreting behaviour. As further models emerged, it was possible to reframe some of these ideas, though they have remained on the fringes of NLP.

Essentially, the Satir Categories describe dysfunctional roles and behaviours. They are dysfunctional in that they tend to block behaviour and learning. Each role demonstrates a different kind of incongruence between intention, body-language and communication style. In mild cases they are just annoying. It is easy to see them as negative aspects of the Four Reality types, and you can sometimes spot a type from what they do that doesn't work.

The Satir types

Virginia Satir described four types—*Blamer, Computer, Placater, Distracter*—in her book *Peoplemaking* (1972). The key section of this was reproduced in Bandler & Grinder (1976: 47–53). Remember that these are descriptions of extreme dysfunctionality. In reality, people may exhibit such tendencies in varying degrees. Briefly, the types are as follows:

Blamer—1st—Unitary

The First position type, the Blamer, lives in a Unitary world, where they are 'right' and everyone else is 'wrong'. This is a deterministic reality, which means that they themselves do not take responsibility. When things go wrong, blame has to be put on someone else. They may blame a specific person, or condemn the unspecified *They*.

Blamer types believe that words have defined meanings, and do not subscribe to the NLP Presupposition that the meaning of their communication is the response they get. If other people do not understand them, that is their fault.

Blamers feel powerless or stuck because they feel helpless up against the principles or rules which determine their behaviour. They perceive themselves as having no options, no escape: this is the only reality there is.

Computer—2nd—Sensory

The Second position type, the Computer (originally 'Super-reasonable') lives in a Sensory reality of facts and data, of detailed analysis, projects and programming. They come across as distant, rather cold and calculating, because they are fascinated by things. Many children pass through a stage of absorbing the *Guinness Book of Records* (see Egan 1997: 84–5); Computer types seem to get stuck there. This is the world of the boffin or nerd; the collector, the birder or train-spotter who is motivated to gather facts, statistics or sightings. Some become scientists who have an insatiable desire to know how everything works, or what the universe is made of. Part of their obsession may be the quest to find even more fundamental particles or building blocks of matter, or to devise ever more unified theories.

If they come across as cold or impersonal, it could be that they are not at home in First position, but live in some alternative reality. The mask or persona they put on may be an attempt to face a world which is rather alien and mysterious to them.

Computer types often feel (if they feel anything at all) that life is rather pointless, senseless, that the universe is without purpose. In their agnosticism or confusion, they believe logical analysis is essential, rational argument the best way to sort things out.

Placater—3rd—Social

The Third position type, the Placater, is very concerned with what others think of them. They adopt a low status in the group, and try to please everyone in it, for fear of being excluded from it. They tend to put themselves down, and make judgments about

themselves being unworthy based on comparisons with significant others. They often have strong feelings about which behaviours are or are not acceptable, and feel hurt when their own
values or feelings are ignored.

Placaters tend to feel undeserving, insignificant, without value,
and adopt a lowly attitude to life. They are motivated to be like
everyone else, and hate standing out from the crowd. Placaters
want everyone to be comfortable, and try to ensure that no-one
rocks the boat. Inside they are in touch with their feelings and
empathise with others in their belief that everything, the world,
other people, the system is unfair, and they feel guilty about this.

Distracter—4th—Mythic

The Fourth position type, the Distracter, is easily bored, and
wants to make things different and exciting. They do this by
injecting random thoughts, actions, ideas into the social interaction. Maybe their minds are working fast and seeing alternative
meanings of events, but they are not informing others about what
they perceive, but just acting as if it is true. Because it is so easy to
restructure the world in this way, there is little challenge, except
that of actually doing something for real. Their fantasies are usually ephemeral, and the Distracter is soon on to the next thing that
offers excitement. Trying to turn their dreams into reality is frustrating and soon becomes boring. They are easily discouraged,
and retreat once more inside their own unlimited mental
universes, where anything and everything can happen, often
chaotically.

Distracters often lose hope because they lack structure, direction
or priorities. The universe appears arbitrary or meaningless, and
they lose their own sense of identity in it.

Leveler—5th—Level III

Satir later added the fifth category, *Leveler*, in *The New
Peoplemaking* (Satir, 1988). The Leveler has qualities of being

totally aware, congruent, 'going with the flow', sometimes demonstrated in the enlightened or charismatic personality who radiates a strong spiritual sense. For most of us, this is something to aspire to.

The Leveler type is the only one which Satir identified as working well. It is associated with Fifth position, although in terms of good communication skills, there is no need for them to be 'spiritual'. What matters is that they can act calmly and see all points of view. Acceptance and tolerance of others are the key attributes. Leveler has the quality of accepting what life offers, and that includes saying 'Yes' to whatever happens. This is not being a Placater and giving in to demands. This is utilising the energy available, rather than being a victim of it. If you have learned any of the martial arts, especially t'ai chi, you will be familiar (as a transient state) with the ultimate Leveler. This is the centred, balanced posture, ready for anything. Only a master will be able to be in Leveler state for any length of time. The universe is constantly shifting and we are thrown off balance. Being familiar with that state as a resource helps us to literally get both feet firmly on the ground.

?—0th—Level I

There is no Zeroth position Satir Category. Could there be such a type? It would have to be someone who is dysfunctional unconsciously on a behavioural level, for example, having no apparent control over their actions. Perhaps someone who is extremely clumsy, or suffering from Tourette's syndrome would be a possible candidate.

Changing the person's point of view

Given these six fundamentally different ways of perceiving the world, it is possible to find ways of moving from any one of them to any other, a simple path of change which is going to produce a change in point of view. These are represented diagrammatically in Figure 11.7. If you start from the premise that people have become stuck in First position, Unitary-mode thinking, then many change techniques are going to be aimed at producing a shift out of that particular point of view.

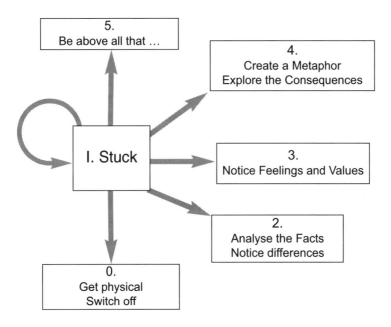

Figure 11.7 Ways of getting moving again

Stay in 1st position

One choice is actually to stay where you are. Amplifying their stuckness encourages change, because every truth fails at some point. You are probably familiar with the loss of meaning when you say a word repeatedly and it degenerates into noise. A similar technique is used in meditation practice, as a way of moving to another level of consciousness.

- Reflect whatever the person says back to them as if they are in a box of mirrors. Repeat their actual words, adding nothing but a questioning inflection. For example, if someone says, "It won't work", echo this with: "It won't work". Then wait until you get a response. Repetition focuses the attention on the arbitrary nature of the present truth. By offering them no opportunity for making excuses, they will soon feel a need to do something different.

- Repeat the word or words the person has used, with a rising inflection. For example, if they say, "I shouldn't have done that", you repeat, "You shouldn't have done that?" with a slight emphasis on the *shouldn't*. If you ask them what is happening and they reply, "Nothing", come back with, "Nothing?" or "And what kind of nothing would that be?" to bring into the open what they seem to be avoiding.

- An approach adopted by many psychotherapists, such as Erickson and Persaud, is to accept what the client says and then take it to an extreme. This keeps the client in First position until it becomes ludicrous or untenable.

- Recap on what has been said, and check that you have it correctly: "Let me make sure I understand you." This is similar to reflecting on the truth.

- "Is this still serving you/the organisation? Perhaps it's time to let go of the old way of doing things." You may want to acknowledge what you have gained from the past.

- "What is the learning in this?" Are they willing to accept what is the case? Can they acknowledge what can be gained from the past.

Move to 2nd position

You could reframe this change as moving from being *you* to being *not-you* (that is, someone or something else). Moving to Second position is about creating alternatives, and widening the scope of what is possible. To assist someone to make the shift to Second position:

- Ask them: "Has this always been true?" This shifts them into second position, as they consider the past. You are challenging the 'eternal' validity of the truth: "Has there ever been a time when something else was the case?"

- Have them expand their awareness by thinking outside the box: "Imagine you are on the other side of this block or barrier. From here, look back and see how you overcame it." Or "Put yourself in X's shoes. How would they see this?"

- Noticing and then varying the qualities of their experience, the submodalities of size, colour, distance, boundaries and so on, will change the meaning of their experiences, and the emotional responses they generate.
- One way of dealing with 'difficult people' is to have them adopt a different persona by getting them to dress up, for real or in their imagination, in some kind of special uniform. They could, for example, wear a hat that signifies a particular role, and which allows them to perform a different role, even if just for a short while.

Move to 3rd position

In Third position you are mentally distancing yourself or dissociating from the experience, and taking on the role of observer or judge. You are thinking *about* your experience, noticing how you are acting, how you are relating to others. You have feelings and make judgments about that other you 'over there' and anyone else involved. It is from Third position that you evaluate what is happening, and decide what to do. To move others to Third position:

- Engage their value system and their judgments: "How do you feel about this?" (This is a counselling-type strategy.)
- Ask: "What matters about this?", "How is this important to you?"
- Get them to prioritise: "What is the most important thing about this?", "What is your highest value outcome?"
- Physically have them move to where they can see themselves 'over there' and have them evaluate their situation. From this position they can respond to themselves. Becoming aware of their dissatisfaction, they may be strongly motivated to change. As an observer they should have sufficient resources to come up with ways of doing something different.

Move to 4th position

In Fourth position people create their own reality by imagining that which does not physically exist, by creating *What If* scenarios and following where their ideas may lead. They envision desired outcomes, reconstruct memories, invent metaphors or make up jokes. It is as though they have a magical gift for rearranging the universe to please themselves—and they are only limited by their imagination. To move others to Fourth position:

- If the person states a limitation, offer a reframe which provides a different meaning for that behaviour, or suggest a context in which that behaviour would have a different meaning.
- Suggest they reframe this themselves: "What else could this mean?", "What does this remind you of?", "What would be a metaphor for this? What might be a more appropriate one?"
- Explore the consequences: "What happens next?", "What might be the implications of this?", "What would happen if you followed this through?"

Although people are naturally creative, some find it easier to fantasize by using a resource in the form of a magical device, such as is used in computer gaming. If they need permission to daydream, then how you say things—your tonality—matters. If you give commands they may feel defensive. It is far more effective if you go into a dreamy state yourself, and then invite them to wonder … "So what would happen if …?", "Just imagine you're … What would that be like …?"

The NLP Teach Me frame ("If I had to stand in for you for the day, what would I need to be aware of, pay attention to?" and so on) gets the person to dissociate from their immediate experience and to focus on several aspects of what they do. As such it changes their perception by getting them to consider several points of view. Bear in mind that some of these changes can be seen as alternating between convergent and divergent thinking, and this can be quite challenging for some people. Helping people shift from a rigid and limited belief system to a more expansive alternative reality is where you demonstrate the art of being an NLP practitioner.

Move to 0th position

One of the most effective ways of getting a change is to move out of cognitive processing (Level II) and engage the physiology (Level I). Many clients are used to sitting in chairs talking about things. Anything that stops them talking and thinking about their woes is more likely to produce a change. For example, get them to engage physical movement: "Stand up, and give yourself a good shake. Jump up and down. Take a few deep breaths ...." Breathing deeply creates a positive physiological change—so that they can let things out. Standing and being centred enables them to feel more alive, better able to deal with life's challenges and to get things done. When people feel good, there is often little that stands in the way. Be a role model for them, and get the benefits yourself!

Several NLP techniques, such as the Circle of Excellence, the Disney Creativity strategy, and timeline work, physicalise spatial metaphors. Simply spreading the contents of your mind out in front of you is a surprising way of doing things. Taking a tour through your experience will give you many different perspectives on the issue. This could be an effective change technique in itself; you may not need to intervene further.

Move to 5th position

Anything which temporarily disengages thinking about issues is going to be appropriate. Trance work, hypnosis, and so on, will take the person to another dimension where reality has a different quality. You could move them to Fifth position by suggesting they "float up above all this ... see everything there and know that you don't have to do anything about it. ... Just accept that this is how it is ... for now."

These shifts are nothing new. What is different is the underlying model which offers a framework for deliberately changing the way people perceive their reality.

Locating resistance

Having a practical model for change makes it easier to explore the different ways of perceiving the world. It also indicates the kinds of resistance you may encounter. There are going to be good reasons why people don't readily make the kinds of shifts listed above. You might think they are showing resistance, but this is more usefully considered as challenging your flexibility of thought! Change inevitably encounters some kind of resistance, and each position will express a different kind of fear. For example, in the Physiological realm, certain fears are hard-wired into us in order to alert us to danger. These fears could be related to sudden movements, loud noises, unexpected touch. We respond to darkness and the creak of floorboards, night-time and the sound of snapping twigs .... Some of these become anchored as phobias. Because they are on Level I, it is possible to change the responses on Level II.

The Four Reality modes show typical kinds of fear (Figure 11.8) which will lead to resistance:

Mode	Fear
1st/Unitary	Loss of control, lacking certainty, not knowing what to do. Chaos, anarchy, heresy, conflicting beliefs.
2nd/Sensory	Failure, getting it wrong, being illogical. Randomness, disorder, irrationality.
3rd/Social	Exclusion, rejection, lack of relationship. Unfairness, unjustness, immorality, violation of values.
4th/Mythic	Confusion, 'not getting it', loss of freedom. The Void, boredom, closure (lack of options).

Figure 11.8 Fears and the Four Realities

Level III fear is associated with loss of meaning, a sense of purposelessness, going into the Void. Perhaps the meaning of life is connected to the need to come to terms with these existential fears.

Dealing with the fear

We live in a culture in which it is the norm to reject ideas until we are really sure they are in our best interests. This means turning down the offers that other people make, saying 'No' to their proposals. Many people are fearful of strangers, of new ideas, of change itself. Once we have built a sufficient fortress of beliefs, we are often reluctant to examine or change them. Whether we call this resistance, hesitation, or reluctance to do anything new, it means we do not learn.

To help people change, you need to acknowledge any fears they may have. Get them to think about the potential gains as well as the potential losses resulting from change. Actually, you may not know for them which is a gain and which is a loss, so avoid mind-reading!

- Help them think through the whole scenario of change. You are going to be asking repeatedly: "And what happens then?", "What else could happen?" You need them to create a richly detailed vision of their vision for their future. As the practitioner or therapist you must have already spent time thinking through a number of possible consequences, seeing things from various points of view, so that what they say will not surprise you.
- Whatever they say, make them right. Accept what they offer, their views, their feelings and so on: "Sure you feel like this. It is to be expected. And there are other aspects which you haven't yet considered ...."

Acceptance and Reframing

Fifth position is about being at one with the universe, being at home in your universe. There is no room for fear, because you have an overview of the whole of your creation. Acknowledging this means accepting everything that happens—the good and the bad (which are merely evaluations on a lower level). Being in Fifth position is an opportunity for examining your attitude to the universe. Accepting the way the world is does not mean you do not want to change it, nor does it mean you have to dwell on its limitations. You created it, and you can reframe your experience at will. When you release your perceptions, your responses to your reality, you can return to your essential nature. This is the way of acceptance.

When you are working with other people, you are going to see in them reflections of your own limitations. This could mean that you do not readily challenge that behaviour, because in challenging it you would also be challenging yourself, and that could be confusing, even painful. Through accepting what the universe offers, you will find opportunities to learn. What will you assimilate into your model of the world? Will you allow yourself to be surprised?

A key piece of working with clients is to accept their reality as valid—for them. When other people seek your help in changing, you need an attitude of acceptance. As Watzlawick et al (1974: 104) put it:

> ... successful reframing needs to take into account the views, expectations, reasons, premises—in short, the conceptual framework—of those whose problems are to be changed. "Take what the patient is bringing you" is one of Erickson's most basic rules for the resolution of human problems.

Acknowledge other people by sharing their reality. Then intervene by moving within that model so that they begin to gain a more integrated concept of their six perceptual positions and learn how they can move between them.

Given this preliminary understanding of the Six Perceptual Positions model, the next chapter explores the Metamirror process which utilises these different frames of mind in a kind of archetypal NLP process.

Chapter Twelve

Exploring the Metamirror

We cloak the beloved in layers of crystal, and see a vision rather than a person for the whole period of our entrancement.

Stendhal

Changing relationships

This chapter looks at a specific technique, the Metamirror, as a way of bringing many of the parts of NLP together, so that you can see how the ideas covered in this book work in practice. This process also offers a paradigm for a generic model for therapeutic change.

The Metamirror is a process for dealing with difficult or unsatisfactory relationships. You undoubtedly can think of people with whom you do not get along, and this bothers you. There are those with whom you have communication problems, experience personality clashes, because they engage in behaviours which you do not like or approve of, or perhaps reflect a side of your personality that you find embarrassing or have yet to face up to. What matters is that thinking about that person creates an emotional response in you which inhibits or limits your behaviour in some way. You feel bad or angry just by remembering that person's put-downs, insults or scathing remarks about your inadequacies or lowly status, or whatever. Remarkably, you still have that response even though that person is no longer around in your life; you could be nursing resentments from your childhood, your schooldays, about people long disappeared or dead.

If you adopt a Blamer view and see the other person at fault, because of their defective genes, flawed character, or because they seem to be from another planet, then there is going to be little you can do to change such relationships. You are not in a position to insist on a radical realignment of that other person's behaviours and personality. Merely hoping that the other person will change could mean waiting for a long time. On the other hand, you could be curious and in taking responsibility for your end of the relationship loop gather more information from a variety of points of view, and then intervene to alter things. Applying the Four Realities model you might notice that perhaps those difficult people have reality mode preferences different from your own, and wonder if this might explain previous misunderstandings.

Projection

This notion that we are more influenced by fantasy has been around for long time, and is especially prevalent when we fall in love. Marcel Proust (in *The Guernantes Way*) (1920–1) put it:

> It is the terrible deception of love that it begins by engaging us in play not with a woman of the external world but with a doll fashioned in our brain.

When you think of any relationship, totally wonderful or otherwise, you get some kind of feeling inside, just by thinking about the other person. A large part of knowing other people comes from what you project onto them. You make generalisations, run scenarios which tell you the kinds of things that those people are likely to do in the future. You also reflect on past encounters, and interpret what happened in the light of the stories and perceptual frames you are currently using to understand your reality. What you are then projecting onto others is actually a statement about your model of the world. As Robert Dilts puts it:

> The idea of the Metamirror was realising that very often what we find difficult in others is precisely that which we have not resolved within ourself. It would not be a chronic sustained problem to us if we had resolved it initially within ourselves. …

> I tend to believe that other people are primarily Rorschach inkblots, that we really know very, very little about the map of the world of another person. And so what happens is that we are projecting onto them in the same way that we project onto an inkblot.

And I can say, having been married to my wife for twenty years, it doesn't change that much. In fact, it is just more confusing when the real person is in front of you because you think you are responding to them. ... The potential of the other person, the potential of my wife, is not my map of her. And my map of her doesn't change just because she happens to physically be standing there. It just gets all confused with her. And so the other idea of Metamirror is the realisation that probably a lot of the difficulties we are having with others are more related to our projection and interpretation, than what is truly their intention, their potential, their identity, and so on.

Dilts (1997a)

The familiar saying "Absence makes the heart grow fonder" is about projection. Without the other person present to remind you of their reality, your mind is free to create any fantasy figure that you would wish to be with. However, when you are reunited, faced with the real person once more, there may need to be some sort of readjustment, in order to update and refashion your internalised image of the other person, the "doll in your brain", to overwrite your distorted memories of them.

The key factor is that you get to feel bad *without* that other person being present. Your thoughts about them affect your state. This suggests that the way to change such relationships is to alter your imagination, the way you think about that person. For the purposes of the Metamirror, the fact that the people in question are no longer around or in your social ambit is irrelevant. (In fact, if they were present, it would probably create more confusion.) If just thinking about someone still bothers you, then use this relationship as the content for using the Metamirror process.

The place to start is with yourself, because this is where you have leverage. You can effect change by re-evaluating and restructuring your memories and impressions. The Metamirror enables you to reframe your experience in a surprising way. You are going to remove some of those "layers of crystal" and move towards a more accepting understanding of that person. In so doing, you alter the nature of the relationship, and the system changes. When you meet that other person again (if they are still around), they are going to be responding to a more congruent version of you. And that will lead to a change both in their behaviour and the ensuing interactions within the relationship.

The Metamirror process provides an excellent opportunity for understanding the application of the integrated paradigm for NLP. The Metamirror process is not taught on every NLP practitioner training, so if you are not acquainted with it, then the best way of understanding it is to do it for yourself. Do this for real with one of your limiting or troubling relationships. Start by being the client, and have someone else guide you through the steps. Follow the instructions as given for the standard technique. I also describe some options for modifying the process.

The History of the Metamirror

The Metamirror was devised by Robert Dilts around 1987 at the time when Judith DeLozier and John Grinder were re-evaluating the basic assumptions and practices of NLP. Their *Prerequisites of Genius* seminar (a fore-runner of New Code NLP) explored the concept using different perceptual positions and perspectives, and of physicalising those positions by spreading them around the room, rather than just holding them in mind. This made for cleaner work, as it was possible to differentiate the various aspects of an issue by locating them in physically separate places. This way of working can be seen as an extension of the Two Chair technique in Gestalt Therapy.

A step along the way was a process they called *characterological adjectives*, a term borrowed from Gregory Bateson. A characterological adjective describes one side of a dependent relationship. If someone says "I'm a prisoner", this presupposes someone else who is a captor. Similarly, for someone to be perceived as 'giving' then other people have to be recipients. From this an exercise was created which involved observing a difficult relationship from the outside. Using a theatre metaphor, you imagine viewing that interaction from the auditorium. First, you put a spotlight on the other person, and notice how they behave in relation to you. Then you train the spotlight onto the person who looks like you, and observe your own behaviour. You describe each side of the relationship in terms of characterological adjectives that suggest how the relationship binds both parties together.

Robert Dilts wrote about the Metamirror process in *Changing Belief Systems* (Dilts 1990: 190–99). He says that "the meta mirror technique creates a context in which we can keep shifting perceptual positions inside and outside the problematic relationship until we find the most appropriate and ecological arrangement of elements in the relational molecule" (page 197). Although Dilts uses a Fourth perceptual position in the Metamirror technique quite appropriately according to the Four Realities model, he does not seem to have appreciated the function of this role, and instead redefined his understanding of Fourth position in terms of an expanded Third position which accounts for group perception (see Chapter Eleven).

The Metamirror process

Choose an issue that is currently real for you, something in your life that you would wish to change. It is a waste of your time working on something totally safe because the result you get will be trivial, reflecting only your unwillingness to explore what really matters. The only safe techniques are those which are totally ineffective! Nor is it worth bothering to construct hypothetical *what if*s in order to ensure ahead of time that nothing will actually change. Doing the exercise for real and finding out what happens will probably answer your hypothetical questions, or you may notice that your problem has simply vanished.

A word of warning: do not choose anything deeply traumatic, such as Post-traumatic Stress Disorder (PTSD), a severe phobia, or any kind of abuse. In such cases you will need help from a qualified Practitioner. Do feel free to work with personal discomforts, annoyances, opportunities for boosting your confidence and self-awareness, in order to discover for yourself how this works.

If you are working with a client and think it appropriate to use the Metamirror, then you need to put a frame in place so that they will be willing to do it. For example, get them to think about one of their relationships—either current, or one from the past—which really annoys them. You will see the changes in their physiology as they do this. When they have got one, ask them to consider: "How is it possible to feel bad about a relationship when the other person is not actually there?"

The following instructions assume you are the practitioner guiding the client through the process. Once you are familiar with doing the Metamirror process—as both client and practitioner— you will be able to adapt it to meet any other particular needs. It also becomes possible to run it for yourself, which means that it will be available to you whenever you want to clarify any relationship. It takes only a minute or so to run, and you can do it anywhere. It is more effective to do it physically in the space around you rather than just thinking it through in your mind. Using spatial separation for the different positions works better because part of the reason you are having a problem sorting things out is because everything is jumbled up. By giving the different points of view their own space you can see how they relate to each other.

Practicalities

You will need sufficient space for getting sufficient distance on the troubling relationship. The client is going to imagine four spots or positions which form the corners of a square about two to three metres along each side. Make sure this space is clear of furniture.

Ask the client to recall a troubling relationship, but tell them you do not need any details of the story, nor any biographical information about the person the client is working on (though it may help to know their gender in order to use 'he' or 'she'). By working *content free* (see Appendix B) the client preserves their privacy, confidentiality is not an issue, and as you are not distracted by aspects of their private life you can concentrate on the process and on observing the non-verbal information that the client provides.

This relationship can be current, or in the past. If it still creates a negative response in them, this is the right one to work on. The person need only recall that relationship briefly and superficially for them to get into that debilitating state. You just need to be able to see the kinds of physiological changes the client experiences, the minimum emotional response that lets you calibrate (observe and remember) their state and body-language.

In order to do any change work with another person, you first need to establish rapport. As you guide the person through the four positions, stand next to them, but do not get in their line of vision. Instead be literally 'on their side'. The other person will need to pause to process things internally from time to time, so pace yourself to the rate at which they can do this.

Steps

1. From a position slightly outside of the working arena, say to the client: "First of all, imagine two spots on the floor, a little distance apart, to represent this relationship. In a moment, you are going to stand on one spot and look at the other person who is on the second spot." Use your arm to gesture approximately where you want them to place these spots. Remember that you are going to need room to introduce two further spots later.

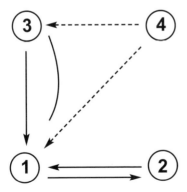

Figure 12.1 The Metamirror Process

Prompt them to move into the space: "Now step onto the spot number 1, First position, and look at that other person. Be yourself, feeling how you feel in this relationship."

You should observe a distinct change in their state—how they look, their skin colour, the expression on their face, their posture, gestures and so on.

"And now, being you in this relationship, give this some words that would sum it up for you." All you need is a few simple descriptive words or metaphors, such as: 'frustrated', 'helpless', 'caged in' and so on. Remember the actual words the client uses.

"OK. That's enough of that limiting experience, so step off the spot, and do something physical such as shaking your arms and legs, just to change how your body is." This is known as 'breaking state'.

2. "Now you are going to do something you may not have done before. You are going to step into that other person's shoes and experience a little of what it is like being them in this relationship with you. Walk over to the second spot, step in and be that other person."

You are asking the client to go into Second position.

"To help you do this, stand as they characteristically stand, hold your head the way they do, gesture and speak as they do. And being them, look at that person who looks like you, over there in First position, and get a sense of how this relationship feels from here. Now give this a few words of description. When you speak, use first person 'I' statements as if you are this person: 'I feel …' whatever."

Remember how they look in Second position, and the descriptive words they use for this aspect of the relationship.

"And now step off that spot and break state by shaking off that feeling, moving around or whatever."

3. "Now you are going to get outside of that particular relation-ship and get some perspective on it, as it were. So step back here into a Third position so that you can see what was going on for you in First position."

Move a few paces back with the client, so that they can com-fortably see themselves in First position. Use your hands to indicate each position: "And as you stand here in Third posi-tion [*indicate with one hand*], look at that you over there in First position [*indicate with other hand*]. How do you respond to *that* you *there?*" Use these exact words.

By referring to them in First position as 'that you over there', and by keeping your hands apart, you will maintain the sepa-ration between First and Third positions. The language you use is neutral in that it does not suggest any particular answer. The client says whatever they feel about it, such as "I feel sorry for him" or "Why doesn't she just get on and do *something!?*" or something much stronger!

You are looking for a definite separation: you don't want the associated feeling response from First position contaminating the dissociated evaluative response that you have here in Third. The client's physiology should be quite different. In Third position they should be judgmental, more objective mak-ing a realistic assessment of that relationship. If they are not, you may need to increase the separation by having them step back a little more, or by having them stand on a chair. Height gives a different perspective.

4. Have them move across from Third position to Fourth posi-tion, to a place where they can comfortably see both First and Third positions.

"From this Fourth position I would like you to symbolically exchange whatever is in Third position with whatever is in First." As you stand beside them, use one of your arms to point at First position, and the other at Third position, and then make the exchange by crossing your extended arms and swapping One and Three. You can make some sort of gentle swishing noise as your arms cross over each other.

5. Having made the change, have them step back into First position, turn to face that other person in Second position and ask: "How is this relationship now?"

There should be a difference. You will usually notice that their body-language has changed as a result of the exchange process in Step 4. As they re-enter First position they will often be more upright, more alive. If not, then you need to go back a few steps to ensure that they had separation. They may need to access some appropriate resources (see the *Variations*, below).

6. Have the client return to Second position, so that they can experience what it is like responding to this revitalised person in the changed relationship.

"Now come here and feel what it is like on the receiving end of the new you." They can give you some words for this experience. These should be different from those before. Draw attention to what has changed. There should be significant physiological differences too.

7. The last step is to have them complete the process back in First position, to be in themselves again: "Finally, come back home to where you belong." And you're done.

As with all techniques, you need to 'pace the client'—which means you go with what is appropriate for them, with what fits their model of the world and belief system.

Understanding the Metamirror change process

The Metamirror process is a systematic visit to each of the four reality modes in turn, to provide their different perspectives on that relationship. Simply experiencing these four points of view is often enough to produce a significant change in the way you perceive yourself in that relationship. In First position you define your reality by describing the relationship as 'troubling' or 'limiting'. This kind of Unitary-mode thinking tends to give fixity or permanence to the words you use, and this creates a sense of stuckness because 'this is how it is'. There is little you can do, because this is how using language produces a relatively stable reality which is both manageable and predicable to a degree.

Moving to Second position is a rare occurrence for most people. Although we often talk about seeing things from other people's point of view, we are more likely to do this from Third position and to criticise or make judgments about events, rather than experience them directly.

Being associated in a difficult relationship produces a certain state in you. In order to experience an alternative point of view cleanly, you need to completely throw off that earlier state, and you do that by making a change on Level I, Body. In other words, you move briefly through Zeroth position to break state. Once you have moved to Third position you are going to be more dissociated, and this kind of dramatic state change will not be necessary.

The Third position has to be far enough away so that you can see yourself over there in your imagination. The important part is that you are not bound up in the emotional response you had in First position which was limiting you in some way. The evaluative response from this judgmental Observer position will probably have a different emotional quality, such as frustration, or the feeling that this has been going on long enough. It should motivate you sufficiently that you realise: "It's time to change!" Trust your judgment and decide to do something different.

Third position is not about action as such, so you move to Fourth position in order to reframe that relationship. You need to do something surprising, engage in some magical thinking that will interrupt the old pattern, because otherwise you will just come up against your conscious limitations again. Exchanging First and Third perceptions in this way is a variation of the technique of scrambling a memory. It is one way of restructuring your experience. But you could use any other random or intuitive way to reorganise your model of the world.

Actually, you have no idea what the change is or how it works. It happens beyond awareness. Neither is it possible to say which part of the process creates the change. Although you may think that swapping perceptions around or adding a resource is the critical step, this is not a helpful way of thinking. You cannot stand totally outside of the system that is you, nor can you isolate one element and identify it as the key. Change is systemic; all the steps interact and contribute.

What you can know is the result of your intervention. Therefore, you need to check that the change has made a difference. Check how you experience both First and Second positions having made the change. The relationship should be less stuck or problematic now. To provide a sense of completion, return to being yourself in First position and integrate the experience into you in some way. Some clients may need to metaphorically collect all their parts up.

Variations on a theme

The standard Metamirror process takes the client to the four separate locations, each with a different function. If you are working with clients who are unfamiliar with the surprising 'weirdness' of NLP, you may need to build up slowly. Start by restricting your explorations to one kind of separation. For example, if they are used to talking about their issues while sitting down, break that habitual pattern by asking them to stand up, and walk round behind the chair, or you could invite them to cross the room and stand and observe 'that person who looks like you' from another point of view. You are helping them to get some distance on their issues. If they are far enough away to leave their debilitating state behind, then they can get into an evaluative mode. Each new kind of perspective is going to produce change if it something they do not usually do.

Using Fifth position

You could also bring in a Fifth position, if it becomes apparent that the person needs more resources. You could suggest that they access a more resourceful self, even a Higher Self if that is part of their belief system, beyond their ordinary cognitive awareness. Fifth position is expansive and in contrast to the focused attention they are paying to what is going on in the relationship square. Therefore it would make sense to change the direction of attention, and 'look the other way' (which is a nice ambiguity). Their mind will know what to do. Once they have accessed this state, get them to connect this larger sense of self to what is happening on the cognitive level.

Modify the process as follows:

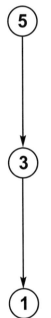

Run the process as far as Step 3. If the client thinks that what they need in First position is some extra resources, then they can find some by acknowledging that they are part of a more universal, 'bigger' reality. Have them turn around so that they are facing the other way, away from First position, and then use the following script:

4. "Now I want you to look the other way, and imagine that you are looking out into the universe. It is as if you are at the narrow end of a funnel, and out there is all the energy, all the light, all the resources in the universe that you can call upon to help you, to be with you and revitalise you. All you have to do is to feel it beaming down into you—and simply accept it. And as you feel all this energy or light streaming into you, becoming part of you ... just turn around, focus on that you in First position, and beam it all into them. You are acting as a relay from the universe to the you in First position" (Figure 12.2).

Figure 12.2
Beaming down
resources

Alternatively, they could make a further separation by stepping into this Leveler or Fifth position and actually experiencing something of this universal state. From there they can beam down the resources to where they are needed.

5. Have them step back into First position, turn to face Third and Fifth positions, and "Simply receive what is being beamed to you. Accept all these resources from your higher self, the universe, and allow them to become part of you."

Adding resources enables the person in First position to feel bigger in some way. If you are working with clients for whom an explanation of Fifth position might hinder the change process, because it does not fit with their beliefs, then referring to a resource state is more neutral. It is simply that place you go to find whatever you need at this time. The good thing is that their mind will supply whatever is necessary, just as long as they are open to accept what comes, however crazy it may seem.

Various relationships

You have relationships with individuals, with groups, with parts of yourself. There is no reason why you couldn't explore any such relationships using the Metamirror technique. Usually, people choose a relationship involving one other person, and this would be the best to use initially. But if the client chooses to work on a relationship with a family or group, or even an organisation, and this makes sense to them, go with it. Consider how you would be a group in Second position. This might be how Dilts' groupmind or 'we' position could be utilised.

You could also use the Metamirror process to explore past or future relationships with yourself, using a kind of timeline experience. Is there an earlier version of you which you are now ashamed of or angry with? Does that younger you need reassurance and encouragement? If this relationship needs resolution or clarification, then because these relationships are also within your mind, you have a way of dealing with them. However you have been representing that relationship, it is always possible to restructure it and thus change its meaning and its emotional response. If you accept the Mythic view that your reality is a figment of your imagination, then you can change any life experience. A computer metaphor would be the process of writing data to disk. Each time you save a document, you overwrite the previous version, retaining only the latest one. When using a computer you are constantly overwriting previous versions, updating them. In a similar way, you could imagine that you are overwriting obsolete memories. If you alter their structure, you change the meaning. What you call your 'past' is not written in stone, but in easily changeable magnetic polarities or the connections of neurons. Your memories of the future (visions, expectations, desired outcomes), as well as of the past are always open to review, revision, and reinterpretation. It is never too late to do this, because everything is available in the present.

The purpose of using NLP change processes is to remove some of the illusions and fantasies you project onto the world. You are still going to be living in some kind of made-up created reality, but you are going to be taking more responsibility for interpreting it according to your current needs. You are also going to be paying more attention to the information that the universe is offering you as a result of expressing those needs.

A basic paradigm for change

The Metamirror process demonstrates the use of the Six Perceptual Positions model. The meaning of a relationship will change when you relate bodily to an issue, adopt different states, move physically from one viewpoint to another. By transforming your internal space into an external environment you engage in a multiple shift in thinking. The main part of the Metamirror process describes a journey around the four positions in a particular order, in order to explore how each position's view adds to the understanding of the issue. States can be changed in Zeroth position, resources can be accessed from Fifth position. In other words, you now have a working space in which you can move from any position to any other position according to the specific need of the client. Exploring an issue from several points of view is going to create some significant change in the way the client frames their experience.

In the realm of change management, McWhinney and his colleagues (1997: 119–199) have already mapped many management change techniques according to the Four Realities schema. By extending this to include 0th/Level I and 5th/Level III Perceptual Positions, it becomes possible to map any management or therapeutic change technique, not just those in NLP. Some have a different emphasis, some go into more detail, others leave parts out. But they can all be seen as traversing paths in the Six Perceptual Positions model. For example, all NLP processes are meant to finish with future pacing and an ecology check, to ensure that the client is comfortable with the change. Exploring the consequences is a Mythic-mode activity, which then becomes an evaluation of the probable outcomes in Social mode. Having gained a positive, motivational response to the change, they are motivated to embrace it, to choose to implement their decision in Sensory mode, which results with a new Unitary truth.

The most common starting place is being stuck in First-position thinking. From there get the person to do anything that will get them to flip the polarity and explore the opposite, to examine 'what isn't', the 'not-self', the universe of other possibilities which they hadn't collapsed into that fixed, unitary perception or truth. Then have them step back and consider, evaluate, how they respond to that issue and the alternatives. Finally, encourage the ironic understanding that their experience of reality is of their own making, by offering alternative meanings, by reframing their experience.

Accepting that the meaning you make depends upon your current way of perceiving the world, means you could be curious and begin to find out how you code your experience using words. Language itself tends to encourage fixity. Loosen up your thinking by finding new metaphors that enable you to make new connections, and thus see the world differently. The art of change is in thinking flexibly, acknowledging that there is no ultimate truth, only your own creative understanding of reality. The more you accept alternative explanations or stories, the less attached you will become to any particular one of them, and the more personal freedom you will experience. And as you do that, the better a role model you will be for others.

Chapter Thirteen

Conclusion

The only way to make sense out of change is to plunge into it, move with it, and join the dance.

Alan Watts

Developing a paradigm for NLP

People have been describing and interpreting aspects of human behaviour throughout recorded history. Each new explanation comes from re-evaluating and revising what has gone before to meet current needs, and to further illuminate our increasing understanding of ourselves. My contribution has been to show how the comparatively recent phenomenon of NLP relates to the ancient wisdom and the archetypal patterns that run through our history of change. Being curious about how NLP works, how it helps people make changes, can be seen as yet another small step forward in our understanding of ourselves.

My particular skill is in noticing patterns, finding similarities in those things which on the surface seem to be quite different, and combining them in interesting ways. In this book I have combined two basic models: the Three Levels model of Body, Mind and Spirit, and the Four Realities model of styles of cognitive processing—Unitary, Sensory, Social and Mythic—to produce a composite Six Perceptual Positions model which offers an elegant and practical framework for change.

This model provides a paradigm for finding a variety of ways in which the practitioner can intervene effectively, and which maintains an element of innovation and surprise. Having discovered how someone is stuck in their perception of their reality, you can help them shift to a different perceptual position. This strategy describes a basic change process used not only in NLP but in other kinds of therapy and change management. NLP has contributed some sophisticated and efficient ways of making some of these shifts.

In this book I have rearranged the jigsaw puzzle pieces provided by NLP—the 'trail of techniques'—to show a simple pattern which demonstrates the Six Perceptual Positions paradigm in use. I have reinterpreted some of the basic thinking and techniques, and reframed them in order to show how they are all part of a larger pattern which provides an understanding of how NLP works. Perhaps you are beginning to discern more of the picture on the box.

Pattern-detecting is one aspect of Mythic-mode thinking. Without an organising pattern or story, information remains just information. You generalise your experience, and act according to the principles and theories you have created, even though you may not be explicitly aware of what they are. With a paradigm in place, you can test out ways of intervening in the world to find out what works. In the early NLP books there is a great emphasis on more or less ignoring *content* and focusing instead on *process*. NLP's original power came from asking "How do you do that?" and in intervening to change ineffective strategies, moving from Unitary to Sensory-mode thinking. NLP's techniques alter *how* people do what they do. However, this was just the first step in changing the way people think about change.

There are six perceptual modes to consider, not just the two concerned with *content* and *process*. This model can be extended to account for Social-mode thinking and to consider the *decision* that has been made, and then re-evaluate that choice. And you can adopt Mythic-mode thinking and wonder about the *meaning* and the *consequences* of that. Although these ways of changing are familiar, they have not been systematically connected before (Figure 13.1).

Perceptual Position	Level	Reality Mode	Focus on:	Relationship:
0th	Body		State, Context	
1st	Mind	Unitary	Content	Sameness
2nd	Mind	Sensory	Process	Difference
3rd	Mind	Social	Decision	Comparison
4th	Mind	Mythic	Meaning	Similarity
5th	Spirit		Acceptance	

Figure 13.1 Positions and Focus

Intervening to create change

Zeroth/Body

Many NLP techniques bypass cognitive processing and work directly with physiological changes. Your state changes according to your posture, breathing, the way you walk and so on. Anchoring also works without cognitive understanding. Copying physiology offers a way to experience something of someone else's state, not only of body, but of mind and spirit.

It is also feasible to change behaviour by altering the context or environment someone is in. For example, using pink or lavender coloured lighting or paintwork calms people down. Putting speed humps or narrow gaps along the road affects driver behaviour.

First/Unitary

Unitary thinking is Deterministic—it's just how things are. Changing a Unitary stance has to be an 'all or nothing' intervention. Because there are no divisions or parts, everything has to change. However, most attempts at changing someone's belief system 'all at once' are doomed to failure. Altering the content of someone's model of the world becomes a battle of wills, dogma, beliefs, and will usually meet resistance.

Second/Sensory

A Sensory system is also Deterministic. Sensory-mode thinking assumes that anything can be broken down into component parts, qualities, or sequential processes or pro-grams (a person's programming is deterministic because *it* is running *them*). You can effect change by rearranging the struc-ture, sequence, or contribution. Intervening here is more suc-cessful because you can change things piecemeal, tweak processes to make them more effective. This is more subtle and more acceptable.

Third/Social

As you move from *Deterministic* to *Free Will* thinking, you take responsibility for your own power to create your reality. You decide how you will evaluate your experience, alter the importance of a particular view.

A Social-mode intervention should aim to change the decisions that the person is making. They have many things to con-sider—their options, values, morality and so on—and these have to be prioritised by evaluation and comparison.

This is the realm of setting outcomes. Deciding on the well-formedness conditions and ensuring proposed changes are ecological are Social-mode judgments.

Fourth/Mythic

A Mythic-mode view suggests an individualistic perception of reality. Any intervention aims to change the meaning of an experience or situation by presenting an alternative interpreta-tion. This results in a sudden flip in perception—a reframe—which alters the meaning and significance of the previous ideas and often results in a release of laughter as the person experiences the incongruity between the two different world-views.

Mythic-mode thinking explores the consequences of actions, and tests scenarios or stories to find out what happens next.

NLP is not just about moving towards openness and creating choice—operating along the divergent Sensory–Mythic diagonal. NLP also has to move towards closure, to define itself, state prin-ciples, select goals, establish its values—which belong to the Unitary–Social diagonal. Social-mode thinking, being more convergent, can lead to other kinds of limitations, which is why you need to be careful when asking for justification, using *Why* questions. The person is well able to find a story to account for their behaviour. Stories which justify what happened produce a sense of closure which deters further exploration.

Evolution

An evolutionary change has occurred within NLP. The early NLP books sometimes invoked magic as a description of how NLP worked. However, the two volumes of *The Structure of Magic* probably disappointed many readers who expected something more Harry Potter-like! Instead they got an essentially Sensory-mode, detailed, analytical model of language. But then establishing your academic credibility for a revolutionary way of thinking may be a sensible first step. Bandler and Grinder's *Frogs into Princes*, *Reframing* and *Trance Formations* demonstrate a far more Mythic-mode way of exploring transformational change. These books are edited transcripts of trainings, less structured, with fewer procedures or recipes, so that readers had to work at making sense of the desultory flow of ideas. They are more intuitive and conversational in style, ideas flow abundantly, and demonstrate Bandler and Grinder accepting what the audience gives them and then taking it further.

New metaphors have been introduced which have expanded NLP's growing subject matter. For example, Richard Bandler's *Design Human Engineering* is a very Sensory-mode metaphor. One Social-mode aspect has now matured into *NLP Coaching*, which has a far greater emphasis on values and personal decision making. And Mythic-mode thinking is harvesting the fruits of Milton Erickson's work, in the creative use of metaphors and storytelling in creating change. As NLP has become more ordered, structured, prescribed (even bureaucratised), the original concept of magic is played down. In seeking academic respectability, NLP has moved to a more scientific and logical rationale which matches the Sensory-mode thinking in learning, psychology and brain research.

Systems of thought unfold as the existing ideas are organised and sorted. To move on it is necessary to see new patterns which allow you to generalise and condense the existing knowledge into some essential paradigms which then provide a basis for further explorations and refinements in processes and techniques. No system exists in isolation. There is much interaction across disciplines. NLP has borrowed from mathematics and physics, from other therapeutic disciplines, from drama and storytelling, and has used appropriate metaphors for illuminating other qualities of human behaviour. NLP has evolved by assimilating a great deal of wisdom from many aspects of human endeavour. In order to take the next step NLP needs to go through a paradigm shift by reflecting on what it has so far achieved, and by getting its act together. The Six Perceptual Positions model offers a practical way of using NLP. It provides a roadmap for the future by taking the essence of the past and re-presenting it for new audiences.

This book offers many refinements to the ideas I wrote about in the first edition of *Understanding NLP*. I am still finding further interpretations of the Four Realities model in a variety of contexts, and my understanding of this pattern is continuing to evolve. I have also thought through other NLP material which was not covered in the first edition. For example, the model presented in Figure 13.1 also suggests a way of understanding language and metaphors, how we communicate and fail to communicate on different levels and in different modes. However, that has to remain for another book.

Thinking takes time. Ideas, connections do not arise all at once, though once you set a frame of inquiry—ask appropriate question— it would appear that ideas arise, happy coincidences occur, just as fast as you can handle them! It was only as I started to work on the chapter on Perceptual Positions that I picked up *Reframing* again, and suddenly made the connection between this and Fourth position. I had sort of known this for a while, but suddenly the connection became much clearer. And then I wondered, why had no-one ever noticed this before? It has been around for twenty years, but the connection was not made. What does this say about how our minds work?

Mythic-mode magic and metaphors

Not everyone finds each mode equally easy to access. In particular, Mythic-mode thinking can be quite challenging, as it means relinquishing the notion of a fixed reality, and instead holding alternative worldviews as being equally valid. One consequence would be having four varieties of NLP! It is also hard to specify guaranteed methods for generating reframes, making jokes, or originating creative ideas. Essentially, Mythic-mode thinking is about making connections and associations at an abstract level which is beyond the immediately apparent world of the senses. Sensory-mode NLP has you noticing differences, constructing effective sequences and procedures. Mythic-mode NLP requires you to work at an abstract, bigger chunk level so that you are looking for metaphors—generalisations and patterns exhibiting a similar structure.

However, you are already using Mythic-mode thinking when you ask yourself or others to explore the consequences of their actions or interventions: "So what would that do for you?" This is a great question because you do not need to understand what they are talking about. People often talk in a kind of private language, use clichés and metaphors which, if you start to unpick them, can be a distraction. The question bounces them beyond that and gets them to compare the present situation with what is likely to happen over time if it continues in a reasonable way. Bandler & Grinder tell the story (1982: 41–42) about door-to-door salespeople who future pace the potential problems their customers might experience as a result of buying from door-to-door salespeople! By telling them what their neighbours might say, they are helping their customers deal with some of the possible consequences that could arise. Being prepared for what may happen not only enables them to react in a more congruent way when something does occur, they also feel grateful to the person who helps them understand this.

The Six Perceptual Positions model is not a description of reality, nor an attempt at defining 'the truth about NLP'! However, in terms of the question "What is NLP about?" it should help. It invites you to re-examine what you have been told NLP is or does:

the descriptions, the details, the presuppositions, and to reflect on your experience using the models and paradigms you are now aware of. It challenges you to go beyond what you already know about NLP, and to create your own processes and techniques. As you sort out your ideas you may well feel confused at first. You could feel annoyed that some of the books you read or courses you attended gave you 'wrong' information, or feel frustrated that other versions of NLP appear 'old-fashioned' or 'obsolete' and are incompatible with yours. This is part of the paradigm shift. What you have to decide is what you are going to do with what you now know. You can put the information to one side with all those other self-help books that you once read but can't remember much about. Or you can accept and integrate this knowledge into your growing wisdom, your own practice of NLP. The decision is yours. The consequences you will discover in the future.

Appendix A

Four-fold Patterns

Four-part models have been around for millennia. Others are being created all the time to explain human preferences. It is possible, in theory, to combine any two dimensions of human behaviour, and produce a four-box model. In many cases, especially in the business world, people recognise four basic types, but have not explored the underlying dimensions.

For example, here are some traditional patterns (Figure A.1) which have been fitted into the Four Realities model in order to show the similarity.

Model	Unitary	Sensory	Social	Mythic
Grail	Sword	Spear	Grail	Dish
Tarot	Swords	Wands	Cups	Pentacles
Playing Cards	Spades	Clubs	Hearts	Diamonds
Seasons	Spring	Summer	Autumn	Winter
Elements	Air	Fire	Water	Earth
Motives	Emergence	Establishment	Relationship	Dissemination
Humours	Sanguine	Choleric	Phlegmatic	Melancholic
Buddhist	Samjña	Rupa	Vedana	Samskara
Gospels	Matthew	Mark	Luke	John

Figure A.1 Variations on four realities

McWhinney's Four Realities model

Much of my thinking has been influenced by Will McWhinney's work. In the 1990s McWhinney put forward a clear and formal explanation of the Four Realities model. This divides the world into two major dimensions: Plurality—the One and the Many; and Agency—Free Will and Deterministic. By combining these two dimensions, he created a map of four cells, which he labelled:

Unitary [U]; Sensory [Se]; Social [So]; and Mythic [M], (Figure A.2).

	Monistic	**Plurality**	*Pluralistic*
Deterministic	**Unitary [U]** Truths Rules Action		**Sensory [Se]** Facts Sensory Information Evidence
Agency			
(Free Will) *Volitional*	**Mythic [M]** Ideas Creations Strategy		**Social [So]** Values Feelings Decision

Figure A.2 The Four Realities Model, McWhinney (1997)

The following table (Figure A.3) links recent management or personality profiling tools to the Four Realities model:

System:	U	Se	So	M
McWhinney	Unitary	Sensory	Social	Mythic
Satir	Blamer	Computer	Placater	Distracter
Jung (Myers-Briggs) Types	Thinker	Sensor	Feeler	Intuitor
Handy Management types	Zeus Power/Club	Apollo Role	Athena Task	Dionysus Existential/ Person
Merill (TRACOM): Types (Robbins & Finley)	Drivers	Analyticals	Amiables	Expressives

Pine & Gilmore:
  Offerings†
  Theatre:
	Commodities
	Platform
		Goods
		Matching
			Services
			Improv
				Experiences
				Street

Belbin: Kinds of work Team members‡	Blue Chair	Green Co-worker Shaper Finisher	Orange Resource Investigator, Monitor Evaluator, Team Worker	Yellow Plant
Pepper: World views	Formism	Mechanism	Systemism	Instru- mentalism

†   Pine & Gilmore also propose a fifth stage or offering: Transformation.

‡   Belbin's Team Role model has more role categories within the *Many* side, because that is what Teams need more of.

Figure A.3 Four-part Personality and Management tools

Notes:
Jung has other categories or types: Introvert/Extravert and Judger/Perceiver. These are basic polarity distinctions:

- Introvert/Extravert is a variation of One—Many
- Judger/Perceiver corresponds to the division Determinism—Free Will.

The Myers-Briggs Type Indicator, based on Jung's model, uses a grid of 16 boxes. Other complex typologies have 8, 9, 12, 16, 64 types. Other instruments are more sophisticated; finer distinctions are made as they focus more on certain aspects of human interaction.

Honey and Mumford's four basic Learning Styles—Activist, Pragmatist, Reflector, Theorist—also seem to fit this pattern (Honey & Mumford, 1986). However, the questionnaire used for individuals for discovering their preference appears to be a mixture of cognitive styles. This is not to say that their descriptions are invalid. It could be that they lack an underlying paradigm for sorting, and use pragmatic judgments based on experience instead.

There are other models which describe a change process, such as that identified by the psychologist B W Tuckman in the 1970s. He proposed four stages of team development which most teams seem to go through in order to function effectively. They are:

- **Forming—Storming—Norming—Performing**

This can be interpreted as follows:

Forming: finding out 'what is'

Storming: realising that there are other points of view, and trying to accommodate them

Norming: group awareness and sharing

Performing: being able to work independently from, yet belonging to the group.

A similar progression occurs within Hersey & Blanchard's Leadership styles (see Blanchard et al, 1985):

- **Directing—Coaching—Supporting—Delegating**

Appendix B

Doing NLP Exercises

Doing exercises

You do exercises in order to develop and practise new skills. Doing NLP exercises familiarises you with a different way of thinking. The advantage of being in a training situation is that you can learn from your 'mistakes', explore what can go wrong, and learn from the experience, before you put yourself in a situation where things may be more critical.

Your personal 'team' in action

When you are doing an NLP exercise or process, it is useful to think of the different roles you need to take on. You need to remember that they are working together to achieve your outcome or purpose and to produce a satisfactory result. That is, you need to demonstrate your own internal leadership, and have all your parts and roles aligned, so that you act with integrity and appear authentic to those you are working with.

Generally speaking, there are three general ways of doing exercises:

1. Internally

Most of the work is done in the privacy of your mind. You notice or pay attention to certain aspects of your experience; you remember, visualise, recall and have feelings about them. You then dissociate, mentally stand back and take a more objective point of view, and deliberately change the qualities, the coding, or the frame of your experience. Essentially, you do the exercise in your imagination, staying inside your head, following the instructions given to you by the therapist or helper. Many of the original NLP exercises were done in this way.

2. Externally

You externalise your inner reality by re-creating it on the outside as a spatial metaphor. Mapping inner reality onto external space provides a spatial separation of the elements, instead of having them jumbled up in your imagination. Once you can see what is there, it makes it easier to rearrange or restructure your model of the world. This way of working allows you to physically move around that space, examine different aspects of yourself, other people and so on. As you move, you see things from different angles and distances. You can step into different roles, or imagined versions of yourself (and others) and work within them. You can step out and notice the results of making changes. You can notice how distance alters a relationship, by moving towards or away from it. Standing on a chair allows you to rise above things to get a fresh perspective. You might literally discover what a fly on the wall would see—though probably not through compound eyes!

3. Serendipitously

Change also happens in a more unstructured way. You set yourself a question, or someone else implants a post-hypnotic suggestion in your mind (actually people are doing this to you all the time—but you don't notice!), and then answers come to you unbidden. The trick is to notice them. You may refer to this as *serendipity*: you find what you are looking for in an unexpected place, or you get creative ideas, make decisions, at times when you are engaged in some kind of everyday activity such as taking a shower or walking the dog. In fact, many people deliberately go for walks in order to think something through. To get the best out of this method, I recommend having pen and paper handy in order to jot down ideas as they come, because they are easily lost.

How to do NLP exercises

Traditionally, in NLP, exercises and processes are done by working in groups of three people. These roles have a number of names:

Person A: the client, subject, explorer, worker.
Person B: the helper, guide, operator, therapist, mentor, coach.
Person C: the observer, 'meta-person' (in NLP jargon).

You take it in turns to take on each of the three Roles. This is what each role pays attention to:

As A: Client or Subject

- Treat the exercise seriously. Use an issue that is real for you, rather than some hypothetical problem. If it is difficult thinking in general terms, consider that "there is a part of me that wants to do X". The more you engage with the issue, the more you gain from the exercise.

- Respect your own feelings. Many of the things you will be asked to do will be unfamiliar, because much of change work is about breaking a pattern and doing something different. Therefore it is likely to feel uncomfortable at first. However, if you have a strong reaction to doing whatever, then respect your self-preservation part and stop. Trust that you have a part which is looking after you and protecting you from danger.

As B: Helper or Operator

- Adopt an attitude of dispassionate curiosity: you are there to witness to the other person becoming "more of who they really are".

- You are not there to demonstrate how clever you are. Think of yourself as a catalyst, assisting the change process. Your job is to keep things on track.

- Before you start, read the instructions. Then give your full attention to the client.

- The primary skill is to establish and maintain rapport with the subject. See Chapter Six.

- During the process, stay out of the client's working space or visual field. If appropriate, be 'on their side' as you go through the exercise with them.

- Do not rush. Take your cue from the client; allow time for them to process. Notice what is happening on the outside as a result of this internal processing.

- Assume that the words the client uses only have meaning for them. By treating their words as meaningless, you can simply use them back to them without causing conflict by reinterpreting or rephrasing them. "So if you had X, what would that enable you to do?"

- If you get stuck, it is all right to tell the client, for example: "Stop for a moment. I am just going to confer with the observer. I'll be back in a moment." Move off-stage to notice what is happening now, and enlist the help of the observer, or refer back to the instructions. The client will be OK. They have had their problem for some time—another couple of minutes won't hurt!

- Only move on when you are sure what to do next. Make sure that you get back into a positive, resourceful state before you re-engage.

As C: Observer or Meta-person

- Make sure you are familiar with the instructions and purpose of the exercise.

- Stay at sufficient distance so that you can see both A and B. Sometimes it is a good idea to switch off the sound and to observe the body-language.

- Make a note of what happens for both A and B. You may want to jot things down.

- If the helper is having difficulties, you will have to decide whether to intervene, or whether to wait until asked for help. Set up a signal for intervening.

- At the end of the round, or the end of the exercise, you may want to give feedback. The only useful feedback is in the form: "This is what you did well. This is one thing you could do better." Do not give advice: "If I were you I'd ..." as this is seldom respectful. There is no value in giving negative feedback; focusing on what doesn't work is not what you want!

Using space

When you work with other people, you need to consider how you are going to use space. If it is not important, as in the first type of exercise above, then you can arrange chairs in an equilateral triangle, so that you are close enough to each other to be able to converse, observe. Sometimes it is better for the observer, Person C, to stand back in order to be able to see both A and B. It may be advisable for C to stay far enough away that they cannot hear the words and have to pay attention to the nonverbal communication.

If you are going to use an External exercise, you need a large space. Generally, the client and their helper will go exploring together, while the observer will maintain sufficient distance to be able to take in all that is happening without being in the way. The operator also needs to be aware of where the subject is placing elements in space, and neither stand in those positions, nor interrupt the line of sight.

As a group

At the end of the exercise it is important to reflect on what happened. However, remember that if you have done a powerful piece of change work, then the client may still be processing and probably want to stay with it. Therefore, do not bring them out of that processing state unless you have to. Then you can give them some kind of instruction along the lines of "And let your unconscious mind continue to process that, as your conscious mind returns to the present, the here and now, knowing that it is OK to continue to change only as fast as you need to."

Reflection is an essential part of learning. You learn from experience when you think about what happened, and begin to make explanatory stories, make further connections, perceive other meanings and draw conclusions. You could also metaphorically or physically stand outside of the exercise space and consider it from the outside. Maybe look at the process, how you did the exercise, and what you could do differently next time.

General guidelines

Follow the instructions
In the early stages, it is better to follow the suggested instructions, as it is probable that they have been developed and refined through experience of what works. The language patterns could be vital to success. If you find something does not work for you, get curious about what you have been doing or why this is the case. First, you need to check that you did what was recommended. Then you will know better where to explore. You may discover something that will work even better, and you can refine your understanding. But if you start by making up your own version, or by improvising, you may be missing something.

Keep to the timing
Decide a time for each round and keep to it. Many exercises do not gain from being longer.

Stay focused

Focus on doing the exercise, and avoid distractions and diversions, such as gossip.

Reflect

At the end of an exercise take time to notice what happened. You may want to consider: "What is one thing I could do better next time?"

Learn from mistakes

Remember, you are all learners. You are not expected to be 'perfect'. Allow yourself to make 'interesting mistakes', as this is the way you learn.

"Less is More"

NLP techniques can be relatively quick, taking minutes rather than requiring a weekly commitment extending over months or years. One reason for this is that they work *content free*. This means you do not need to know the details of the client's problem. The practitioner's skill is in observing changes in the client's physiology—their skin colour, facial expression, body-language—from the outside, which lets you know that you are getting results.

Working content free

Your first task as the helper is to keep the client on track. Then you need to use the evidence of your senses to notice the client's state at any moment, to notice the extent to which they are changing, which you can observe from their nonverbal communication. It usually does not help knowing any details of their issue, other than the barest minimum. If you were to know the content it would set up associations in your own mind, and this could get you reminiscing about your own similar experiences. Then you might be tempted to offer advice, empathy, or think that "the same thing happened to me". (It didn't!) It does not help the other person if you get emotionally involved. They have to sort it out themselves. You need to stay objective and keep the process moving.

Future pacing

At the end of the process, check that the changes will be maintained. NLP refers to this as *future pacing*. Ask the client to imagine a time in the future where a similar situation would arise (and the old habit would have kicked in if they had not changed). As they imagine this future event, check their physiological indicators again, to see whether the new, improved state still holds. If it doesn't, then you will need to make further interventions. If it does, your work is finished. Pause to allow time for the client to get to know themselves in this changed state. Remember Dorothy's initial disorientation in the Land of Oz. A strange new colourful world takes a while to get used to.

You may also find the essence of your vision, or the metaphorical meaning as more important. Instead of taking the vision literally, find out what that kind of vision means to you. What is the connection between that story and what you would like to be true in your physical reality?

About the Author

Peter Young is very much a Mythic-mode thinker, and enjoys exploring ideas, metaphors and stories in novels and cinema as well as in management and therapeutic models of change. He has been studying NLP since the late 1980s, and has been evolving his 'Understanding' model since 1998. The Six Perceptual Positions model is only the beginning of the story. There is a great deal more to explore in terms of the *processes* and *stories* of change, and the ways in which conflict can be clarified and resolved. We still have a long way to go in our society for people to learn to recognise, appreciate and accept the variety of ways in which people create their unique models of the world.

Contact Information

Peter Young's website:
    www.storying.co.uk
has further information about his books and articles, and a list of NLP websites.

Previous books by Peter Young:

Understanding NLP: Metaphors and Patterns of Change, 2001, Crown House Publishing, Carmarthen.

The Spanish edition:
    El Nuevo Paradigma de la PNL: Metáforas y patrones para el cambio, 2002, Ediciones Urano, Barcelona.

Change Manager, Part of the Q-Learning *Be your best … and beyond series*, 2003, Hodder Headline, London.

Bibliography

Andreas, Steve and Andreas, Connirae, 1989, *Heart of the Mind: Engaging Your Inner Power to Change With Neuro-Linguistic Programming*, Real People Press, Utah.

Ardui, J, and Wrycza, P, 1994, Unravelling Perceptual Positions, in *NLP World*, Vol. 1, No. 2, 1994, 5–22.

Ashby, W Ross, 1952, *Introduction to Cybernetics*, John Wiley, New York.

Bandler, Richard, 1985, *Using your Brain—for a Change*, Real People Press, Moab, UT.

Bandler, Richard and Grinder, John, 1975, *The Structure of Magic I: A Book about Language & Therapy*, Science & Behavior Books, Palo Alto.

Bandler, Richard and Grinder, John, 1979, *Frogs into Princes: Neuro-Linguistic Programming*, Real People Press, Moab, UT.

Bandler, Richard and Grinder, John, 1982, *Reframing: Neuro-Linguistic Programming and the Transformation of Meaning*, Real People Press, Moab, UT.

Bandler, Richard; Grinder, John; and Satir, Virginia, 1976, *Changing with Families*, Science and Behavior Books, Palo Alto.

Bateson, Gregory, 1972, The Logical Categories of Learning and Communication, in *Steps to an Ecology of Mind: A Revolutionary Approach to Man's Understanding of Himself*, Ballantine Books, NY Chandler Publishing Company.

Belbin, R Meredith, 2000, *Beyond The Team*, Butterworth Heinemann, Oxford.

Bennis, Warren and Biederman, Patricia Ward, 1997, *Organizing Genius: The Secrets of Creative Collaboration*, Nicholas Brealey Publishing, London.

Berne, Eric, 1964, 1968, *Games People Play: The Psychology of Human Relationships*, Penguin Books, Andre Deutsch, Harmondsworth.

Blanchard, Kenneth et al, 1985, *Leadership and the One Minute Manager*, Fontana/Collins.

Blanchard, Kenneth; Oncken, William Jr and Burrows, Hal, 1989, *The One Minute Manager Meets the Monkey*, Fontana, NY Quill.

Bodenhamer, Bob and Hall, L Michael, 1996, *Figuring Out People: Design Engineering with Metaprograms*, Crown House Publishing, Carmarthen.

Bodenhamer, Bob and Hall, L Michael, 1999, *The User's Manual to the Brain: The Complete Manual for Neuro-Linguistic Programming Practitioner Certification*, Crown House Publishing, Carmarthen.

Buzan, Tony and Buzan, Barry, 2003, *The Mindmap Book*, revised edition, BBC Publications, London.

Caine, Michael, 2003, Talking on a BBC Radio 2 programme to celebrate his 70th birthday.

Campbell, Joseph, 1949, *The Hero with a Thousand Faces*, Fontana, HarperCollins Publishers, London.

Clarke, Arthur C, 1982, *Profiles of the Future: an Inquiry into the Limits of the Possible*, Victor Gollancz Ltd, London.

Dearden, Robert F, 1984, *Theory and Practice in Education*, Routledge and Kegan Paul, London.

de Bono, Edward, 1991, *Six Action Shoes*, HarperCollins, London.

de Bono, Edward, 1992, *Serious Creativity: Using the Power of Lateral Thinking to Create New Ideas*, HarperCollins, London.

DeLozier, Judith and Grinder, John, 1987, *Turtles All The Way Down: Prerequisites to Personal Genius*, Grinder, DeLozier and Associates, California.

Dilts, Robert, 1990, *Changing Belief Systems with NLP*, Meta Publications, Cupertino, California.

Dilts, Robert, 1997a, unpublished transcript, ITS Master Practitioner Training, London.

Dilts, Robert, 1997b, *Visionary Leadership Skills*, NLP University, Santa Cruz, CA.

Dilts, Robert, 1998, *Fourth Position*, NLPU website: www.nlpu.com Article of the Month.

Dilts, Robert; Epstein, Todd and Dilts, Robert W, 1991, *Tools for Dreamers: Strategies for Creativity and the Structure of Innovation*, Meta Publications, Cupertino, California.

Dilts, R and DeLozier, J, 2000, *Encyclopaedia of NLP*, http://www.nlpuniversitypress.com.

Egan, Kieran, 1997, *The Educated Mind: How Cognitive Tools Shape our Understanding*, The University of Chicago Press, Chicago.

Faulkner, Charles, 2003, A brief meaning of everything—a talk given at the ANLP Conference, April 2003.

Gibbons, Stella, 1932, *Cold Comfort Farm*, Penguin Books, Harmondsworth.

Gray, John, 1993, *Men are from Mars, Women are from Venus*, HarperCollins, London.

Hall, L Michael, 2000, *The Spirit of NLP: The Process, Meaning and Criteria for Mastering NLP*, Revised Edition, Crown House Publishing, Carmarthen.

Hall, L Michael, 2002, Always Ask 'Why'?—The Redemption of Why, *Anchor Point*, Vol 16 #5, May 2002, pp. 24–29.

Handy, Charles, 1978, 1985, 1991, *Gods of Management: The Changing Work of Organisations*, 3rd edition, Business Books, Random Century Limited, London.

Heinlein, Robert A, 1961, *Stranger in a Strange Land*, GP Putnam and Sons.

Heinlein, Robert A, 1980, *The Number of the Beast*, New English Library, London.

Heller, Joseph, 1961, *Catch-22*, Transworld Publishers, London.

Hofstadter, Douglas R, 1985, *Metamagical Themas: Questing for the Essence of Mind and Pattern*, Penguin Books, London.

Honey, Peter and Mumford, Alan, 1986, *Using Your Learning Styles*, Peter Honey, Maidenhead.

Huang, Al Chung-Liang, 1973, *Embrace Tiger, Return to Mountain: the essence of T'ai Chi*, Real People Press, Moab, Utah.

Huxley, Aldous, 1954, 1959, *The Doors of Perception*, Penguin Books, Harmondsworth.

James, Tad and Woodsmall, Wyatt, 1988, *Time Line Therapy and the Basis of Personality*, Meta Publications, Cupertino, CA.

James, William, 1890, 1950, *Principles of Psychology*, Volume II, Henry Holt & Co, New York (1890), Dover Publications (1950).

Johnstone, Keith, 1979, *Impro: Improvisation and the Theatre*, Methuen Drama, London.

Johnstone, Keith, 1999, *Impro for Storytellers: Theatresports and the Art of Making Things Happen*, Faber & Faber, London.

Jung, Carl Gustav, 1971, *Psychological Types*, The Collected Works of C G Jung, Volume 6, Routledge, London.

Kopp, Sheldon B, 1971, *Guru: Metaphors From A Psychotherapist*, Science and Behavior Books, Palo Alto.

Korzybski, Alfred, 1958, *Science and Sanity: An Introduction to Non-Aristotelian Systems and General Semantics*, International Non-Aristotelian Library Publishing Company.

Kuhn, Thomas S, 1970, *The Structure of Scientific Revolutions*, 2nd edition, enlarged, The University of Chicago Press, Chicago.

Lawson, Hilary, 2001a, *Closure: A Story of Everything*, Routledge, London.

Lawson, Hilary, 2001b, Stephen Hawking is Wrong, *Prospect Magazine*, November 2001 www.prospect-magazine.co.uk/

Lee, Harper, 1960, *To Kill A Mockingbird*, Arrow, London.

Mamet, David, 1991, *On Directing Film*, Faber & Faber, London.

McCarthy, Bernice and Morris, Susan, 1994, *The 4MAT CourseBook*, Vol. 1, Excel, Barrington, Illinois.

McWhinney, Will, 1995, The Matter of Einstein Square Dancing with Magritte, *Cybernetics & Human Knowing*, Vol 3, No 3.

McWhinney, Will, 1997, *Paths of Change: Strategic Choices for Organisations and Society*, Sage Publications, London.

McWhinney, Will; Webber, James; Smith, Douglas and Novokowsky, Bernie, 1997, *Creating Paths of Change: Managing Issues and Resolving Problems in Organisations*, Sage Publications, London.

McWhirter, John, 2002, Remodelling NLP, Part 13A, *Rapport* #56.

Pepper, Stephen, 1942, *World Hypotheses: A study of evidence*, University of California Press, California.

Persaud, Raj, 2003, *From the Edge of the Couch: Bizarre psychiatric cases and what they teach us about ourselves*, Bantam Press, London.

Pine, B Joseph and Gilmore, James H, 1999, *The Experience Economy: Work is Theatre & Every Business a Stage*, Harvard Business School Press.

Ramachandran, Vilayanur, 2003, *The Emerging Mind: the BBC Reith Lectures 2003*, Lecture 2, Profile Books, London.

Robbins, Harvey and Finley, Michael, 1997, *Why Change Doesn't Work: Why Initiatives Go Wrong and How to Try Again—And Succeed*, Texere Publishing, London.

Robbins, Tom, 2000, *Fierce Invalids Home from Hot Climates*, No Exit Press, Harpenden.

Satir, Virginia, 1972, *Peoplemaking*, Science & Behaviour Books, Palo Alto.

Satir, Virginia, 1988, *The New Peoplemaking*, Science & Behaviour Books, Palo Alto.

Schwartz, Peter, 1991, *The Art of the Long View: Scenario Planning—Protecting your Company Against an Uncertain World*, Century Business, London.

Smallwood, David, 1997, 7% 35% 55%, *Rapport*, #37 Autumn 1997, p. 13.

Tagore, Rabindranath, 1916, *Stray Birds*, [translated from Bengali to English by the author], The Macmillan Company, New York.

Treasure, Mike, 2002, Joined up NLP—a talk given at the ANLP Conference in Northampton, May 2002.

Tuckman, Bruce W, 1975, *Measuring Educational Outcomes*, Harcourt Brace Jovanovitch, New York.

Vogler, Christopher, 2000, *The Writer's Journey: Mythic Structure for Storytellers and Screenwriters*, 2nd edition, Pan Books.

Watzlawick, Paul, Weakland, John and Fisch, Richard, 1974, *Change: Principles of Problem Formation and Problem Resolution*, W W Norton & Co.

Woodsmall, Wyatt, 1999, 'Logical Levels' and Systemic NLP, in *NLP World*, Vol 6, #1, March 1999, pp. 51–78.

Yapko, Michael, 1994, *Suggestions of Abuse: True and False Memories of Childhood Sexual Trauma*, Simon & Schuster.

Young, Peter, 2001, *Understanding NLP: Metaphors and Patterns of Change*, Crown House Publishing, Carmarthen.

Young, Peter, 2003, *Change Manager*, Part of the Q-Learning *Be your best ... and beyond* series, Hodder Headline, London.

Index

USA, Canada & Mexico orders to:
Crown House Publishing Company LLC
4 Berkeley Street, 1st Floor, Norwalk, CT 06850, USA
Tel: +1 203 852 9504, Fax: +1 203 852 9619
E-mail: info@CHPUS.com
www.CHPUS.com

UK, Europe & Rest of World orders to:
The Anglo American Book Company Ltd.
Crown Buildings, Bancyfelin, Carmarthen, Wales SA33 5ND
Tel: +44 (0)1267 211880/211886, Fax: +44 (0)1267 211882
E-mail: books@anglo-american.co.uk
www.anglo-american.co.uk

Australasia orders to:
Footprint Books Pty Ltd.
Unit 4/92A Mona Vale Road, Mona Vale NSW 2103, Australia
Tel: +61 (0) 2 9997 3973, Fax: +61 (0) 2 9997 3185
E-mail: info@footprint.com.au
www.footprint.com.au

Singapore orders to:
Publishers Marketing Services Pte Ltd.
10-C Jalan Ampas #07-01
Ho Seng Lee Flatted Warehouse, Singapore 329513
Tel: +65 6256 5166, Fax: +65 6253 0008
E-mail: info@pms.com.sg
www.pms.com.sg

Malaysia orders to:
Publishers Marketing Services Pte Ltd
Unit 509, Block E, Phileo Damansara 1, Jalan 16/11
46350 Petaling Jaya, Selangor, Malaysia
Tel : +03 7955 3588, Fax : +03 7955 3017
E-mail: pmsmal@streamyx.com
www.pms.com.sg

South Africa orders to:
Everybody's Books CC
PO Box 201321, Durban North, 4016, RSA
Tel: +27 (0) 31 569 2229, Fax: +27 (0) 31 569 2234
E-mail: warren@ebbooks.co.za